REPORTAGE PRESS

ABOUT THE AUTHOR

Rob Crilly is a freelance foreign correspondent. For five years he lived and worked in East Africa, travelling through war zones in Sudan, Somalia, the Democratic Republic of Congo and northern Uganda, reporting for *The Times*, *The Irish Times*, *The Christian Science Monitor*, *The Daily Mail* and *The Scotsman*. Born in 1973, he was educated at the Judd School, Tonbridge, and Cambridge University. Before moving to Africa he spent five years working for British newspapers, most recently as Edinburgh Bureau Chief of *The Herald*.

SAVING DARFUR

Everyone's Favourite African War

BY ROB CRILLY

REPORTAGE PRESS

REPORTAGE PRESS

Reportage Press
26 Richmond Way, London W12 8LY, United Kingdom.
Tel: 0044 7971 461 935
Fax: 0044 20 8749 2867
Email: info@reportagepress.com
www.reportagepress.com

Published by Reportage Press 2010

British Library Cataloguing in Publication Data.

A catalogue record for this book is available from the British Library.

ISBN: 978-1-906702-19-9

Cover design by Henrietta Molinaro.

Layout by Florence Production, Ltd.

Printed and bound in Great Britain by The Good News Press Ltd, Ongar.

Endorsements

"Rob Crilly has had the moral and intellectual courage to find the Darfur that lies beyond the slogans and celebrity campaigns. His book is a haunting and brutally honest account of international failure and African suffering. Above all it is faithful to the trauma of those for whom nobody really speaks. Lucid, engaging and written with love for the entire continent of Africa." – FERGAL KEANE, BBC News

"Crilly takes you to Darfur, into a vast landscape of heat and dust and horrific war. But as he leads you from plains to mountains and into camps and villages, all your preconceptions are turned upside down by the fiendish complexity of this war. This book peels off the labels that have been stuck on Darfur by outsiders and exposes the stubborn realities beneath the surface." – RICHARD DOWDEN, Director of the Royal Africa Society

"Saving Darfur is an engaging and insightful look into one of Africa's most intractable conflicts. Rob Crilly has as good a grasp of the people and the politics of the region as anyone writing on the subject today. This book's triumph is the author's ability to make the complexities of the crisis accessible, through the eyes of the people who have watched and suffered as the atrocities unfolded. If you're looking for just one book to bring you up to speed on Darfur, this is it!" – MARTIN GEISSLER, ITV News

"While I disagree with much of Mr Crilly's analysis, he provides us with a solid journalistic account of his first-hand experiences in Darfur." – MIA FARROW, actress and activist

"Rob Crilly tells the story of Darfur up close, focusing on the people who have fought and suffered. Neither cynical nor moralising, he brings to life its protagonists – rebel fighters, Arab militiamen, displaced villagers, foreign aid workers, diplomats and campaigners. Saving Darfur delves beneath the stereotypes to tackle the complexities of Darfur and Sudan, illuminating both the ordinariness and the bizarreness of this extraordinary African war." – ALEX DE WAAL, author of *Darfur: A New History Of A Long War*

"The crisis in Darfur is complex, multi-layered and has its roots deep in history. It is not, as it is often portrayed, a straightforward issue of good versus bad. Rob Crilly has spent more time than any other journalist I know travelling in and out of the region to piece together his analysis; his vast experience informs this book and lifts it head and shoulders above other attempts to explain what has plunged Darfur into disaster." – ADAM MYNOTT, BBC News

"Few correspondents have covered Darfur more diligently, authoritatively and comprehensively than Rob Crilly . . . The Darfur that emerges is not a simple question of bad guys and good guys, or evil presidents and tragic victims, but a place of nuance and complications . . . (Crilly) pulls us through this maze with the sure string of a series of ripping yarns and the kind of gritty reporting that is, sadly, so rare these days. This debut from one of our best correspondents presents a compelling read for the lay reader, and is a must-read for those who (often mistakenly) think they already know what Darfur – and much of modern conflict – is all about." – ALEX PERRY, Time Africa Bureau Chief, author of *Falling Off the Edge: Globalization, World Peace and Other Lies*

For Mum and Anna

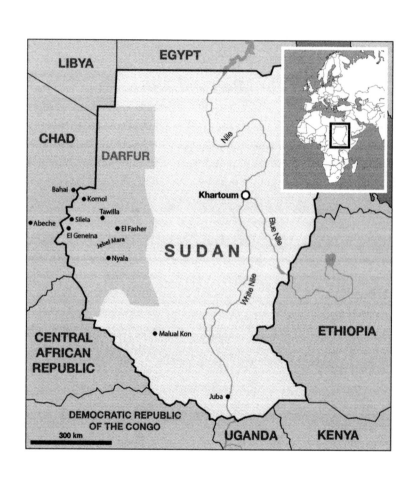

Contents

INTRODUCTION: JANJAWEED RAID

Live in East Africa long enough and you learn there can be good gunfire and bad. The pop, pop, pop of an AK-47 might mean a wedding or it might mean a funeral; a murder, a celebration or a war. So the sound of shooting in the Darfur city of El Fasher did not have me unduly concerned. It was that sort of place – dusty, gun-ridden and lawless.

"Should we be worried?" I asked the man sitting across the table from me at the Humanitarian Aid Commission (HAC). He didn't answer. Instead, he dashed to the windows at the back of the office, closing the shutters as the sound of gunfire drew nearer. His already dingy office was plunged into darkness. Then it dawned on me. As a senior government official in this war-torn region, the commissioner was a likely target of whoever was moving through the market just outside. His office was not the place to be.

The commissioner clearly agreed. After a hurried consultation with his assistant he raced for the door, pausing only to remove his natty red tie. In a town where men wear the traditional white flowing jalabiya, a shirt and tie means only one thing – government official. He may as well have knotted a target around his neck.

Outside in the courtyard, the commissioner jumped into a pickup and roared away. The women who had earlier been serving tea and the men sitting on string chairs had all disappeared. The place was empty. I was alone.

By now the popgun clatter of AK-47s had been joined by the boom of heavier calibre weaponry. Sudan's security services were fighting the intruders using anti-aircraft guns mounted on pickups – "technicals". Their fist-sized rounds were designed to blow planes from the sky and were devastating when used on humans. The noise was all around me. I phoned a friend who was working for a charity to find out what was happening.

"Yes, the United Nations has just radioed a warning to avoid the vicinity of the market," he told me by mobile phone.

The commissioner's office was in the centre of the market. It began to dawn on me that I had been abandoned on a battlefield, and there was nowhere to run. Walking into the market would have been suicidal; hiding out in a government office seemed little safer.

In front of me an open gate led on to the main road where two pickups raced past. They were filled with men in khaki uniforms, their faces wrapped in scarves and shades. The sound of shooting raced past with them.

Someone was shouting at me from the far side of the compound, at the end of the one-storey building where the government's aid officials were based. An old man in a dirty robe was waving his arms wildly, urging me to take cover in a doorway. I still had no idea who the attackers were. They could have been rebels or government- there was no way of telling from the brief glimpses as their cars raced past. There was nothing for it but to sit tight and hope the raiders were not intent on looting the HAC offices.

I ran towards the old man, stumbling along an uneven dirt path, and threw myself through the door. Inside was cool. It was much like dozens of Sudanese government offices that I had already seen. It was plain, the walls were bare and a single empty desk commanded the room. There was no computer, no paperwork or pens. Just the desk and a selection of armchairs. Three Sudanese men were also sheltering there, mobile phones glued to their ears. One, his leathery face screwed tight in concentration, did his best to provide a commentary in broken English. "It's unknown robbers," he said.

I sat down heavily in a chair and was engulfed by a cloud of dust. Outside the gunfire had intensified. Engines screamed. There were shouts in Arabic. My new friends told me the fire fight had started in the city centre before spreading through the market to the area around us as the gunmen used the road outside as their escape route.

"It is Janjaweed," added my commentator, before moving the phone from his ear to his mouth, Sudanese-style, to ask a question. He moved the handset back to his ear and then turned back to me: "They have not been paid so they have come to the market to steal their wages."

In eight trips to Darfur this was my first encounter with the Janjaweed. It wasn't a meeting I had sought. Even their name, meaning 'Devils on Horseback', seemed designed to inspire fear. And they had lived up to its promise. The camps around El Fasher, the capital of North Darfur, were filled with tens of thousands of women and children widowed and orphaned by the mobile killers. The victims were always from the black, African tribes, mostly the Fur, the Zaghawa and the Masalit – the peoples whose menfolk had risen in rebellion against the government back in 2003.

The Janjaweed – mounted Arab militias whose traditional role had been to protect the tribe and their livestock – were the government's response. They formed a cheap and effective counter-insurgency force. They had murdered, maimed and raped their way through the civilian population as part of a scorched earth policy aimed at starving the rebels of support, emptying villages and filling the aid camps. Some estimates put the death toll at 400,000. More than two and a half million people had been forced from their homes. In September 2004, four days after Colin Powell, US Secretary of State, declared the slaughter of African tribes to be a "genocide", I swapped my mother's house in the rolling southern English countryside of Kent for Kenya, and a new life as a foreign correspondent.

Even before I set off, foreign editors were calling asking how fast I could get to Sudan. Harrowing reports of mass killing had started emerging from the refugee camps in Darfur and across the border in Chad. Darfur was already the biggest story in my new patch and, over the next five years, I would spend more time on it than anything else.

It wasn't that Darfur was Africa's bloodiest war. The death toll in the Democratic Republic of Congo's lingering civil conflict passed five million in 2008. Somalia's hungry and war-ravaged country had not even had a government since 1991. In northern Uganda, a cultish rebel army had kept swaths of countryside shrouded in fear for more than two decades, with 20,000 children abducted to join its ranks. Even the civil war in South Sudan, responsible for two million deaths, easily surpassed Darfur on a crude index of misery.

None, though, could match Darfur for profile. Celebrities were queuing up to highlight the cause. George Clooney had travelled backwards and forwards to Chad, Southern Sudan and Darfur, and lobbied politicians in Washington and London; Don Cheadle, star of Hotel Rwanda, co-authored a book on the subject; Mia Farrow had turned herself into a one-woman lobby group, spending weeks at a time on the Chadian border and posting furious diatribes against Khartoum and its biggest foreign ally, China, on her campaign website. Darfur even made it into the 2008 presidential debates. In between questions about economic bail-outs and health care reform, the then Senator Barack Obama used the example of Darfur to answer a question about when he would use US firepower in situations where American national interests were not at stake.

"We could be providing logistical support, setting up a no-fly zone at relatively little cost to us, but we can only do it if we can help mobilize the international community and lead," he said. "And that's what I intend to do when I'm president."

What I wanted to know was, of all the wars in Africa, why did we care about this one so much? Maybe because it seemed so simple. Anyone who tells you they "get" the intricacies of Somalia's never-ending clan wars or Congo's shifting mosaic of militias is probably bluffing. In contrast, Darfur was easy. It was a holocaust. The good guys were African. The bad guys were Arab. And the bad guys were really bad – the Sudanese government had even given shelter to Osama bin Laden in the 1990s. Then there was Darfur's timing, emerging on the tenth anniversary of the Rwandan genocide, in which a million people had died and the world had agreed never to let happen again.

There was just one problem. As the bullets flew in El Fasher, the accepted analysis suddenly felt out of kilter. The city was a government garrison town. Armed police and soldiers guarded every road intersection and ringed the airport. What were the Janjaweed doing attacking their own side? Sure, they wanted to be paid, but why not rape and pillage their way through the camps around the town where 150,000 of their enemies were camped? From my vantage point (admittedly crouched low in an armchair, well away from the now-shuttered windows) the war was slipping out of focus. Black and white certainties were mixing into grey.

What follows is my attempt to get under the skin of the Darfur conflict, to explain for myself what is really happening in Sudan's western desert region. My journey takes me into the rebel-held mountains on a donkey and to the jungles of Southern Sudan; there are lessons learned from a teddy bear named Mohammed. It is unashamedly a reporter's account. There are better histories of Darfur. Other writers explain more successfully the anthropology of the war, its ethnic element and the politics of Khartoum. There are better books for dates, names and places. But in a conflict where so many people around the world claim to speak for the suffering people of Darfur, this is an attempt to broadcast the real voices from the aid camps, the rebel villages and the Arab camel markets.

Along the way, there is criticism of some of the organisations that have done such a great job of keeping what should be an obscure African war on the news pages. Their generalisations have helped raise awareness of the slaughter, but polarised the search for answers. There are a few suggestions for how we could do a better job of finding peace. That said, I never came to Africa to change the world or even to save Darfur. It was the search for adventure that brought me and my notebook to El Fasher. This was a real story. Something that mattered to millions of Darfuris. After five years doing most of my journalism from a desk, this was a chance to get under the skin of a place, its people and its wars.

There were big questions at stake, too. Darfur itself may have been an obscure battleground, but it was playing host to some of the big themes of the early twenty-first century: the role of China in Africa, the West's relationship with the Arab world, and how global warming was emerging as a new source of conflict.

Few might have heard of Darfur's Abbala or Fur tribes, but conflicts in desert lands dominated by oil and Islam were already familiar territory. Events here would shape attitudes towards international justice, peacekeeping missions and the way we view the world. And it was on my doorstep.

The shooting died away after about twenty minutes. Gradually the sound of engines rumbled off into the distance and the marketplace fell silent. Inside the bare, brick building the four of us waited for an hour before venturing outside. The marketplace was deserted. Its rickety wooden stalls were overturned and shell casings lay in the middle of the road. The next day I learned that the fighting had claimed the life of one person. Four more had been injured. There were short reports on the wires, but the mainstream media ignored the story. I didn't even try to file. One person dead was nothing compared with a genocide. Why would my editors care about one life lost as a messy, awkward aside to the main conflict? It was a digression, an irrelevance. It seemed little more than a sad loose end.

That wasn't true, of course. A town had been terrorised and a man lay dead. This book is my attempt to tease out those loose ends, to complicate, and correct, the story of Darfur.

PROLOGUE: THE DARK COUNTRY

There wasn't much to see from the night sky as the plane began its descent into Khartoum. Our route had taken us first over Southern Sudan, one of the least developed places in the world. Beneath us there were no landmarks or roads, let alone twinkling street lights or illuminated advertising hoardings. As the sun dipped below the horizon, the land below disappeared. The ground was simply swallowed into nothingness. Then, as my Kenya Airways 737 continued north towards the capital, the land beneath us would have turned to desert and the blackness stretched on into the distance. We could have been flying through outer space, such was the absence of humankind's impact on the invisible land somewhere underneath. Even as I felt the aeroplane dropping towards its destination, there was not much more to see. The darkness crept right up into the city. The black desert vacuum encircled Khartoum and extended far into its streets and suburbs. Lights flickered here and there. Headlamps moved in straight lines. There were even primary colours shining out from the fairy lights of a funfair. But this was not like arriving into London, Paris or Brussels, their prosperity beaming into the sky from millions of lightbulbs. It may be old-fashioned, if not racist, to refer to Africa as the Dark Continent, but arrive at any African city at night and it is difficult not to be struck by the darkness of night when electricity is a luxury not everyone can afford. Here and there, I could spot patches of pitch black amid the speckling of white and yellow: maybe these was slums, or stretches of the Nile, or camps where thousands of people had fled the country's various conflicts.

The land that awaited me, I knew, was one of turmoil, unrest and war. Much of its existence since independence in 1956 was defined by civil war in the south of the country. In recent years, the west too had erupted in violence as years of rivalries had coalesced into a rebellion by Darfur's tribes. This was the land hidden in the shadows beneath me.

In some ways, though, the darkness revealed the strands of history that formed modern Sudan. Like a photographic negative, the story of Sudan, its influences and its depths, were mapped out by the black swaths – the bits you couldn't see, rather than the bits you could. The rivers and the desert were what shaped the land and its people. Even its name comes from the Arabic, Bilad al-Sudan, or "land of the blacks", the derogatory name once applied by Muslim geographers to a swath running from the Red Sea to the Atlantic.

Humans have lived here from the time of the Stone Age, settling around the Nile in the northern part of modern Sudan and opening trade routes with Egypt. The relationship would define much of Sudan's early history, as the pharaohs increased their influence over the area that would come to be known as Nubia. The two countries became interdependent, as each developed hand in hand, shaping the other's art, culture and religious life. The Sudanese are still proud of the fact that their country has more pyramids than the more famous tourist attraction of Egypt. The influence would dwindle over time, but modern Sudan's history remains heavily dependent on that of its northern neighbour.

The country we now know as Sudan was formed in the early part of the nineteenth century. Egypt was then a province of the Ottoman Empire and its governor, Mohammed Ali, looked to the south for slaves and minerals. His well-trained troops had little trouble taking control of Sudan for the Ottomans, but the reign of the Turkiya, as they were known, was characterised by brutality. The result was decades of simmering unrest, which came to a head in the 1880s with a nationalist revolt led by Mohammed Ahmed bin Abdallah, a humble boatbuilder's son who proclaimed himself the long-awaited Mahdi or messiah. The Mahdi's army captured Khartoum in 1885, killing the British hero, General Charles George

Gordon. A decade later, British forces retook the city, and established an Anglo-Egyptian condominium over Sudan, run jointly by the two powers. The country's western boundary was not fixed until 1916, when the independent sultanate of Darfur was annexed after its leader declared loyalty to the Ottoman Empire during the First World War.

Rapid economic development arrived with the British. Railways and the telegraph were extended. Cotton was grown for Britain's textile industry and dams were used to expand the area under irrigation. But not everyone benefited. North and South were administered as separate states. The South was seen as a backward region, best closed off to develop at its own pace. So while a small Northern elite was being given the chance to ready itself for power, with the colonial government increasingly governing through indirect rule, the south remained isolated and under-developed.

When independence arrived in 1956, the seeds of civil war had already been sown. Southerners, a mix of Christians and people with traditional, animist beliefs, feared independent Sudan would be dominated by Muslim Northerners, whose political elite had strong ties to Egypt. The result was a civil war that festered until 1972, before reigniting a decade later. Independent Sudan has always been a country at war with itself. The conflicts have consumed resources and lives, hampered development and contributed to political turmoil at the centre, dominated by coups, counter-coups and leaders prepared to change ideologies rather than release their grip on power.

In 1969, Colonel Jaafer Nimeiri led a group of army officers to power and immediately began nationalising industries according to a mix of socialist and pan-Arab policies. He remained in power until 1985, by which time he had forged an alliance with the Muslim Brotherhood and given up his leftist programmes for an Islamist agenda. He imposed Sharia law on the country, further alienating southerners who did not share the religion of the North. Inevitably, his reign ended with a coup, followed by elections and three years of coalitions, a worsening economic climate and continuing war in the South.

The country I was now arriving in had been governed since 1989 by President Omar al-Bashir, another army officer who had seized power in a coup. Like a later model Nimeri, he used Islam as the glue to bond his country – the biggest by area in Africa – during the fight against southern rebels, and was pouring oil revenues into the struggle.

The lights below me were an indication that this wasn't the poorest country I had visited in Africa. The black holes in between were a reminder that the wealth was concentrated in a few hands.

1. EMPIRE OF SAND

The horse was not much to look at. The ten-year-old dappled mare was podgy and well past her racing prime. Riyah spent her days in the shade of a dusty stable on the outskirts of Khartoum. Goats nibbled at shoots of grass sprouting through the sand beneath her hooves and a camel spat at strangers who strayed too close. The place was modest – a jumble of wire fencing and a thatched roof to keep off the blistering sun – but Riyah had once commanded the attentions of the world's most wanted man. For Riyah, which means "the wind" in Arabic, used to be the favoured plaything of Osama bin Laden. When he took time off from milking the profits of his African construction firms or building a global network of fanatics from his base in the Sudanese capital, he loved nothing more than a day at the races or riding off into the desert sands on Riyah's back.

She was a sorry sight by the time I ran my hand through her silvery mane. And the friend who had promised to care for the horse when Bin Laden left Sudan had had enough of her. To Issam al-Turabi she was a mongrel, and he was getting sick of feeding and caring for his old friend's horse. She was practically worthless, the result of a breeding experiment, and a dud on the track. The skittish mare was used to only a little exercise, the occasional trot at a nearby riding school.

"When he first met me at the races – he knew my father, of course – he asked me to buy him some good, well-bred horses, so I bought him some thoroughbreds. But then he started bringing Arabians to breed with these Sudanese thoroughbreds. So this horse," said Issam, pointing to Riyah, "is a distorted breed."

1

The son of Sudan's foremost Islamic scholar – the man reckoned to be the power behind the throne and credited with turning the country into a pariah state as it lurched towards Islamic extremism – and the terrorist struck up a friendship based on their mutual passion for horses. They would go to the Khartoum races together on a Friday, cheering on Bin Laden's stable of horses or picking out potential studs from the field. This was strictly good, clean fun, however. There would be no betting and occasionally Bin Laden would put his fingers in his ears when music played over the loudspeakers. At other times he would walk away from the sound, which he considered "haram", or banned, by Islam. In the evenings, they would walk for hours unrecognised through the city's sand-filled streets, exercising their horses.

Bin Laden was long gone by 2005 and my first visit to Sudan. He had been expelled in 1996 by a government under intense pressure from the US. The world was just starting to get wind of the Yemen-born millionaire's global jihad. Two years later terror cells linked to Al Qaeda would bomb American embassies in Kenya and Tanzania. Worse was to come in New York. Yet his old pal said he found it difficult to reconcile the tall, gentle, quiet man he took to the races with the architect of 9/11.

"At the time I knew him, he was just a wealthy Saudi man and a good Muslim," said Issam. "It all changed when he was thrown out of here. If he had been left here, I think he would have just got old and fat and not been any trouble."

I doubted that, but thanked Issam all the same. Finding Riyah had given me something of a thrill. Running my hand along her flabby neck, it was possible to imagine a time when Bin Laden was virtually unknown, discussing form and weight at the racecourse. At the same time, Riyah was a stark reminder of the friends Khartoum once kept. Along with Bin Laden's old home – still dotted with bullet holes – and the roads his companies built, there was no forgetting the regime's dalliance with evil. Much of the government was the same as when Bin Laden had strolled the sand-fringed streets with his horse. Only Issam's father, its ideological guide, Hassan al-Turabi, had fallen from favour.

The sun was beginning to dip below the horizon by the time we began the short drive back to the city centre from the suburb of Manshiya, beside the Blue Nile, where Riyah was stabled. Al Siir Sabil Nasr, my driver and fixer, had become less talkative as the afternoon passed. Now he was intent on the road ahead. It wasn't often he hurried anywhere, but as we headed for my hotel in downtown Khartoum the speed of his battered yellow taxi increased alarmingly. Over the next few years, as Al Siir and I became friends, I would learn to read him better. He would display a very Arab, very humbling, hospitality, treating me to fish breakfasts beside a dried-up canal in Omdurman, or spicy fried chicken lunches with mounds of rocket and a bowl of chilli dipping sauce. In turn, I would speak with his boss if he needed time off, visit his relatives in hospital and once help haul his car from a hole on a construction site. He got me out of scrapes – and sometimes into them. We would have blazing rows and then make up like an old married couple. But this was my first trip and I was still to work out the intricacies of Sudanese life, and the best way to get along with Al Siir.

"There's no rush," I said confidently.

"It is Ramadan, Mr Rob," came the reply. "I must break my fast. Please understand."

The clock was ticking towards 6:30pm and I realised the streets were almost empty. The only other cars around were driving just as fast as Al Siir's decrepit Toyota. Everyone else was already home preparing for darkness to fall and the chance to end their fast. It was a stupid first timer's mistake. I had kept Al Siir out far too long. At least we were only a block from the street of my dingy hotel. Al Siir put his foot to the floor as we raced towards a set of traffic lights, which were just turning red.

"Al Siir, those lights are . . ." was all I managed before I was cut off by the squealing of brakes, the smell of rubber and then, finally, the inevitable crunch.

One of Khartoum's tiny minibus taxis – known as amjads – was by now buried deep into the wing of Al Siir's taxi. Its driver was screaming abuse at Al Siir who, in turn, was pouring forth a stream of spittle-garnished Arabic consonants.

3

Al Siir turned to me and lowered his voice to a pleasant tone: "It is OK, Mr Rob. He is saying he is very sorry, it is his mistake and he will take care of it. There is no problem."

I had my doubts, but there was little to add to the discussion. I quietly took my leave of the scene. The day had brought the first of many lessons. Khartoum worked to a foreign timescale. I was still in Africa, but this was an Islamic, Arab city which marched to the beat of the Muezzin's call rather than the tick of a clock. People rose with the early morning call to prayer and in Ramadan sat down to eat when the sun slipped beneath the horizon, just as they did across the Middle East.

The fact that Khartoum was Africa and Arabia rolled into one didn't seem to matter much in this sophisticated city. But elsewhere the differences between Arabs and Africans – real or imagined – had killed thousands.

* * *

Khartoum is a city of sand. Golden Saharan sand edges every street. Fine grey dust blows in on each breeze. Piles of red builders' sand lie beside long-since abandoned construction sites, sending unwary pedestrians sprawling. The stuff is everywhere, in every room, in every shoe, coating every surface. It gets between teeth and up noses. In the rains it turns thick and sticky, but never washes away. During the haboob season, great desert storms roll in, dumping their dusty cargo on a city that long ago gave up any fight against the sand. Khartoum's sandy suburbs stretch in all directions, eventually merging with the desert. It is every bit as much the city built on sand as the city beside the Nile, the point where the waters of the Blue Nile and White Nile mingle before raging on to the north.

The heart of the city beats beside the confluence of the two mighty rivers. Everything else takes its bearing from here. To the north-west is the old capital, Omdurman, with its souks, crowded alleys and ivory workshops. Its bazaars are crammed with obscure treasures: black Bakelite telephones and colonial swords are piled beside pots of leopard claws or baby crocodile skins fashioned into ashtrays.

To the north is one of Khartoum's suburbs, where the sprawl of the city has grown into the more spacious district Bahri or – in more prosaic terms – Khartoum North. But the real city, Khartoum proper, nestles right at the bond between the Blue and White Niles (which may have been rather better named the Brown Nile and the Greyish Brown Nile, such is their murky appearance).

It was here that an old fishing village expanded rapidly in the first half of the nineteenth century, as boats of ivory hunters and slave traders passed through looking for booty. Cargoes of textiles arrived from Egypt and gum Arabic in caravans from Darfur. Khartoum became a bustling frontier crossroads. The riverbanks were still shaded by palms and crocodiles lurked in the shallows, but its position, shielded on two sides by wide stretches of water, made it an ideal location to defend. So when British forces arrived in the 1880s to put down a rebellion that threatened the hold of its Turco-Egyptian proxies over Sudan, this was where they hunkered down.

Charles Gordon's forces faced the devout army of the Mahdi, a long awaited saviour who promised to reform Islam and repel the colonists. London expected Gordon to evacuate the city. Instead he attempted to hold Khartoum against the uprising, digging a trench and building walls to defend the open stretch between the two rivers. The Mahdi sat tight waiting for the river levels to fall. Eventually he pounced, prompted by the approach of a British relief column. The city was levelled in waves of looting and destruction. General Gordon reputedly died on the steps of the governor's palace, overlooking the Blue Nile.

Modern Khartoum grew from the ashes with the return of an avenging British army in 1898. The conquerors immediately placed their mark on the city as it was rebuilt in a series of inter-locking Union Flags. One theory has it that the imposing new metro-polis was designed as a symbol of British dominance. Or that the arrangement of cross roads and diagonals may have been easier for a single machine gun position to defend. Some of the original layout can still be seen in the grid of streets intersected here and there by diagonal roads in clumsy, confused six-way junctions. Elsewhere it has disappeared beneath modern blocks of soulless sand-coloured government offices. Roads have been widened to ease congestion – although with little effect. Cars cram every junction in a cacophony of blaring horns. Here and there the sleek shiny glass of new hotels catering to business travellers catches the light, reflecting the sun on to the hordes below. They share the skyline with hundreds of minarets. This is a claustrophobic place, full of noise and chaos.

It is only along the rivers' edges that the hectic pace fades. Here stand the whitewashed walls of the Republican Palace, seat of President Omar al-Bashir, and where the governor's residence once looked across the water. Palm trees shade the pavement. Strollers can watch wooden-hulled boats flit across the water just as they have done for centuries. It feels cooler here.

Everywhere else there is only the dry heat of the desert – and Al Siir's little car had no air-conditioning. We drove around with the windows open, but it was like sitting in front of a hairdryer. There was no cooling breeze as we motored around town on my first day, only a hot torrent of air, tightening the skin on our faces as the hours wore on. That was the least of my worries, though. There were no seatbelts. The handbrake had long since packed up, and it was difficult to tell if there was more than one gear. Yet, somehow, the rickety Corolla wouldn't give up. Speed was out of the question, of course, and we would trundle around the city's new roads in second gear, infuriating drivers of big, white 4x4s with blacked-out windows and gleaming saloons – the visible signs of a growing middle class getting rich on oil money.

I was to take many of these tours with Al Siir and we always found ourselves struggling with the combined, hypnotic effect of hunger and heat. Afternoons slowed. All the hustle and bustle of Khartoum life ebbed. Shops shut and streets emptied. We should have been strolling by the river or seeking out the shade of the city centre's colonnaded pavements. Not arranging appointments and office hopping. Everyone else was adapting to the heat. Where there would normally be men sitting on stools, sipping thimble-sized glasses of sweet tea spiced with ginger and discussing events of the day, there were instead just men sitting on stools, staring into space.

Only the police seemed to be going about their work as usual. Every bridge had a guard post with a couple of officers and a machine gun on the roof of a pickup. Each corner in the down-town area around my hotel had a gleaming new car marked "tourist police". It felt good to be in Khartoum at last. For a year I had pottered back and forth to the Sudanese embassy in Nairobi enquiring as politely as I could whether my visa was ready for collection. For a year the pleasant lady in the visa office said she was still awaiting approval from Khartoum. The press attaché apologised repeatedly for the delay. Ever since arriving in Kenya in 2004 I'd been itching to travel to Darfur. By this time the conflict – or its latest reincarnation – was a year old. Journalists from all around the world were riding with the Janjaweed, interviewing rebels and flying in United Nations helicopters. They were telling their readers or viewers about a terrible genocide unfolding in Sudan's western region. They reported on exotic-sounding Arabs who swept through villages on horseback, slaughtering poor African tribesmen who were trying to eke a living from their dust-filled fields. Thousands of refugees had fled across the border to Chad, while those left behind were crammed into miserable aid camps. It was my job to be there to see it for myself. But without a visa I couldn't get in.

Precisely twelve months after applying I received a phone call from the press attaché asking me to submit a fresh application. "Don't worry Curly, this time it will be approved," she said mysteriously, not even adding the customary insh'Allah – God willing. Sure enough, within days I had my visa.

But arriving in Khartoum was just the start of the journey to Darfur. Any foreigner has to first register with the Police Department of Aliens, a drab building with a sun-drenched courtyard surrounded by piles of sand. Chinese construction workers loitered by a couple of broken plastic seats as their fixers scurried around sorting out paperwork.

Al Siir and I had had a couple of false starts. The building had apparently moved since the last time Al Siir had visited. Then we had to find a photocopier so I could supply a copy of my passport and visa, freshly stamped at the airport. It was the sort of tedious

7

bureaucratic hurdle that would become routine in Khartoum. Everything seemed to take twice as long as expected. Al Siir and I had already begun to fall into a pattern that we'd repeat many times as I returned again and again to the city. Exasperation with his inability to find our intended destination soon turned to relief as he disappeared into a dark back office to find a friend who could hurry through the process.

The Chinese workers – perhaps building one of the new bridges across the Nile or engineers working in Sudan's booming oil industry – showed no signs of moving from their seats. From the crowds of fixers waving passports and forms at the counter in front of them it looked like they were in for a long wait. Al Siir was back within five minutes waving my passport, now bearing a little blue sticker.

"You see Mr Rob, Al Siir has friends everywhere," he said, grinning proudly as we set off for his car and the next stop en route to Darfur.

This funny man, with a stiff-legged walk and bald head, had come highly recommended. His English was good and he seemed to know almost everyone worth knowing – government officials, dissidents and rebel leaders were all in his contacts book. Occasionally we would have our differences. There were times when he would lead me into offices for interviews with people I had never heard of, much less requested a meeting with. He had a certain way of doing things and it wasn't to everyone's taste, but soon we established our working relationship: I did as I was told and kept the crisp $100 bills coming.

After the Department of Aliens came the Department of Foreign Correspondents and Journalists. Its entrance was gloomy and easy to miss in an anonymous downtown block. Bare wires hung from the ceiling and a smell of urine wafted through the hallway. Water dripped down the steps as we made our way up to the second floor. A doorway, the entrance to an office, stood open. A man was asleep at his empty desk, his head resting on his hands. Journalists and aid workers in Sudan were constantly worried about the threat of phone calls being intercepted, emails read and dispatches scrutinised. I wasn't sure there was much to fear.

The office I needed was housed at the end of the corridor. This looked an altogether smarter affair. The lights worked, the armchairs were leather and air-conditioning units hummed busily.

Now came the tricky part of obtaining permission to work as a journalist – filling in the "Purpose of Visit" section on my application for a press permit for Darfur. I could lie outright, pretending to be covering a trade conference or writing a travel piece. Not that anyone would believe I was there reporting on anything but the war. But how to phrase "reporting on genocide" in a way that would be acceptable to the very regime responsible? It would be a difficult subject to broach, but a fellow journalist in Nairobi, a frequent visitor to this office, said it would be straightforward. Just say you are going to report on the humanitarian situation, he said.

A stern looking woman, swathed in scarves, was looking me up and down. "Yes, Mr Andrew said you would be coming," she said from behind her desk, where she fiddled with a mobile phone. "He is a very funny man. Very funny, makes us all laugh all the time."

She looked at me expectantly. I couldn't shake the feeling I was missing something.

Tea was fetched as we began chatting about Khartoum, the weather and my friend – anything other than Darfur. More forms arrived to be filled in. I handed over five photographs and eighty dollars and was asked to wait. There was more tea and chat and, eventually, a freshly laminated press card arrived. The travel permit, it seemed, would take more time. No-one seemed very sure exactly how much time. Four days was mentioned, but this seemed to be nothing other than the best time to check back in with the officials. The waiting would always be the worst bit. With a notebook full of ideas, the last thing any journalist wanted to do was kick their heels in hot, dusty and expensive Khartoum.

Over the years the waiting would get easier. It would become a chance to hang out with friends, talk to diplomats and aid workers or work on features. Only once did I ever lose my cool. On that occasion I had been waiting three weeks in Khartoum in the hope that my travel permit might materialise. Each day Al Siir and I made our way to the second floor office and each day one of the assistants, Mohammed, told us, "Tomorrow, insh'Allah."

Eventually, I could take it no more. Every day was costing me a couple of hundred dollars and resources were running low. I snapped.

"What do you mean tomorrow, insh'Allah? You tell us this every day. What is it with Allah? I'm waiting for a human being to stamp my form and you tell me it will happen insh'Allah," I said, the decibels rising as a theme started to develop. "Don't you think Allah has better things to do with his time than oversee the application process for a foreign journalist?"

It was not a clever thing to say. Immediately Mohammed's face clouded. I didn't need to look at Al Siir to know that he was staring at me, shocked. I'd crossed any number of boundaries. There is never any need to be rude to officials who are simply doing their job. I was questioning Mohammed's desire to help me, in a country where hospitality is the measure of a man. That would have been offence enough. But to question his appeal to Allah was crass and the height of Western hubris. And for good measure I had alienated someone I would have to deal with every time I returned to Khartoum.

The travel permit never materialised. It turned out a young British journalist had failed to register with the authorities when she arrived in one of Darfur's regional capitals before flying straight into a disputed area. She was arrested and questioned on her return, then kicked out of the country. For the time being, all journalist travel requests were being turned down. It was not Mohammed's fault – or Allah's for that matter. Each application would pass through half a dozen other government departments for approval. National Security was the only one that really mattered. A fresh government offensive in Darfur, rebel gains or another journalist overstepping the mark would mean applications could simply disappear. A flat rejection would have been considered rude. Mohammed had been displaying excellent manners with his assurances of "Tomorrow, insh'Allah."

That first day had been a long and tedious one of form filling, waiting for officials to be free and the constant nagging feeling that best laid plans were going astray. As a freelancer, every day that I sat and waited was a day without earning. The trick was to have a couple of features up my sleeve that would keep the cash rolling in. One idea had been to track down Bin Laden's horse, a tale which earned me enough to make the effort of finding Riyah well worthwhile – even if one newspaper turned down the story when I couldn't get hold of photographs showing the Al Qaeda leader on horseback. Another idea materialised as Al Siir and I puttered around the streets of Manshiya trying to find the stables.

In the distance, spanning the waters of the mighty Blue Nile, stood Khartoum's newest bridge. It would be a matter of some hooplah when President Omar al-Bashir opened the span a year or so after my visit. Bridges were crucial to the city's functioning as cars sped between Khartoum proper, the historic capital of Omdurman standing on the far side of the White Nile, and Khartoum North, an expanding suburb across the Blue Nile. The new Manshiya Bridge was the latest in a rash of construction projects designed to ease transport flows in a chronically congested city. Yet the flag fluttering from its highest point was not the familiar red, white, black and green of Sudan: it was the red of China.

"The Chinese are here and we are very pleased," said Al Siir as we gazed across the water at the graceful arc of the bridge's steel frame. "It is all around us. It is good for business for all of us."

So it seemed. The dragon economy was never far away in Khartoum. There were the contractors waiting to register as aliens, minibuses covered in Mandarin script whizzing through the busy streets, and Sichuan and Cantonese restaurants were springing up across town. To the north, Chinese engineers were damming the Nile with a \$2bn hydropower project that would, it was said, eventually double the country's electricity supply.

China's arrival was part of a continental pattern. At the turn of the millennium, China had launched itself on a grand African adventure, drilling for oil, digging mines, building bridges and selling plastic nick-nacks from Mauritania to Mauritius. Underlying

China's interest was the scramble for Africa's resources, needed to fuel the rapidly expanding Chinese economy. In Sudan, of course, that meant oil. From a standing start in 1999 the country had grown to be sub-Saharan Africa's third biggest producer. Its 450,000 or so barrels a day may be dwarfed by production from Libya and Nigeria, but were still enough for the Chinese to invest heavily, keeping one eye on total reserves estimated at six billion barrels. As much as eighty percent of Sudanese production was being shipped to China. In return, Chinese engineers were building dams, roads and refineries – much of it paid for with oil profits or loans from China.

Sudan's oil cash had also brought a flood of investors from the Gulf States. The smart offices of the oil companies along the Nile – their walls of glass and brushed metal taking on the colour of the sky in a striking change from Khartoum's overwhelming dusty beige – were now being joined by fancy hotels and chic coffee shops. The smell of money was everywhere in an economy that had grown in spurts of up to nine percent in recent years, according to official figures which were probably a shade exaggerated. On later visits I'd sip cappuccinos in the city's first 5-star hotel. A second, built with Libyan cash, opened on the banks of the Nile not long after. "Executive" homes were springing up in neat new neighbourhoods. The government was fond of pointing out that investment had quadrupled in a decade that coincided with the flow of oil. There were still beggars on street corners and poverty lurked in every back alley, but Khartoum's new city all seemed a long way from the misery of Darfur. The investors did not seem to be put off by American sanctions or the prospect of further international intervention. They had no doubt factored the risk into their margins. Materials were more expensive and sometimes took longer to arrive, but the returns in a country still hugely underdeveloped made it all worthwhile, they told me. Darfur was barely mentioned at investment fairs held in the vast Friendship Hall (built with Chinese cash, naturally) next to the Nile. Businessmen from Saudi Arabia, Qatar and the United Arab Emirates looked at models of the new Khartoum – all skyscrapers, golf courses and smiling residents – and slick video presentations, before writing large cheques. Most seemed to think Darfur was a long way from Khartoum.

"We have the problem of Darfur and to some extent it has affected direct investment," said Eltegani Ahmed, an adviser to the Ministry of Finance. "But I feel we are close to finding a solution and this is reflected by the foreign investors coming here."

Economists warned me that Khartoum's boom rested on shaky foundations. The country's economy was still one based largely on agriculture and the oil money would not go far in such a vast country. Investors had arrived from the Gulf States in years when oil prices hit record highs and they needed a new destination for their cash. They would likely leave when times got tough. The oil itself would not last long and the reserves had probably been overestimated. And the composition of much Sudanese oil made it difficult and expensive to refine. Then there was the added complication that the government was in the North and most of the oil was in the South, one of the factors in the twenty-year civil war that had been ended with a peace deal months before my first visit. None of that really seemed to matter for the time being though, as a gleaming new city grew beside the Nile.

If the mobile phone masts stretching into the sky represented a new, cash-rich facet of the city, the minarets stretching to heaven represented another. The worship of dollars still lagged far behind the worship of the Prophet. Alcohol was banned, women who failed to cover their heads were flogged and contact between unmarried couples was restricted. Much of expat life revolved around finding a drink. Anyone with a friend at one of the embassies or in the United Nations could rely on regular shipments. Anyone else had to rely on all sorts of tricks. There was only one rule: don't talk about it.

The most civilised way to enjoy a beer was to frequent one of the restaurants that had perfected the sly art of serving foreigners. Waiters at one place would quietly ask whether any Sudanese would be joining the table. If not, an empty bottle of non-alcoholic Becks would be placed on the table along with an overpriced glass of the real thing. A police officer casting an eye over proceedings would assume all was in order. Another place operated a "bring your own" policy, whisking away bottles of wine from customers' bags and returning with a filled jug. But my favourite trick was also the most nerve-wracking.

It had been a long day writing for *The Irish Times*, covering the visit of Dermot Ahern, the Irish foreign minister. He had arrived with a small press pack from Dublin, who were understandably in need of some refreshment by the time evening wore around. Khartoum being my patch, I assured them I knew exactly where to go. Friends had told me about another restaurant with a cunning subterfuge. You just had to know what to ask for, apparently. The six or so of us sat down at the table and all eyes turned to me. I called the waiter over and did as instructed.

"We'd like a pot of your special tea," I said confidently.

"I beg your pardon?"

"Erm, a pot of your special tea please."

Confidence was draining from my body. Had I been the victim of a terrible practical joke? Were the police even now on their way to detain a stupid khawaja, the local word for a foreigner? I shifted nervously in my seat as my new friends tried not to catch my eye. It was difficult to tell who was more embarrassed.

After an awkward interlude the waiter returned with a teapot filled to the brim with Tusker, a watery Kenyan lager. It was far from ice cold. And it cost about $10 a pint when served in a teapot, but it went down pretty well nevertheless.

The alcohol stopped flowing after my first few visits. The police either got wise or stopped turning a blind eye. For the most part, though, Sharia law rarely seemed to interfere with expat life. Bacon had to be smuggled in and greetings in public had to be limited to a stiff handshake rather than a kiss (Mai, the bubbly assistant at the Department of Foreign Correspondents and Journalists, even stopped shaking my hand after a while, as part of her plan to become a better Muslim and find a husband), but Sharia law was, by and large, for Muslims. Khawaja women were not expected to wear the veil. The only rule was to behave in a way that would not

14

cause offence. Most Sudanese were far from extreme in their Islam, though most took a conservative view of personal morality.

Driving with Al Siir on that first visit we passed a pasty-looking female pedestrian. She was wearing a long skirt that trailed on the ground and nothing but a low cut vest on her top. Her arms were completely bare and there was a generous flash of cleavage as we both craned our necks to stare.

Al Siir could barely contain his disgust as he slowed the car to a crawl and asked between clenched teeth: "This is how women dress where you come from?"

* * *

If there was one way to get to the heart of Khartoum's flirtation with Islamic extremism, it was to meet the man who did more than anything to define Sudan's reputation as a haven for terrorists. Hassan al-Turabi, father of Issam the racing enthusiast, had once been the ideological guide behind the throne. He was the hardline theologian who kept the government of Omar al-Bashir pure. Most analysts regarded him as the man who controlled the army officer's strings, and the de facto leader of the government as it institutionalised Sharia law and turned the world against Sudan. By the time I met him, Turabi had fallen out of favour. He had been in and out of prison for years and placed under house arrest from time to time. Frankly, I was unsure what to expect as Al Siir and I turned up at the door of his whitewashed villa in Riyadh, one of Khartoum's confusing array of suburbs that all looked the same – wide roads and tall walls hiding spacious houses.

What I found was a warm and engaging figure full of grandfatherly charm. Rather than a cardigan, he wore a traditional jalabiya and a white turban wrapped loosely around his head. His feet sported a pair of slippers with a leopard skin print. Members of his political party were just leaving as we settled down in his sitting room. It was a struggle to remember the long list of crimes attributed to his time in power.

"Ah Crilly, this is an unusual name. This is not English, I think," he said with a giggle. Mango juice and bottles of ice-cold water were offered around as he chit-chatted about this and that, the weather and the British fondness for tea – shared by the Sudanese. It was a struggle to slot the first question between his rapid words, punctuated with more giggles. Eventually, though, he launched into a broad ranging discussion that took us through Sudanese history, the Irish Question and his love of prison life. The twinkle in his eyes disappeared only when we reached Bin Laden's stay in Khartoum.

"I personally did not invite him," he said, a brief flash of irritation disappearing in more giggles. "I didn't know he was here. He was from a Saudi building company. In those days Saudis could come without visa. We welcomed them because they had a lot of money. He came here and started building roads and investing in farming. He was a very quiet person. He was not in the papers and didn't appear at political rallies. He just stayed at home with his wives . . . plural."

More giggles. This was the official version of the Bin Laden story. I had heard the same from government ministers and Turabi's son. In it, the Saudi Sheikh, as they like to call him, was nothing other than a businessman investing in Sudan. His Al Hijira construction company was responsible for building a modern highway from Khartoum to Port Sudan on the Red Sea Coast. And he had interests in thousands of acres of sorghum, gum Arabic and sesame. If he turned to violence it was only after he had been asked to leave the country by a government acting under intense American pressure. So runs the Sudanese version. The Americans had funded the Sheikh for years in his anti-Soviet struggle in Afghanistan and then created a terrorist by chasing him around the globe. The man who lived in Sudan was a quiet, studious Muslim. Pious, maybe, but not a terrorist.

"It wasn't my idea for him to leave. He should have stayed. It would have been better for us – we would have more roads," said Turabi, with more giggles as he enjoyed his own joke.

Turabi's mental gymnastics were typical of a man who had

made countless twists and turns in pursuit of power. Principles regularly came and went. Acolytes were cultivated then ditched. He was the radical ideologue who eventually declared women need not wear the veil; the Islamist who opposed the fatwa against Salman Rushdie. His highly educated, tactically astute mind allowed him to reinterpret Islamic teachings to his own advantage, apparently at will. There was only ever one end in sight, an Islamic state, but how to get there was a route apparently open to a considerable degree of flexibility. He spoke perfect English – the result of studying law at the London School of Economics, followed, incidentally, by a PhD at the Sorbonne – but you could never be sure quite what he meant or where his quixotic mind was headed. His inner thoughts and his place in Bashir's regime through the 1990s remained opaque.

In 1989 Omar al-Bashir, a brigadier in the army, led a small band of officers to power in a bloodless coup that ended one of Sudan's brief experiments in democracy. Turabi needed Bashir for his influence over the military and as a figurehead to convince Egypt and Saudi Arabia that the new government was anything but an Islamic takeover. At the same time, Bashir needed Turabi's political nous and spiritual leadership. Once in power the conspirators immediately set up a Revolutionary Command Council to give the new regime secular colours, and Bashir ordered the arrest of Turabi, leader of the National Islamic Front (NIF). The deception was complete. By day Turabi read his Koran, but by night he slipped out of Cooper Prison – the high-walled British-built jail that acted as a graduate school for many of Sudan's political elite – to attend meetings of the new regime. For months the pretence continued. Turabi, along with another key figure, Ali Osman Mohammed Taha, was released into house arrest where he continued to shape policy. For a man of his intellect and ego, this stint away from the limelight could not have been a happy time.

Eventually he could resist no more. Turabi came out of the shadows in 1990 to declare Sudan's support for Iraq's invasion of Kuwait. The following years marked the country's transformation into a pariah state. In theory, his Popular Arab and Islamic

17

Conference was part of an attempt to reconcile Sunnis and Shias, uniting Islam and developing an alternative world order to the American-led version. In practice, it hosted Islamic radicals and terrorists. The Palestinian Liberation Order, Hamas and Egyptian Islamic Jihad were among the groups hosted by Turabi. Foreign fighters flocked to Bin Laden's training camps. This was also the time when Carlos the Jackal, the Marxist terrorist and one of the world's most wanted men, lived in Khartoum before eventually being handed over to France.

Yet still Turabi insisted Sudan was not a terrorist proving ground, but rather a friendly Muslim nation looking after its brothers.

"They were not terrorists. Most of them were post-Afghan people, some of their countries refused to receive them back. So, some of them came to Sudan because they thought they could get a job here. Some of them were doctors, so they could get work in any place, actually."

There were more giggles and I was momentarily wrong-footed. Was he making a jokey reference to Ayman al-Zawahiri, once the leader of Egyptian Islamic Jihad. He had been in Sudan during the Bin Laden years. Today he is better known as one of Al Qaeda's senior lieutenants. He is also a surgeon.

I tried to catch Al Siir's eye, but he was fixed on Turabi. He certainly would have known his words were lies. In 1993 he had tracked down the office of Islamic Jihad, a place that many diplomats suspected existed but no-one had ever seen. He had even toured one of the Jihad camps in the desert outside Khartoum where young Sudanese men were given forty-five days of basic military training and a dose of religious fervour. He had needed official permission to visit and there was no evidence of the Al Qaeda instructors that the outside world feared were radicalising a generation of Sudanese. But there was still enough evidence to conclude that Islam and the gun were being taught as the solution to Sudan's problems.

Those were Turabi's glory days. Fellow ideological travellers arrived from around the world to sign up to his alternative world order. By the time I met him, Turabi was out of power and his influence seemed shot. He had fallen out with Bashir as the result of an internal power struggle within their National Congress Party. The army general had offered his mentor's head up to the West as evidence that Sudan had ended its flirtation with extremism. He had been in and out of prison again, between further periods of house arrest. But now the government of his old ally seemed content to allow visiting journalists to pitch up at his stucco and brick mansion and spend a couple of hours chewing the fat with a man who once controlled every aspect of political life. They clearly thought he was no longer a danger.

No-one knew where the bodies were buried better than Turabi. And no-one understood the government and its actions in Darfur better either. To understand Khartoum's actions and its drastic counter-insurgency actions, he explained, it was important to understand the background and instincts of the man he once put at its head.

"The government is a military government. Omar al-Bashir is still in uniform, so he thinks that anyone who resists must face disciplinary action, but he cannot fight the Darfuri people because his army is mostly from Darfur. So he started attracting the nomads from there, arming them with tragic consequences."

Darfur is not just a marginalised patch of desert on the edge of the country, he continued. To Khartoum, all the country is a patch of desert on the edge of the country. It had already allowed southern rebels the option of independence as part of a peace deal to end two decades of civil war. Rebels in the east were agitating. No-one wanted to see Darfur going down the same road towards greater autonomy or there would be little left of Sudan. Darfur, with its cattle and camels, was actually a vital part of the country's economy. Without it, the new city growing beside the Nile would lose a chunk of its economic foundations. Khartoum – with its fancy hotels, expensive coffee shops and smart malls – was looking more and more like a city state at the heart of a crumbling order. Sudan was not so much a country, but an empire built on sand. Its leaders had one objective: to survive. That meant keeping their empire

19

functioning. In short, they governed as if they were under a constant state of siege. One tactic was to use Islam as the glue that bound their people together. Another was to divide the opposition using tribal lines or whatever else they could find. They had done it in Southern Sudan and they were doing it again in Darfur, said Turabi, a mischievous glint returning to his eye. The key was for the rebels to stick together as Darfuris, he added, and not get bogged down in details.

"We are close to them all and we tell them to come as one front with one paper, one set of demands: immediate settlement of the humanitarian problems with the refugees and the internally displaced persons (IDPs) and the crimes committed against them, and a transition to a share of power and wealth," he said, using the UN's term for people who are refugees in their own country.

The old Islamist was at it again. He was out of power and out of prison, but apparently still not finished. One of the rebel groups, the Justice and Equality Movement (JEM), was headed by Khalil Ibrahim, a doctor and one of Turabi's former protégés. He shared much of his teacher's Islamist ideology and had risen through the ranks of his Popular Congress Party. No-one could ever prove a direct, controlling link, but many of JEM's public pronouncements sounded as if they could have come from the man sitting in front of me. The government had long fingered Turabi as the brains behind the rebels, but the evidence was difficult to find. Turabi always denied anything other than a historical connection.

"The leader was a member of the same party as me. We broke away on this matter of federalism and the doctor thought there was no point in forming a party as it would be banned, so he took up arms instead."

Things would change in the years after my first visit to Khartoum. Turabi was arrested in the aftermath of a rebel attack on Khartoum as security forces tried to prove what everyone suspected: that Turabi was using Darfur to regain a toehold on power. That detention lasted a day. Then he was picked up again, this time in 2009, for suggesting that President Bashir should give himself up to the International Criminal Court to save Sudan from international isolation. There seemed little evidence that Turabi was directly manipulating the Darfur crisis. The only thing that had changed was the government's level of hysteria. The conflict was closing in on their power base in Khartoum – the rebels had reached the gates once and the international community seemed intent on arresting the president – and the empire of sand looked as if it could crumble. Turabi and other high-profile dissidents were obvious targets. Darfur, which had long been the secret to economic, political and military power, was not an irrelevant border zone.

* * *

First was the light, a blinding flash that confused and disoriented anyone within hundreds of metres. Next the thunderous roar of a cruise missile strike ripped through the industrial area of factories and workshops clustered on the edge of Khartoum North. Then came the dust, the flotsam and jetsam of what used to be a pharmaceutical factory. Finally, the air came alive with the sound of gunshots as police and soldiers fired into the sky, protecting against further attacks.

Ismail Idriss al Haj told his story from a bare room above a manufacturing works just across from the remains of the Al Shifa pharmaceutical plant. Today he is completing his national service. In 1998 he was finishing his schooling and lived in a hut next to the plant where his father worked as a watchman. On 20 August he did what he did everyday, perched himself on a small stool beside the road outside the Al Shifa works, talking with his father while they waited for dinner. He had no idea that Bill Clinton's Operation Infinite Reach was about to go into effect. It was directed against Al Qaeda assets following the deadly attacks on US embassies in Africa a few days earlier. More than 200 people died in Nairobi and eleven in Dar es Salaam when suicide bombers struck simultaneously.

The US needed a target and they found one in Al Shifa. It was believed to be processing VX nerve agent and to be linked to

Bin Laden. Thirteen Tomahawk missiles zeroed in on Khartoum at the same time as seventy-five missiles rained down on Al Qaeda training camps in Afghanistan. The redbrick wall of the plant protected Ismail from the blast.

"Five minutes earlier I had been inside but had just left, so it was as if Allah saved my life," he said, ten years later.

The ruins have barely been disturbed since the day the plant was bombed. Looters have tried to salvage roof tiles and twisted girders, but most of the wreckage remains. It is both a silent memorial to the one person who died and a useful propaganda tool for a government keen to remind the world of its victimhood at the hands of the US.

The creaking iron gate is open to anyone wanting to visit – mostly white men, journalists, said the plump wife of the site's guard. For a few crumpled Sudanese pound notes she pointed out what was left of America's military hardware: a small torpedo-shaped helium canister and a bent disc of metal. All around is the rubble. Broken tiles from the old shower block squeak and grate underfoot. A few blister packs of pills peek from beneath crushed brickwork. The plant's four-storey office block is still standing, but is nothing more than an empty shell. In the middle of the site, a twisted concrete roof is barely held aloft by bent pillars, their steel reinforcements sticking out like cracked ribs. Broken plastic bottles of children's paracetamol syrup that now hold only dust lie beside bottles labelled "ciprofloxacin" – an antibiotic of last resort.

The plant's owners and the Sudanese government denied any terrorist link. Western diplomats echoed their claims, saying the site was crucial for producing malaria medicine and drugs to fight tuberculosis. Over the years the evidence presented by American officials has dwindled, to the point where the Sudanese chairman of the plant saw his US-based assets unfrozen.

The site is a reminder of what happens to pariah states. Hosting Islamic terrorists and preparing the ground for a global Jihad is not the way to ensure a fair hearing. Khartoum may be guilty of many things, but Al Shifa was not one of its crimes. It was the people of Sudan who suffered as a result and it conveniently left a burning sense of injustice and victimhood that the Sudanese government can turn on at will.

"My father was a guard and had worked as a labourer even as it was being built. He knew all the rooms, all the places and never saw anything like that," said Ismail. "I don't understand why they would do this to us. The Americans must not like us."

2. DARFUR ON A DONKEY

The donkey was having a better day than its rider. For four hours we had climbed mountain passes, stumbled through dried-up river beds and picked a path across steep valley faces. Somewhere ahead my guide was steering his ride around rocky outcroppings and over tree trunks with ease. Even my rucksack and computer satchel strapped to the back of his makeshift saddle did little to throw him off course. It was a different matter behind, where a temperamental donkey and a tired journalist were locked in a one-sided battle of wills. The donkey had long since realised that a heavy stick wielded by an Englishman with a love of animals was unlikely to cause him any pain. He went where he wanted. So it was a jolting, neck-jarring trek as we struggled up into the mountains, occasionally slithering backwards in a cloud of dust as we picked the wrong path. Every bone from shoulders downwards was aching. Every joint had long since seized.

But then as the air cooled and the track rose higher something changed. My white donkey picked up his pace and passed the guide, Mohammed Abdul Wat, who tried to catch at his reins. My obstinate steed knew something I didn't – journey's end was in sight.

Before us lay the Jebel Mara, the heart of Darfur. It was the visual equivalent of a damp towel across the brow. Rows of trees thick with fruit were arranged in neat order – apple trees in an orchard stretching far into the distance, alongside an orange grove with tiny green fruit just starting to swell and ripen. A crystal clear stream rose from the rocks to one side. It probably even burbled as it disappeared into the terraced valley below, filling irrigation channels which then carried their glistening load into fields freshly planted with potatoes and onions. Villagers bent double between the rows straightened and waved as they realised visitors were arriving.

Something clicked. This picture of Darfur started to make sense of the war. This was not the Darfur that I'd seen on half a dozen previous trips, or watched on my television or discussed with humanitarian workers in Khartoum. That was a land of dust and heat and flies; where millions of people needed convoys of food trucks just to stay alive and where the sun dried every ounce of life from the soil. The Darfur stretching out in the valley before me and my truculent donkey might as well have been filled with milk and honey. A dense covering of trees rippled in a thousand shades of green as a breeze caught their leaves. It was a place where the sun's energy brought life to fertile, volcanic soil. As my mind took in the sights and sounds of this new Darfur, the region's miserable conflict became a little easier to understand. After the sandy wastes of North Darfur, the choking grey dust of West Darfur and South Darfur's yellow, empty plains, this land of plenty suddenly looked like a place worth fighting for.

Not that I had time to reflect on any of that, for with a turn of speed that resembled a tractor in low gear the donkey was off down the steep downward track that led into the village of Gorolang Baje. Children carrying empty plastic jerrycans on their way to the stream scattered screaming. Somewhere behind me Mohammed was roaring with laughter.

"Why are you going so fast?" he called after me, before laughing all over again. "The village is not going anywhere."

The donkey stopped only after barging his way through a flimsy wooden gate and burying his head in a juicy mound of hay piled on the ground in what appeared to be a stable-yard. Moments later Mohammed trotted into the dung-filled enclosure, swung his leg over the saddle in a single graceful movement and landed on the ground just beside me.

"This is the place of my brother," he said, his thick glasses now covered in fine dust accumulated during the journey. With a nod at my ride, he added: "He knew his way."

My dismount did not go unremarked among the crowd of children who had followed the wild donkey and its white rider into the village. I had to lean on Mohammed's shoulder as my aching body slithered out of the saddle and down to the ground amid shrieks of laughter. My hips and knees felt as if they had fused into solid lumps of bone, and it was all I could do to lower myself on to a reed mat. More laughter. I muttered something that I hoped was amusing about being a weak whiteman, and slept.

This was indeed journey's end. After the spectacular journey in, the town itself was not much to look at. Gorolang Baje was a one-car sort of town and the car was a broken-down pickup, its wheels replaced by bricks. It was the sort of town that is common all across Africa – a town that was in the process of being reclaimed by nature, with a post-apocalyptic feel. The brick-built houses along its main street were crumbling to dust. Where once trucks and cars might have laboured up and down its hills, donkeys and camels were now the only form of transport. What must at one time have been neat little shops and teahouses were now tatty and threadbare, selling little more than boxes of matches, tiny tablets of soap or packs of chewing gum lined up on wooden benches. And the newest homes had given up on new-fangled technologies, such as corrugated iron, in favour of thatch. It reminded me of towns in Somalia and the Democratic Republic of Congo where signs of development – the old Greek-run general stores, the Italian salt works or the railways – were gradually being eaten away by the jungle. A place where time seemed to be running backwards – and where you would not have been surprised to turn a corner and find the Statue of Liberty sticking out from the sand, a reminder of a lost civilisation, which had sunk back into Africa's wilderness.

Getting here had been half the adventure. In Nyala, the capital of South Darfur, I had managed to convince an aid worker to sign me on to one of the United Nations helicopter flights to the market of Feina, at the edge of the mountains. Heavy fighting a year earlier had forced most of the NGOs out of the Jebel Mara. An aid worker died during the evacuation when a helicopter crashed and few had dared to go back. The flights in and out were supposed to be for humanitarian staff, but with a bit of persuasion and plenty of reassurances that the government would be none the wiser, a friendly charity had smoothed my passage. Once in Feina it was a case of liaising with a permanently-drunk rebel commander and then finding a man with a donkey willing to guide me through the dried up wadis – stony riverbeds that fill with water once a year – and over rocky hills.

It could not have been a better introduction to the conflict in Darfur. As we clip-clopped our way along dry riverbeds, we passed destroyed village after destroyed village. Each looked the same. Piles of stones were all that were left of the houses. The thatch had been burned away leaving only a rubble-strewn battleground. Along our route there must have been a dozen ghost villages which were nothing more than stony fields. Boulders, rocks and pebbles that were once organised into walls had given up any purpose and sunk back down to the earth; the mango trees that would once have been prodded by children with long sticks trying to reach their fruit stood unpicked, their crop rotting on the ground.

Silence is rare in African villages. There is always a crowing cockerel, blaring radio or generator throbbing with noise to disturb the calm. In Sudan there is usually a gaggle of children on hand to shout khawaja at any white visitor. But these villages offered no noise to interrupt the gentle clip-clopping of the two donkeys.

Mohammed had a one-word explanation for each of the silent ruins. He simply pointed at each deserted, dead village and said: "Janjaweed." This was the handiwork of the feared Arab militias responsible for much of the violence in Darfur. Twice we stopped as planes flew overhead. They could have been Sudanese armed forces – lumbering old Antonov cargo planes used as unsophisticated bombers by soldiers opening the cargo doors and kicking out drums packed with explosives and wire – or they could have been United Nations planes. We couldn't tell. The Sudanese air force had begun to disguise their aircraft by painting them white, the same as aid agencies. There were constant reports of government planes overflying the Jebel Mara in acts of intimidation.

There were few travellers on the road that day. At first we passed children with their donkeys and cows going backwards and forwards to waterholes. The children sucked on mango stones and waved. Then, gradually, the people and the water dried up, as the land turned to rock and the villages turned to ruins. We passed one village that was still standing and stopped to pick up a handful of kisra – a thin, rubbery bread made from fermented sorghum with a sour, unappetising flavour. We handed our water bottles to a tough-looking woman who filled them from a murky well. But mostly it was just Mohammed, me and the donkeys inching into the hills.

The Jebel Mara massif stretches 3000 metres into the sky above the arid Darfur plains. The extinct volcano has a certain romance among the aid workers, journalists, analysts and activists who follow Darfur. As I was learning, it was not the easiest place to reach in Sudan, lending the tales of green valleys and orange groves something of a mystical aura. Even Darfuris tell stories of mythical creatures that live in the depths of its central crater lake. Then there is its history as a stronghold of the Fur tribe, who knew they could always rely on its life-giving volcanic soil for sustenance. In times of trouble their royal family would fall back into the mountain fortress confident they could see off rivals. Now those qualities – fresh springs, fertile soil and defendable heights – had made their traditional homeland a glittering prize in Darfur's desert war.

Today, it is no-go territory for the Sudanese government. The hills are a rebel redoubt, where the Fur, who make up one faction of the Sudan Liberation Army, organise their soldiers and protect their civilians. For journalists, it is a chance to get away from the government-controlled areas into a different part of Darfur; one where rebels are running the towns and villages and are responsible for trying to help displaced civilians. This was a place to try and answer some of the fundamental questions about Darfur: Who are the rebels? What are they fighting for? Are they any better than the government at delivering aid to people bombed from their homes? In short, are they the good guys?

Few journalists had ever made it in to the cradle of the rebellion. I wanted a Jebel Mara dateline more than anything else.

General Elsadig Elzein Rokero announced his presence by clearing his throat, looking slightly baffled by the stranger lying sprawled on the mat before him. His tall frame was dressed entirely in green and topped off with a scarf bound around his face and wrapped into a turban, in typical Darfuri style. His eyes, nose and half a moustache were all that were visible through the cloth, which kept out much of the dust and created a romantic air of mystique at the same time. The twin tools of his trade were obvious – a Thuraya satellite phone tucked in his breast pocket and a Vietnam-era submachine gun which hung at his side. These were pretty much all he needed to control his rebel army. This was the man I had come to meet, someone I hoped would help explain Darfur's conflict from the rebels' perspective and flesh out some of the reports floating around that they were picking up support from their former foes among the Arab tribes.

If this was true then it would undermine the guiding narrative of the conflict, one that had gained currency at the start of the war and been repeated parrot fashion by journalists, myself included. In short, the accepted view was that this was a conflict between the Arab nomads of Darfur and the settled, African farming tribes. It had started in 2003 when the Fur, Zaghawa and Masalit peoples took up arms against an Arab government in Khartoum that they believed had deliberately marginalised Darfur and its population. The sophisticated view would include details about long-standing tribal disputes over land and water, all exacerbated by global warming and the spread of the Sahara sands from the north. In response, the government armed its Arab allies, deploying the dreaded Janjaweed militias mounted on camels and horses, who then embarked on a terrifying orgy of destruction as they battled the rebel movement and targeted their civilian supporters in a scorched earth campaign. Villages were burned and looted, just like that road of stones into the Jebel Mara. Women were raped in a deliberate, organised attempt to destroy an entire way of life. The result was hundreds of thousands dead and millions more packed into aid camps, reliant on humanitarian agencies for food, water and medicine. This was a "genocide" according to the United

States government, directed by a homicidal regime against black, African tribes.

In many ways it was the perfect story. On the one side were the rebels from a forgotten people, abandoned and neglected by their government. They were fighting for a better deal for their community. On the other were the Janjaweed – Arabic for "devils on horseback" – backed by their Islamist masters in Khartoum. The government was already reviled for its accommodation with terrorists during the 1990s and for its role in an earlier civil war in the south of the country. Now they were doing the same thing in Darfur with a proxy army of rapists and murderers. This was a simple conflict between good guys and bad guys, so the accepted wisdom ran – easily differentiated as black or Arab, David or Goliath. The Africans were a peaceful farming people. The nomadic Arabs, with their love of guns and horses, were trying to take Darfur for themselves as part of a grand Arabisation project. In a continent of messy, difficult wars, this was a simple conflict. Darfur had managed to capture the imagination of the West and its pack of journalists based in Nairobi in a way that Somalia, northern Uganda and the Democratic Republic of Congo never had.

As I sat on a reed mat somewhere in the heart of the Jebel Mara, I hoped General Rokero might begin to fill in one side of the story and help guide me through this black and white analysis, which had become the official version of the conflict.

He was the same age as me and in another life he might have been an oil engineer, the career for which he had trained, but instead he had joined the SLA and risen to become its chief of staff and then its general secretary of humanitarian affairs. In our previous conversations – conducted hundreds of miles apart by satellite telephone – he had spoken of Arab fighters defecting from the government side to join the rebellion, and as we discussed the war he repeated the claim.

"Every day there are new Arabs coming so I can't know exactly how many we have now," he said quietly, in slow but perfect English. "If I had to guess I would say maybe 4000 are here in the hills."

As we talked, I did my best to rehydrate my shattered body. General Rokero had arrived with a plastic jug filled with ice cold water. It had come from one of the huge clay pots that are found throughout Sudan, often at the side of the road in the shade of a palm. They keep water cool in ingenious fashion. Their porous walls allow the water to slowly soak through, evaporating on the outside and sucking heat from the water inside: a sort of simple fridge. (I would discover by the end of the trip that these open clay vessels were also useless at keeping bugs at bay and would pay the price once back in Khartoum – but for the time being it seemed as if this was the greatest invention ever.)

Refreshed, it was time for a tour of Gorolang Baje and a stroll into the hills around the town and back. The paths crunched underfoot as each step sank into the black volcanic gravel that passed for soil. The town was something of a command post for the SLA rebels who control the Jebel Mara mountains. They come and go, collecting orders from General Rokero and taking tea in the gloomy, bare-walled shops that dot the tumbledown market. We stopped at one of the low-roofed buildings where a man in a stained jalabiya was stirring a steaming pot of ful – a dark brown sludge of stewed beans – and settled ourselves on a wooden bench. The Darfuri way is to add plenty of peanut oil to the ful and eat it with flat, white bread dipped in chilli powder and salt. It was my first meal of the day, and the hearty gloop was tastier than it looked. Outside the sun was starting to sink below the mountains. Inside the only light came from candles as General Rokero began to introduce me to his comrades.

Tusher Mohammed Mahdi, with his white scarf hiding most of his face and neat moustache, looked like any other commander. But once upon a time he would have had only one reason to venture into this mountainous rebel enclave – to kill as many of the guerrilla fighters and their supporters as possible. For Tusher used to lead a band of Arab fighters, armed, financed and encouraged by the Sudanese government. He came from the Um Jalul, one of the most traditional of all the nomadic camel owning clans of Darfur and also one of its most feared – if any clan can be described as the core of the Janjaweed, it is the Um Jalul. Their leader, Musa Hilal, is known widely as the most important of the Janjaweed commanders and now holds a position in government close to President Omar al-Bashir. Tusher was one of a number of Arab commanders who had forsaken tribal loyalty to join the rebels after a series of broken promises.

"In the beginning we were proud to fight because the government was telling us that all this land would belong to us. But later we discovered that would not be true," said Tusher, cradling an AK-47 rifle in his arms.

His weapon was much cleaner than the battered, scratched Kalashnikovs carried by other rebels, an indication of the way Khartoum distributed thousands of new rifles in Darfur as the conflict escalated. Tusher described how government soldiers would arrive with crates of ammunition and trunks of cash before each assault on rebel positions or their civilian supporters.

"The government had vehicles and artillery and air coverage," he continued, his teeth shining white in the gloom. "After the government bombed the area we would go in. We would burn and loot everything. The government told us to do that."

In this way, Tusher's 150 or so mounted raiders attacked seven or eight villages – he can't quite remember the number and would rather forget their names – as part of Khartoum's proxy army. In time, though, the promises of more cash began to dry up. A Sudanese officer told Tusher that the fertile land of the Jebel Mara would never be given to the Jalul and rumours began to fly around that other Janjaweed brigades were being paid more cash. Gradually their food and money had run out and his fighters went hungry. Eventually, waving a grubby white rag, he led thirty of his disenchanted men to an SLA checkpoint. They were debriefed and questioned for days, before each was handed a copy of the Koran and welcomed into the rebel movement.

Tusher said he only had regret for the way he had been duped and that he fully signed up to the rebel programme of fighting for the rights of the marginalised people of Darfur.

"It made us feel bad that we had believed the government's lies. We were told that the SLA wanted to kill us and take our animals. That's why we did what we used to do," he said.

Now Tusher takes orders from General Rokero, a man who would once have been his sworn enemy, and is tasked with defending part of the southern reaches of the mountains. A handful of Arab commanders told similar stories of government promises broken or lamented how the conflict has made their livestock worthless by closing down routes to markets and grazing land.

They did not sound like a people who had been engaged in a genocide, intent on asserting the right of their Arab tribes to trample all over the land, waterholes and women of an inferior African people. The men before me were Africans in every sense. Their language was Arabic but their skin was just as dark as their newfound comrades, and their people could trace their African roots back at least five centuries. As they talked, they sounded more and more like men who were watching their traditional way of life crumbling as the Sahara continued its unrelenting spread from the north, and had leapt at a government offer of land, money and influence to put down the insurgency. When the promises were exposed as lies they no longer had the stomach to fight neighbouring tribes they once thought of as brothers. They may have taken the government's dollars, but they now felt victims of the war every bit as much as the Fur.

We left the commanders squatting on tiny wooden stools drinking tea, and made our way to the compound of simple buildings where I was to spend the night. A chicken had been slaughtered and its tough, sinewy flesh was being boiled slowly into a sweet stew. It was late and my belly was full of the bean porridge, but I forced down handfuls of meat and sucked on some bones, knowing that chicken was a rare treat in this part of Darfur. General Rokero wished me well and disappeared off into the night, leaving me to bed down in a shed filled with sacks of food aid and plastered in what smelt like donkey dung. My empty plastic water bottles seemed to have disappeared from my pile of dusty belongings. I would learn later that these were a valuable commodity in the remote mountains, but all I could think about was how I was going to endure another energy-sapping, dehydrating ride back over the mountains without any water.

The cool Jebel Mara air was welcome as I wrapped myself in a sleeping bag. At first the pitter patter of insects dropping from the rafters and landing on my simple bed kept my eyes from closing, but then the aches and pains of a long day in the saddle took over and I slept.

* * *

Most of Africa rises with the sun and goes to bed as it sets. Sudan is different. The country's oppressive heat means its people use the cool evening hours of darkness to meet friends, share dinner or play football and then rise late the next morning. And so it was that I enjoyed a lie-in followed by breakfast of leftover chicken stew. General Rokero found me as I sipped a sweet cup of tea that would leave a sugary fur on my teeth for the rest of the day.

He had already lined up the day's first agenda item – an interview with two women who had been raped. I had mixed feelings about the meeting. I've lost track of the number of raped women pushed in front of me by charities, women's groups and rebel commanders in East Africa. Would my papers be interested in another tale of misery? Was it still shocking enough to make it on to the pages? Anyway, I had nothing else to do, so agreed to meet them.

The women were already tucked away in the dung-scented store-shed where I had spent the night. Here they could tell their stories out of sight and out of mind of a society where rape brings disgrace to their families and shame to the entire village. Both were sixteen and were sitting quietly in the gloom, their pink and lilac headscarves almost shining in the halflight. They had been captured by government soldiers in an attack on the rebel town of Deribat about three months earlier. Each had escaped only after an SLA counterattack on the town.

Awatif Ahmed Salih wrapped her scarf around her face as she told her story, using it to blot the tears that rolled down her cheeks. She had been alone at home as the Antonov cargo planes had dumped their crude bombs on the town. The attack followed a familiar pattern: after the planes came the pickups, about twenty of them, some mounted with heavy machine guns, along with Janjaweed militia riding horses and camels. Human rights monitors who interviewed some of the survivors estimated that thirty-six people died. Awatif survived the initial assault, but was picked up by gunmen as they swept through the town and taken to an administration block close to the market. There she was locked in a room with about a hundred other women. An older woman told her what to do to survive.

"There were men coming and going all the time so the idea was to keep your eyes down so that they would not pick you," said Awatif quietly in her native Fur tongue. She kept her eyes lowered as she spoke, meeting my gaze only occasionally.

Younger soldiers had been sent to select women for their commanding officers from the pitiful harem of sex slaves. One by one they would arrive and then leave with a prize of war. Awatif kept her eyes locked on the ground, but the tactic failed her. As darkness fell outside her prison, a soldier dressed in khaki grabbed her by the wrist, tied a blindfold over her eyes and loaded her into a truck.

"I was cursing and making a lot of noise because I thought they were going to kill me," she said. "When I realised what was happening, I was telling them to kill me."

After a two-hour drive bouncing along rutted tracks she was delivered to a commander. Maybe he manned a checkpoint or ran an army base, she could not tell. Her blindfold was removed by a man wearing a khaki uniform decorated with stars once she was safely inside a camouflaged tent. She spent the night being raped over and over again. In the morning, once more blindfolded, she was driven back to Deribat to the waiting women who all had similar, miserable tales. That evening, the junior officers returned and the cycle was repeated. It stopped only after three nights when rebels attacked government positions in the town. The women simply ran. They did not stop until they reached the mountains of the Jebel Mara.

Her story, spoken with the quiet dignity of someone who has suffered and survived, illuminated one of the true horrors of the conflict in Darfur. It showed how rape was being used as a weapon. These were not soldiers who had gone berserk; men out of control and high on bloodlust. It seemed to be a coordinated assault on the women of Darfur. Whether it was part of a genocidal plan to kill off certain tribes or not, the result was suffering on an enormous scale. Awatif's words, I knew, could tell this story better than any UN report or Oxfam press release, but they also carried a risk – that she would never be able to marry, that she would be reviled as a whore, or raped again, if the world knew her story. But Awatif had already made up her mind.

"I want you to use my true name because I have told you the truth of what happened," she said, fiddling with a tiny wooden copy of the Koran hanging around her neck, her eyes meeting mine to emphasise her determination. "This will be a message to other women over the world to support the women here."

As we sat in the dusty store room, surrounded by sacks of grain and the smell of donkey dung, I knew there was another problem with the interview. This was a sixteen-year-old girl brought to me by an SLA commander who seemed to have a canny understanding of how the international media worked. Could she be a stooge, a convincing actor with a tale cobbled together to cast the Janjaweed and government soldiers in a negative light? Her story certainly held together under two hours of questioning, going over the same ground again and again. The crucial evidence, though, came days later when UN officials confirmed hearing similar accounts from survivors of Deribat. Their investigators interviewed girls as young as thirteen who were targeted by government soldiers during the attack. Two pregnant women were raped, causing them to miscarry, and a group of fourteen women was held for a week and raped day after day by up to four men at a time. Their report concluded that rape was being used as a deliberate tactic of war.[1]

---

1 – *Eighth periodic report of the United Nations High Commissioner for Human Rights On The Human Rights Situation in The Sudan: Women Abducted, Raped and Kept as Sex Slaves Following the December 2006 Attacks on Deribat,* August 20, 2007

About 3000 of the survivors of Deribat had made their way to Gorolang Baje in the days and weeks after the attack. No-one would read the fancy UN document here. They didn't need to. Habiba Mohammed Elhag, the rebel contingent's women's officer, said she was trying to help dozens of women who told wretched tales of being raped by government soldiers.

"They did it because they want to destroy the kindness and the hearts of the women," she said. "This is the kind of war that we are fighting."

The families who fled Deribat joined another 4000 or so already camped out in the little town on the hill, seeking safety deep inside the SLA stronghold. Others were arriving daily from areas to the east of the Jebel Mara which were still under attack. Few men made the journey: most had already signed up to join the rebels or had been killed to ensure that they would never fight. Gorolang Baje, like many places in times of war, had seen the makeup of its population skewed wildly. Now it was largely a town of women and children. A tour of their makeshift camp was to be the final part of my itinerary, but General Rokero seemed to have other ideas. He wanted to sit and discuss the politics of resistance. Then it was time for tea, sitting on plastic chairs outside the little shed where the two girls had cried their tears. All the while the sun was getting higher in the sky and I could feel my forehead reddening despite a thick covering of sunscreen. There was still a four-hour donkey ride through the mountains to come and with government planes criss-crossing the area I had no desire to be out after dark. Try as I might, though, my host was in no rush to take me to the camp. Instead we sat and sipped our tea – taken sweet and served in thimble-sized glasses – in the neat compound, while behind us I could see smoke rising from cooking fires lit by the displaced families.

Just as I was beginning to despair of ever seeing their homes, General Rokero jumped to his feet and announced the tour could begin.

The camp could have been anywhere in Darfur. Its simple shelters were built from sticks covered with sheets of plastic or thatched roofs. Women sorted sorghum laid out on the ground. Others were weaving circular table mats from brightly-dyed straw – the sort of thing that would sell for twenty dollars in Khartoum's craft shops. They all said they wanted to go home, but none knew when that might be. "Only Allah knows," said one toothless old woman. Above them all fluttered an SLA flag – coloured green, black, white and yellow – mounted on a pole that would once have carried the Sudanese flag.

In some ways it was typical of other tours of other aid camps in other parts of Africa, where mothers watch boiling pots and their barefooted children race around daring each other to get closer to the white man. In other ways it was far more depressing.

The reason for our delay quickly became apparent. Children began streaming into the camp from all directions, laughing and shouting. Each carried a home-made banner, often little more than a piece of white paper covered in childish writing. "Go on International Criminal Court," read one. "Welcome UN," said another. They had been busy with biros as I waited for my tour of the camp, and now it seemed that I was in the middle of a not very spontaneous demonstration demanding international intervention to end the war in Darfur. Their message could be summed up in one simple phrase: "Come and Save Us."

A force of African Union (AU) soldiers had already been deployed to Darfur but had struggled to make any difference. Many – particularly among the Fur – now blamed them for making a miserable situation worse by brokering a peace deal that had been rejected by key rebel leaders. The AU was as much part of the problem as part of the solution. So the people's cry was simple. Only well-trained American and British soldiers wearing the blue helmets of the UN could save them, they thought. It was an unrealistic dream. What the villagers here didn't know was that the force being negotiated in far away places like Addis Ababa, New York and Khartoum would still be made up almost exclusively of Africans – the Nigerians, Rwandans and Senegalese who were failing to stop the attacks. That was the only way the Sudanese government was likely to let in peacekeepers wearing the blue of the UN.

Around us dust rose into the air as pair after pair of feet tramped the volcanic soil, until we were surrounded by three or four hundred women and children, shouting, singing and screaming. It made for an impressive and intimidating sight. They were all looking in my direction, as General Rokero turned and whispered: "Now perhaps you can say a few words."

This is not unusual territory for a journalist in Africa. A tour of a village can quickly take on the status of an official visit as dignitaries line up for introductions, goats are slaughtered and visitors' books opened expectantly. A few words are then required in return. The trick is to limit your speech to a few platitudes layered with generous thanks to your hosts. And so it was that I offered my gratitude to the people of Gorolang Baje for their hospitality, before explaining how moved I had been by their stories and expressing my fervent hope that they would be able to return to their homes soon. General Rokero was translating my words into Fur and it seemed to do the trick. Most of the crowd were smiling. A few cheered and clapped.

Not everyone was satisfied, however. "You have heard our problems," said one elderly woman, as she grabbed my arm. "When will you help us?"

This again was a familiar predicament. So I began to explain how I was not an aid worker or a UN official with the ability to order up trucks of food or helicopters for the wounded, but a journalist with no power other than the ability to take their stories to the outside world. Maybe then things will start to change, I suggested, looking out across the crowd of children, their eyes wide with hope as they held their handwritten signs calling for the UN and ICC to save the people of Darfur. It was one of the most depressing sights I had even seen. In some ways it is easier to deal with misery, with mothers holding skeletal children as they tell how their village was burned and their menfolk killed. It is a tale I have heard all across Sudan and all across Africa in slightly different forms. It is the bread and butter of being a foreign correspondent. After a while it goes down into the notebook without even triggering any emotion. What is infinitely more difficult to deal with is hope:

the belief that the outside world can solve the problems of Darfur; that the soldiers of the UN will one day ride to the rescue; or that the ICC will end Sudan's culture of impunity. In short, the faith that people in faraway lands give enough of a damn to really make a difference. That was the sentiment that lay in the simple banners displayed by the children. They had hope in institutions many in the West had given up on long ago. They believed that outside help could save their lives, rebuild their villages and send them home – yet for four years nothing had changed in Darfur, despite countless UN resolutions. I doubted my reports in British, Irish and American newspapers would help the people who stood before me.

I had come for an adventure. It was a tale to tell back home of riding into the sunset with rebels, or a chance to lord a Jebel Mara byline over my rivals in Nairobi. Changing the world or saving Darfur were not part of my agenda.

My donkey was waiting to carry me back over the mountains. It was almost time to leave, after forty-eight hours learning some of the truth about the Darfur war. It was beginning to look less like a desert struggle between good guys and bad guys and more like another one of Africa's very messy conflicts where everyone is a victim and everyone is at the mercy of outside powers. The Arabs who had fought as Janjaweed had lost just as much as their enemies among the Fur rebels and, as usual, it was the women of Darfur who had suffered most – detained for days at a time and used for sex. Part of me knew that I had been used by General Rokero's spin machine, which had laid on the demonstration in front of me as part of their campaign for UN peacekeepers. And I also knew that if the war was no longer about good guys versus bad guys then an international intervention force would struggle to know where to intervene. Who should they keep apart when the old distinctions were disintegrating? It seemed that nothing much was going to help these people.

None of my misgivings mattered to the woman who was still clutching my arm. To her it was enough that a white man had visited their shattered community, eaten their food and listened to their stories. In return, my platitudes satisfied her and her friends. They began ululating and dancing as more children joined the throng, banging drums, coconut shells and anything else they could find. More dust was kicked up into the air. The din was deafening. I felt like a liar.

3. WAR BY PROXY

It was only after a couple of hours waiting for Africa's most wanted man that the problem became clear. Joseph Kony, leader of the murderous Lord's Resistance Army (LRA), was a man of mystery. The only known image of him was a faded black and white photograph taken two decades earlier. Since then he had lived the life of a fugitive, roaming the tropical jungle along the borders of Southern Sudan, northern Uganda and the Democratic Republic of Congo with his band of rebels, as they raped, murdered and mutilated their way across a war-ravaged land. For journalists, securing an audience with Kony had become – like a cave-side chat with Bin Laden – something of a holy grail. Scores had tried and failed.

"So how are we going to know it's him?" I asked the handful of journalists waiting with me.

We had been promised a sighting of General Kony by the United Nations. A week of satellite phone calls and messages relayed back and forth across the Sudanese forests had apparently secured a meeting between the UN's humanitarian co-ordinator, Jan Egeland, and the reclusive guerrilla leader. For the officials, it was a chance to persuade Kony to give up some of the child soldiers and sex slaves he had captured from Ugandan villages and coax him deeper into a shaky peace process; for the altar-boy turned self-proclaimed prophet, it was a chance to play statesman and gain legitimacy. For me, it was a welcome distraction from Khartoum where I had been stuck more than a week waiting for a travel permit that would never arrive. My plans for that particular trip to Darfur were shot.

Yet as I delved further into Kony's story and his role in Southern

Sudan, it gradually dawned on me that his war had parallels with the one being fought far to the north-west in Darfur. The LRA was a proxy army, rather like the Janjaweed. Both had backers in Khartoum and the deal that eventually brought an imperfect peace to the jungle where I stood might have lessons for Darfur: understanding Kony might help me to understand Darfur.

Getting here had been just as troublesome as reaching Darfur. Two helicopters had delivered us to a remote village in Southern Sudan. From there we transferred to Land Cruisers which ferried us along tracks turned into bogs by weeks of rain. Our first sight of the LRA was a checkpoint manned by their young, dreadlocked footsoldiers. The place looked deserted until half a dozen figures loomed out of the shadows at the side of the road. They wore rubber boots and slung their AK-47s over their shoulders as they ordered us out of the vehicles before checking impatiently through our bags, demanding satellite phones be turned off for fear their GPS settings could reveal the location of their base. They may have been in their teens but they were tough and disciplined.

Beyond the checkpoint lay Ri-Kwangba, a sad collection of straw-covered huts where the rebels had been given safe haven. This was their jungle home while peace talks continued to end Uganda's long running civil war. The sickly smell of rotting maize – a sweetener delivered to keep the LRA talking – hung heavily in the humid air. A dozen or so gunmen, mostly in their teens, stood watching their visitors without saying a word. Some wore football shirts in the purple of Barcelona or with the image of David Beckham plastered across the silky fabric. Along with their skinny shoulders, it was one of the few reminders that these were still boys. Their blank-eyed stares gave them the appearance of a soulless robot army. The silence was broken only by the occasional sound of a ripe mango crashing from branch to ground.

Time was ticking slowly by. Nothing much stirred as the sticky heat grew. We did our best to find shade and a comfortable place to sit.

It took a sudden movement, a rustling in the bushes somewhere near the tree line, to bring us to our feet. A column of rebels was moving towards the huts. They were led by a tall man clutching a satellite telephone. Was this Kony?

"Is it him, is it him?" I was hissing at the reporter next to me, fearful that a sudden move might spook the shadowy leader before he even arrived.

"I can't quite see," she whispered back. "No. False alarm. That's Vincent Otti."

Kony's deputy leader had arrived as part of an advance guard to negotiate the exact terms and conditions for the meeting. He arrived to an electronic fanfare of satellite telephones all ringing at once. "No, no, no it's not him," I could hear my colleagues saying into their phones.

One of the other journalists had jumped the gun. Kony's arrival had been trumpeted on the wire and across the internet, before we had realised it was actually Otti. The reporter in question slipped away embarrassed to a quiet corner, but he had my sympathy. How on earth were we to recognise such an elusive character?

Excitement over, we went back to waiting. By now it was four o'clock. The helicopters were running out of the daylight they needed to fly and there was no sign of Kony. Otti was deep in negotiations with UN officials. He would talk with Jan Egeland before disappearing behind a bush every so often to call his master on a satellite phone, before reappearing and repeating the cycle

The wait was agonising. Only a tiny number of people had ever set eyes on the man who had led a child army in a campaign of devastation. As a result, he had become a figure of legends rather than facts. He was the altar boy who had grown up to become a rebel leader. He was the wizard who used magic to protect his brainwashed adherents. He was the deluded man from the bush who wanted to rule Uganda according to the Ten Commandments.

His followers believed Kony received instruction from God and treated his orders accordingly. He had a reputation for bloodlust incredible even by Africa's warped yardstick. Lieutenants who disagreed with their leader were never heard from again. Villagers suspected of informing had their lips sliced from their faces. Anyone caught riding a bicycle had their legs amputated in order to deter others thinking of racing to raise the alarm ahead of an LRA attack. His army of child soldiers – abducted, brutalised and purged of compassion until they became part of a zombie-like killing machine – had somehow managed to inflict heavy losses on the Ugandan military and evade defeat for twenty years. Defence analysts spoke admiringly of the LRA's bushcraft and ability to outwit the national armies pitted against them.

The sun was inching lower. Our numbers were thinning. The UN's media minder had already dragged several of my colleagues off to one of the helicopters. Spending the night stuck in a damp, malaria-infested rebel camp with only maize porridge and mangoes to eat was not on anyone's schedule and the first chopperload of hacks had left disappointed. I'd stayed by the skin of my teeth – and the fact that I was writing for four different newspapers. We had twenty more minutes before the second helicopter was going to have to leave. After a long day of anticipation it looked as if Africa's most secretive rebel commander had given us the slip.

None of us waiting in the humid clearing expected Kony simply to stroll out of the jungle wearing wellingtons and green fatigues, clutching a battered diary held together with elastic bands. There was no puff of smoke or bolt of lightning to herald the arrival of a monster. And I understood now why Kony was reluctant to appear in public. The legend crumbled as we peered at a frail man who shied before the reception that awaited him. His bloodshot eyes avoided the gaze of the curious onlookers like a nervous child on his first day at school, or a drunk in an alley. An aide carried his white plastic chair. Behind him a bodyguard of seventeen boy soldiers carried more chairs and a solar panel, essential for charging the satellite phones that co-ordinate Africa's deadly conflicts.

He hurried inside a tent set aside for the meeting (where his garden furniture had been arranged) and spent twenty minutes talking to the UN officials before emerging to conduct an incoherent press conference.

"We talked about peace talks that are taking place in Juba," was how he summed up the meeting. To a question about the abducted children in his ranks, he answered that it was impossible to release any because: "We don't have any children in our movement, there's only combatants." Everything else he said was lost in half sentences that petered into silence and anxious whispering into his aides' ears.

He had been scarcely more fluent inside the tent, apparently, struggling to keep up with the discussion and relying on his deputy, Otti, to do most of the talking. "It was as if he'd been chewing the root," said one of the UN officials with a smile.

I'd come away with a scoop. I could call myself one of the few journalists to have met Kony and to have peered into those wild eyes. But my brief glimpse into Kony's crazy world raised more questions than it answered. As he disappeared back along the jungle trail to wherever he had come from – and the journalists boarded the four by fours that would take us out of the jungle – one question stood out: how had this confused shell of a man managed to bring the Ugandan government close to defeat and spread war across central Africa for twenty years?

The answer to the riddle of Kony, like Darfur, lay in the bitter civil war that had raged across Southern Sudan for half a century. The region had been a battleground ever since independence in 1956. The South, administered almost as an independent country by the British, accused the North of neglect. The latest round of fighting erupted in 1983 when the North suspended Juba's Southern assembly and imposed Sharia law on a people who didn't share Khartoum's Muslim faith. Army battalions in the South mutinied and took to the bush, forming the SPLA under the leadership of John Garang. They were a secular, guerrilla force drawn from a people practising Christian and traditional, animist beliefs. They adopted classic hit-and-run rebel strategies, harassing government supply lines and snatching arms, rather than conquering and defending territory.

The discovery of oil added more fuel to a tinderbox of grievances. Where once the conflict had been characterised by the battle for scarce resources in a hungry country, the civil war eventually became a struggle for control of six billion barrels of oil buried beneath the surface of Southern Sudan. Almost two million people had died by the time the war ended in 2005 with an agreement to allow the South a referendum on independence and a share of the oil money.

Meanwhile, successive regimes in Khartoum came and went. Each struggled to hold together the vast empire bequeathed to them by the British. Jaafer Nimeiri clung to power until 1985, his military apparently unable to put down the Southerners. It was his lurch from Marxism to Islam and the introduction of Sharia law that reignited the latest incarnation of the conflict. He eventually lost power in the same way that he seized it, swept aside in a military coup. The generals then gave up power a year later in elections won by Sadiq al-Mahdi, the great-grandson of the Mahdi whose fanatical followers had killed Gordon of Khartoum. His favoured tactic was to arm the Arab tribes along the disputed boundary with the South. He, in turn, was swept aside in 1989, just as he prepared to sign a deal with the SPLA rebels, by the coup that propelled Omar al-Bashir to power. But while the cast changed, one thing stayed the same: Khartoum's reliance on hired militia leaders to wage war on the South, just as they would later in Darfur. One of them was Kony.

* * *

The story of how an Islamist government in Khartoum came to back a rebel leader whose proclaimed intent was to rule according to the Ten Commandments was not one I would find in Sudan. Rather, the setting was the garden of a nondescript bar nestling in the lush, green hills of the Ugandan capital Kampala – the sort of place where the tea comes milky and the furniture runs to flimsy white plastic chairs.

The slate sky was threatening a tropical downpour as I introduced myself to Colonel Patrick Opiyo Makasi. He was that rare thing: a defector from the senior ranks of the LRA. He knew how Khartoum had bankrolled and trained Kony's fighters. Free from the men who had kidnapped him as a child and brainwashed him into becoming a killer, he was ready to talk. First, by way of introduction, I asked Makasi how he escaped from his LRA base, across the border in the Democratic Republic of Congo.

His answer was brief, and delivered in the matter-of-fact tones of someone who has lived his life in a waking nightmare. For five days he struggled through the thick Congolese bush. He skirted prides of lions as well as elephants and buffalo with nothing other than a bottle of orange squash, diluted with rainwater collected from tree hollows, to sustain him. All the while he didn't know whether he was being pursued by his old comrades. A shot to the back of his head, he explained, would be the first he would know of capture. Nor could he predict what reception would await him when he tried to turn himself in to Congolese authorities.

"I was worried. I got there and I didn't know what was going to happen to me because it was not our country. I don't know them," he told me softly in the uncertain English he had learned at school.

After surviving the wildlife of the Congolese jungle, he turned himself in at a police station in the tiny town of Dungu. He was right to be nervous. The town had endured repeated LRA raids. Its burned-out pharmacy and bullet-riddled buildings were evidence that Kony's modern day slavers had passed through its dirt trails, seizing children as conscripts for his army.

"The only thing I told them was I came here and I wanted to go to Uganda, our home," he told me, slurping at his milky tea.

In the end he needn't have worried. The local police simply handed the defector on to UN peacekeepers, who in turn passed him to Uganda's military intelligence, which was desperate for the insider information that Makasi carried with him. Now he lived as part prisoner, part guest of the Ugandan government.

He was a valuable catch. While there are plenty of young escapees in rehabilitation centres or aid camps scattered through northern Uganda, most held junior positions as soldiers, porters or, occasionally, wives to commanders. Senior officers tended to leave the LRA without their heads, executed as traitors. Makasi was different. He had risen from child soldier to become Kony's right hand man. As director of operations, he spoke with the LRA leader on a daily basis and was charged with converting his master's wishes into plans. Few knew Kony or the LRA's secrets so well. Ambushes, redeployment, raids – all were passed by the man sitting in front of me.

Makasi, a slight man of thirty-two, apologised immediately for his awkward English, explaining that his schooling had finished at the age of twelve when he was snatched from the Ugandan town of Gulu. Reading, writing and arithmetic gave way to lessons in using the AK-47 he was given. In fits and starts, casting a wary eye around the garden for eavesdroppers, he explained the gradual process of turning a frightened little boy into a soldier.

"We stayed together and became like family. Even those who were in the bush were like your brothers," he said. "Because you are young you see some commanders like fathers. Things are happening fast and you need the others to help you. You follow what the commander says because there is no-one else to listen to."

Makasi proved adept at soldiering and rapidly caught the eye of his seniors. They gave him a new name, Makasi, meaning "difficult to break" in the Congolese language, Lingala. Kony too noticed Makasi's evident toughness and quiet thoughtfulness, and he was soon promoted to the leader's inner circle, where he remained for years.

That ended the day his leader ordered the death of Vincent Otti, the man I had met in the jungle clearing and one of the key LRA negotiators. His undoing was to push too hard for peace. Knowing that Otti was one of the few people who could persuade Kony to give the talks a chance, Makasi realised that any hope of the war ending was ebbing away. No-one expected the rebels' director of operations to defect. So Makasi simply sauntered out of the camp in Congo's Garamba National Park. He was carrying nothing except a GPS handset and his bottle of cordial, looking for all the world as if he was just off for a ramble in the thick bush.

Makasi was frank about Sudanese support for the LRA. Crates of AK-47s, heavy machine guns and even surface-to-air missiles were delivered by the militia's sugar daddies in Khartoum. Some of the weapons could have been picked up anywhere in the Horn of Africa. But others among the armaments he described were far more sophisticated than those in general use, including the SPG9 armour-piercing, recoilless rifle, and SAM7 anti-aircraft missiles. I asked how he could be so specific.

"I know that because we were staying with them around their [the Sudan Armed Forces'] camp and we were the ones who would collect them from their lorry," he said. "We were on the side of the Sudan government."

He didn't know how much weaponry arrived in that last shipment. All he knew was that it took Makasi and his comrades eight months to bury the arms in caches dotted across Southern Sudan.

Khartoum's role was not limited to that of gunrunner. Before 2000, senior commanders would also be flown to Khartoum for instruction in warfare. They would be taught military tactics and given instruction in new weapons and bomb making techniques. Each officer would also learn how to turn raw recruits into soldiers. Some returning officers even claimed to have been sent to Iraq and Iran for training, said Makasi.

The role of the LRA, as Khartoum saw it, was to disrupt the SPLA supply chain, hinder the delivery of humanitarian aid (which was routinely commandeered by the rebels) and generally act as a nuisance to Khartoum's enemies. It was a partnership built on a common enemy – the alliance between the Ugandan president, Yoweri Museveni, and the Southern rebels. Khartoum had an ally against the SPLA, while the LRA was strengthened in its main objective of overthrowing the Ugandan government.

Makasi's inside information helped explain how Kony – the addled, confused man I had met two years earlier – had managed to outwit the Ugandan Popular Defence Forces for so long. He wasn't just a madman. And it would be wrong to see him as merely the commander of a rag-tag bunch of ill-equipped children. His forces might not be impressive and motives remained opaque, but his connection made him a player in a regional conflict, able to call in weaponry and training from a wealthy, well-armed and generous benefactor.

The softly-spoken former rebel also explained why the peace talks being hosted in Juba were doomed to failure. He said that Kony would never come out of the bush so long as he was wanted by the International Criminal Court (ICC) in The Hague. Judges there had issued a warrant for his arrest in 2005, on thirty-three charges of crimes against humanity and war crimes. Kony believed he would be arrested and hanged in The Hague, explained Makasi, if he ever dared appear at a signing ceremony. In fact, judges at the ICC do not have the power to impose the death penalty.

Finally, Makasi got on to Kony's relationship with God. "To describe him is very difficult for me. He is not mad," said Makasi, who knew Kony better than anyone. "But he is a religious man. All the time he is talking about God. Every time he keeps calling many people to him to teach them about the legends and about God. Mostly it is what he is talking about and that is how he leads people."

* * *

The night after meeting Joseph Kony I slept in a $200 tent, an indicator of the money-making machine that Southern Sudan had become. For that sort of cash you might expect hippos grazing in the river beyond the terrace and a valet to bring jugs of steaming water for morning ablutions before disappearing off for a morning game drive. That's what $200 would get you in neighbouring Kenya. In Juba, the capital of South Sudan, it paid for a camp bed, a fan and an electric socket in a bare tent. The water in the communal bathrooms was cold.

Yet row after row of tents was full. They were filled with demining experts ridding the country of the lethal crop of ordnance buried in the soil, and aid workers come to rebuild a land shattered by civil war. Oil company executives were in town to meet government officials, while young men in dark glasses and khaki shirts were busy setting up private military companies to protect the incomers. With few permanent buildings left after twenty-one years of war, Juba had been turned into a tent city as every type of prospector arrived trying to strike it rich.

This was still a shattered place. The South's infrastructure had been shot back to the Stone Age. Average life expectancy was forty-two. More schools seemed to assemble under shady trees than in brick buildings. Hospitals were little more than bombed-out shells, their patients left to convalesce in the open air. Everything in the markets had to be trucked in from Khartoum or – more likely as the Southerners forged links with neighbours – Uganda and Kenya. Journalists were fond of saying that Southern Sudan had only ten kilometres of tarmac road (if the airport runway in Juba was included). It was too good a statistic to check and it sounded right – if not a little generous. We all used it.

But now Juba was a boom town, built on the wealth buried in the ground. The region may have been desperately under-developed, but things were changing. Government officials dreamed of building power stations, international sports stadiums and ringroads with their income from Sudan's oil reserves. These were the spoils of war. No wonder the conflict had been so long, difficult and bloody. With enough oil to rebuild the economy of the entire pariah state, Khartoum had been prepared to resort to centuries old tactics of divide and conquer. And with its own forces of limited value in such hostile territory so far from the centre of its empire, it instead offered slaves and booty to traditional tribal militias prepared to do the government's bidding.[2]

* * *

Adut Mou Tong was thirteen when the horsemen swept through the town of Aweil. She was too far from her traditional round tukul home to shelter out of sight. Instead she fell to her knees in the street as gunfire sounded all around. Heavy hands lifted her on to her feet and then hauled her on to the back of a horse. She had been captured by slavers from the North. A young woman, not yet married, she made for a valuable bounty of war.

---

2 – *For a full account see* The Root Causes of Sudan's Civil Wars (African Issues) *by Douglas H Johnson, Indiana University Press*

Nineteen years later she remembered shaking with fear, but little more of her journey. Only that it ended in the Jebel Mara mountains of Darfur, where she was kept by the militiaman who had snatched her. There she was expected to wash, clean and cook for the household. It may be difficult for Western ears to understand, but she bore no ill will to the horseman who snatched her. Life would have been little different if she stayed in the town of her birth – treated as a skivvy before being sold as a wife, she explained, in the Arabic she learned in the North.

"When I was taken the man did not mistreat me," she said. "I was like a family member and treated like his own child."

At the age of fifteen, she was given to a relative as a bride.

"I was frightened, but I knew that if I refused then I would be punished with death. But after I accepted he treated me so well. I had all my needs. I was fed, I had fine clothes and the children were taken care of," she said. "I fell in love with him."

We met in the dusty town of Malual Kon, a remote outpost of northern Bahr el Ghazal, a state which lies alongside the frontier with the North. She had been returned as a woman to the land of her birth as part of a government programme to repatriate women taken as slaves. Her prominent teeth, elegant, elongated limbs and ink-black skin marked her out clearly as a member of a Southern tribe.

Throughout the 1980s and 1990s, mounted Arab militia from the North – known as Murahaleen – raided many villages in this part of the South. One of their roles was to protect slow-moving trains which were used to re-supply government garrison towns in the South. Their reward was to keep the spoils of looted villages. Along with cattle, they transported men, women and children – mostly from the Dinka tribe – back to the North to be kept as slaves.

Their motivation was more economic than ideological. As nomadic herders, the Arab tribes had lost cattle to severe drought in the 1970s and pastures to vast mechanised farming schemes taken up with gusto by Khartoum. Life had become a lot tougher for the peoples along the unofficial frontier between North and South. Sharing pasture with their Southern neighbours, as they had for centuries, had become much less attractive. So if the government was going to offer guns and loot to drive away the Southern tribes, many among the Misseriya and Riezegat Baggara were only too ready to sign up.

And what they couldn't carry off, they destroyed. Young men were shot dead to prevent them joining the rebels, and villages were razed.

Adut was taken at the height of the Murahaleen raids in 1986 and 1987. No-one knows exactly how many were snatched, although field studies by the Rift Valley Institute recorded the names of 10,000 people who had been abducted during twenty years of fighting. The plight of the slaves touched a nerve in the West. They became a rallying point for a new type of Sudan activist. Evangelical charities and African-American groups, in particular, began raising money to buy back slaves from their Muslim masters. The going rate was fifty dollars a pop. Christian Solidarity International, based in Switzerland, calculated it had "redeemed" some 60,000 Southerners, but said that was well short of the 200,000 or more slaves snatched. Schools and churches ran fundraising drives, donating pocket money and Sunday collections to the cause.

Suddenly the Sudanese civil war – an obscure conflict in a faraway land, where Africans were killing Africans – had made it into newspapers across the US. Even Michael Jackson was sucked into the circus, promising to travel to the region to help the captives after being told of their plight by the Rev Al Sharpton. (In the end he didn't make it.)

By 2002, though, the redemption programmes were widely discredited. Gullible charities were accused of helping fund Sudan's bloodshed by paying armed groups to free individuals posing as slaves. Humanitarian organisations on the ground concluded that the true number of abductees was far lower than the number being "redeemed". Witnesses to redemption said rebel commanders were sometimes posing as slave traders to collect suitcases stuffed with cash.[3] This is not to say that villagers had not been taken – just

---

3 – *The Great Slave Scam by Declan Walsh*, The Irish Times, *February 23, 2002*

that the facts were being distorted and the true picture lost in the rush to do the right thing.

I had travelled to Malual Kon in 2005, soon after the peace deal had been signed, to investigate slavery and a fresh round of abuses. The tiny, dusty village was brutally hot. I spent the afternoons sitting in the shade of a tree, drinking as much water as my body would tolerate and waiting for the 45°C temperatures to ease. During the rains – due a month or so after my visit – the town would become a swamp. The rain was vital to life, transforming the South's yellow into green, replenishing lakes, rivers and pastures. But at the same time it would bring death, summoning fetid swamps heaving with malaria.

Adut was eight months pregnant when Khartoum's Commission to Eradicate the Abduction of Women and Children (CEAWC) came calling. She had left her four children at home, in their traditional mud-thatched hut, while she visited a neighbour. There was a rap at the neighbour's flimsy, wooden door.

"Mummy, you are needed," called Adut's eldest daughter.

By the time she scrambled outside, her daughter had already been bundled on to a waiting cattle truck. With half a dozen CEAWC officials ready to use force, Adut had no choice but to clamber aboard as well.

"They took my children, then they came to get me," she said, two months after being dumped in Malual Kon, deep in territory governed by Southern rebels. "I wasn't even allowed home to get my things."

She said the two-day ride from the North to the South over bumpy, pot-holed dirt roads in a packed truck was a living hell. "It was so bad. Everyone thought I would have to give birth in the truck," she said.

While other women and children were eventually reunited with long-lost families, no-one had been able to trace Adut's relatives in the South. For weeks she eked out an existence doing menial work – cooking and fetching water. Previously a victim of war, now she was a victim of peace.

Returning the abductees allowed the Khartoum government in

the North to counter criticism that it was implicated in slavery. It had set up CEAWC in 1999 to trace and return Southerners taken from their homes. But not all were slaves. Many Southerners travelled to the North voluntarily, refugees from the civil war, ethnic clashes and hunger.

The Southern rebels were also keen for their people to be returned. With a census and referendum looming, they wanted to boost their population and ensure the region got its fair share of resources.

Adut had been dumped in a town that might as well have been another planet when compared with the fertile Jebel Mara. Malual Kon's entire population of 5000 relied on aid agencies for food and women spent up to six hours queuing in unbearable heat at the town's water pumps to fill their jerry cans. The only things that seemed to prosper were the goats, which played King of the Castle on mounds of rubbish in all temperatures. Adut told me she just wanted to go back to the North.

"I am not happy here. If I get the chance I will go back to find my husband, but I cannot get a permit to leave," she said, as flies hovered around her face. She waved them away with a flick of her thin wrist. A light-skinned baby, the son of her Northern husband, slept contentedly on her other arm.

In his low-roofed brick office, Peter Lual, secretary of the local Sudanese Relief and Rehabilitation Commission, refused to regard returnees like Adut as anything but delighted. "They come here willingly and are happy to be reunited," he said. "We are encouraging these people. These are our brothers and sisters – we may not have much food here but we cannot turn them away."

He was lying and we both knew it.

"Now," said Lual, "Who told you these lies that they were forced to come here and cannot leave? Give me your notebook, I want to see."

My notebook contained the names of four women I had interviewed in the relative safety of the UN's compound. Each had told a similar story to Adut – and each was keen to talk in the hope it might help them get back home. All but one insisted I use their real name so that relatives would know where they were. None of them would have wanted Lual to know their names.

My flight aboard a tiny UN plane was leaving in an hour and Lual knew it. "You won't be getting any plane today," he said grinning. "Now give me their names."

I cursed my naivety. Why hadn't I just telephoned this rebel-turned-administrator on his sat-phone once I was long gone? I made a mental note never to sit at a Sudanese official's desk and accuse him of human rights abuses. Particularly if he was the sort of official that still dressed in fatigues and was probably familiar with the operation of a Kalashnikov.

"You are not going anywhere until you give me that notebook," repeated Lual.

I refused, casting an anxious eye at the militiaman standing just outside the doorway, throwing a shadow across Lual's gloomy desk. For good measure, I added that I was writing a balanced article and had offered ample opportunity for him to counter the allegations. I stood up.

"You can't do this to an international journalist," I said, pushing back my rickety wooden chair, unsure exactly what he was and wasn't prepared to do to me. "If you want me, I'll be at the UN compound." Then I walked straight out of the door.

I left, as planned, on the scheduled flight, wondering what would happen to the women I had interviewed. Each had told me they were trying to return to the North or track down relatives they had not seen in years. Two nights earlier, another woman brought back from the North against her will gathered her child and a handful of possessions and slipped away in the night. No-one knew where she went, but Adut told me she had an idea.

"There are trucks from the North that come here," she said, her unlined face breaking into a conspiratorial smile, "so there are ways to get home."

* * *

57

The peace that returned Adut to a home she didn't know arrived in bright sunshine to the sound of cheers and ululating women. Thousands of people crammed into Nairobi's national football stadium to witness the final signing of the Comprehensive Peace Agreement (CPA), some three years in the making. The occasion was predictably chaotic. Dignitaries lined up to make their lengthy speeches, while spectators – daubed in war paint, wearing headdresses of feathers or waving the colours of the SPLA – danced for hours on end. It was January 2005. After twenty-one years and millions dead there was much to celebrate in a deal to end what we journalists were fond of calling "Africa's longest running war."

The crisis unfolding in the west of Sudan was forgotten for the day as Sudan's first vice-president, Ali Osman Mohammed Taha, and John Garang, leader of the rebel army, signed the agreement. Colin Powell, US Secretary of State, was there to witness their signatures. His role was far from honorary. The administration of George W. Bush had made finding peace in Southern Sudan one of its key foreign policy objectives and America had done more than any other nation to keep pressure on the two warring sides. At one point the two teams of negotiators even began applying for US visas to make the trip to the White House for the final signing ceremony. In the end, though, it was the Washington press corps who had to dig out their khakis and sunglasses to accompany Powell to Africa.

The deal was a huge success for the US administration. It was a trophy that could be handed to Bush's core supporters in the religious right, who had coalesced around the issue of slavery. The war's simple narrative, widely reported as a Muslim North fighting rebels from the Christian South, was easily understood. Intervening to win greater autonomy from Khartoum's Islamists – a regime that had once harboured Osama bin Laden – was attractive to a Western audience who had watched Al Qaeda terrorists crash passenger jets into the World Trade Centre. The reach of dangerous idealogues such as Hassan al-Turabi had been curbed.

No-one doubted that the road ahead would be difficult. There were potential landmines among the terms of the CPA. Combining rebel cadres and government forces into joint units would be a major headache. The deal also allowed the South to hold a referendum on independence in 2011. Garang was known to be opposed to breaking away, but his death less than a year later in a mysterious helicopter crash brought a real possibility that Khartoum could eventually lose a sizable portion of its empire. The CPA had also left the exact demarcation of the North-South boundary for another day, something to be decided by an independent commission. The oil-rich town of Abyei, claimed by both sides, was left in no man's land for now. And what would happen to the Arab horsemen that Khartoum had used to fight the war? The proxy fighters had no seat at the table during negotiations between the Northern government and Southern rebels. And above it all floated the spectre of Darfur, another tragedy casting a long shadow over the day's celebrations

For its supporters though, imperfect as it was, the CPA was the framework that would also help find a solution to Darfur's bloodshed. It set out the terms by which regional opponents could gain control over their land and rebels could take their places in government – positions once reserved only for Muslims. Refugees in camps in Ethiopia and Kenya could begin making plans to return home as donors fished for their chequebooks.

With the war in Southern Sudan over, President Bashir would have no further need for the likes of Joseph Kony. Funding and arms had already been cut off as peace talks progressed. In the months ahead, the plan was for the new regime in South Sudan to reach out to their old enemies in the LRA. Bundles of cash – $20,000 at a time – were delivered by former Southern Sudanese rebels to persuade Kony and his negotiators to keep meeting Ugandan government officials.

Only by then it was too late; Kony had all the negotiating skills of a cornered animal.

* * *

59

Khartoum's proxies may have been cast adrift, but Raymond Kpiolebeyo's story was proof that they hadn't decommissioned their weapons. For eight days he was marched at gunpoint through the steaming Congolese jungle. For seven nights he didn't know whether he would live or die as he slept with eight other prisoners pinned under a plastic sheet weighted down with bags and stones to prevent escape. Their sweat condensed on the sheeting inches above their faces, dripping back and turning their makeshift prison into a stinking sauna. He had been kidnapped by the LRA even as its leaders claimed to be preparing to sign a final peace deal.

"They told us that if one of us tried to escape we would all be shot," said Raymond, speaking through a translator in the headmaster's office of the school where he taught.

The twenty-eight-year-old teacher's home town of Doruma, a few miles from the border with South Sudan, had been hit by a raiding party looking for porters, sex slaves and soldiers. I had arrived in Doruma, among the frontier towns of the DRC, almost two years after I had looked into Joseph Kony's eyes. This was June 2008 and Kony had recently failed to arrive in Juba, where he was expected to consign the LRA to history. A final peace agreement with the Ugandan government awaited his signature. (His aides said a bad dose of diarrhoea was keeping him away, but I couldn't help thinking that the flushing toilets and $200 tents of Juba were a better place to convalesce than the middle of the bush.) I was in Doruma looking for evidence that supported a confidential United Nations report compiled by officials with MONUC – the French acronym for the peacekeeping operation. It said the LRA had cynically used the peace talks to organise itself into a more effective fighting force. The 670-strong band of fighters had more than 150 satellite telephones, many bought with cash meant to aid communications during the talks.

"Simply put, Kony now has the ability to divide his forces into very simple groups and to reassemble them at will. When put together with his proven mastery of bush warfare, this gives him new potency within his area of operations," the report said.

The LRA was given tons of food by a charity, Caritas Uganda, to discourage the looting of villages, and sacks of dollars by Southern Sudan's new leaders, whom they once fought.

The report concluded, though, that Kony was stronger than ever: "Recent abduction patterns suggest that he is now in the process of perfecting the new skill of recruiting and controlling an international force of his own."

Instead of waging war in northern Uganda where his struggle began, or South Sudan where he did Khartoum's bidding, his rebel force was snatching children from four countries. His rein of terror now took in the Central African Republic and the Congolese jungle.

I stepped off a United Nations helicopter in Dungu, a remote town deep in the Congolese jungle, another hour or so from the Ugandan border. The town was being turned into the frontline against Kony's army. Engineers had been extending the airstrip and helping the Congolese dig in. From here there were limited options for reaching Doruma or Duru, the other town where we had heard of attacks. Both were a day's motorbike ride away, along narrow trails through the heart of the jungle. This was deep inside LRA territory and too far from help to make visiting safe. Flying to Duru was impossible – its landing strip was the main road and no-one had used it in years. But a Canadian pilot who ran an air service for aid agencies reckoned he could take us to Doruma, where he had heard a teacher had escaped from the LRA.

We flew out of Dungu the next morning, skimming low over its meandering river. Our low altitude afforded an astonishing view of the town's one landmark – a Gothic castle shrouded in palms and creepers, but still standing as testament to the extravagance and hubris of Belgian rule, as well as the possibility of what might be, if only the Congo could shrug off its neighbours' wars. All around, people were living in thatched huts. Malnutrition was rife. Yet it was easy to imagine candle-lit champagne receptions on the now overgrown lawn that stretched to the river's edge.

Men with motorbikes were waiting for us as we landed in Doruma, the arrival of a plane being rare enough to herald a pay day. Our time was limited by a climate of heat and humidity which combined daily to bring afternoon storms, and we were soon riding pillion on our way to the town's school. The wheels slithered over roots and kicked dust in the air as we raced along red dirt tracks at speeds that suggested a helmet would have been a good idea.

Kony had arrived in the north-eastern DRC about two years earlier, disappearing deep into Garamba National Park. His arrival was part of a gentleman's agreement with the Congolese government: he would be afforded safe haven for the duration of the peace talks, so long as his followers left locals alone. As we travelled through the small village of thatched huts and occasional colonial-era brick buildings with terraces, it became clear that Kony was anything but a gentleman. Villagers told us they kept their children close to home, away from the jungle tracks used by LRA raiders travelling back and forth from Southern Sudan. Raymond's story provided confirmation.

After walking ten hours a day for six days with a sack on his back and another balanced on his head, Raymond arrived at a well-ordered camp filled with children – some the offspring of women kept by commanders and some being trained with guns.

"They were mobile. All the time they were organising," he told me, sitting in front of a calendar bearing the image of the DRC's president Joseph Kabila, and the slogan 'Now let's build our country.' "Some were leaving for other villages and others were arriving."

The camp was a bustling town. Thatched huts stood in neat rows, while labourers farmed sweet potato, maize and beans. At night a television set charged by solar power would be brought out and the young soldiers cheered as they watched noisy American war films. Anything starring Chuck Norris was a big hit, apparently.

After six nights living in Kony's jungle headquarters, Raymond had the chance of escape.

He was woken by a tap on the head from another prisoner – the pre-arranged signal to leave. The two tiptoed over sleeping soldiers before breaking for the thick bush around the camp, just as Makasi had done. He was one of the lucky ones. We heard that five families in Doruma had children snatched just before our visit with little hope of seeing them returned.

At the same time I was haring around the little Congolese town, keeping an eye on the gathering clouds, Southern Sudan's proxies were also off the leash. The Misseriya, the Arab horsemen who did Khartoum's dirty work, were closing in on the disputed oil town of Abyei.

Funded and used by Khartoum, they now felt abandoned for a peace deal that brought them nothing. A few months earlier I had interviewed one of the Misseriya leaders at his Khartoum villa. We met in its cool, airy courtyard where he explained that the oil money was being divided between North and South, with little coming to his forgotten people straddling the border. General Mahdi Baboni Nimiri, a former army chief of staff whose father was the famed paramount chief of the Misseriya, insisted his warriors would not use violence to re-start the war, but his frustration was obvious.

"We have no development, we need hospitals and schools," he said. "So peace has not brought the benefits that other people got. For us peace is strategic. We will not fire the first shot but we will defend the land."

He cut a formidable figure even as he sat in a simple wood-framed chair, a booming voice and aura of greatness marking him out as an impressive commander. His men were among some of the militias that went into Abyei with Sudanese Armed Forces in May 2008, taking on the former rebels of the SPLA. Some 60,000 civilians fled the town, which was half razed. The market was completely destroyed and compounds belonging to the UN and aid organisations were burned. Once unleashed, the proxies have a nasty habit of sticking around, just like in the DRC.

Sitting on a low bamboo bench in the shade of a mango tree, Christine Kutiote described how her thirteen-year-old niece, Marie, was taken as she tried to cross the river for a visit. Now she keeps her own four children close at hand.

"I'm a Christian and I pray for them and that security will get better," she said in the local Zande language, as a priest translated her words into French.

Her low, simple home told a different story. Its mud walls bore a pattern of white spots used by witchdoctors to ward off evil. They have little else to protect them. There is no army, only a handful of unarmed police officers, and help can arrive only by plane or motorcycle, bumping for six hours along swampy tracks from Dungu, where peacekeepers are based. If there were lessons to be learned from this miserable place it is that proxies tend not to go away when they outlive their usefulness. They live on as a forgotten tangent to the main story of Christian rebels fighting Muslim soldiers. Khartoum's actions in Darfur seemed to mirror their tactics in the South, where they had armed militias in what other commentators called "counter-insurgency on the cheap". President Bashir was not the first to do it. The British had used the same tactics; so too other Sudanese presidents following independence. Giving friendly militias the chance to loot and steal seemed to be the way a government with a thin grip on its vast country fought for survival: offer land, money, animals, anything, to tribes prepared to join the cause. At the same time, a simple narrative of centre against periphery, of Muslim against Christian, had attracted unprecedented international attention and forced America to act. Straightforward stories suited journalists and readers alike. But maybe they also attracted simple solutions that overlooked the side issues – such as the proxies. They had no place at the negotiating table and no part in the peace. I was standing in the Democratic Republic of Congo, but Darfur and its proxy war seemed to make a little more sense.

Christine was paying the price for Southern Sudan's proxies. Her little family were victims of someone else's war: inspired in Uganda, funded by Khartoum and still being fought in her backyard.

4. DODGING ANTONOVS

The border was not much to look at. Our 4x4 plunged down into the first of three powder-dry wadis and then lurched up the other side, before repeating the same lolloping motion two more times. The land on either side of the frontier looked the same: a desiccated, dirt poor desertscape where only gnarled thorn trees and tough old goats seemed to survive. But to the rebel commander sitting beside me on the back seat of the car it was home. "Welcome to your second country," said Al Tom Ibrahim Jabarallda, who asked me to call him Tommy. He spread one arm out of the window to gesture at the parched land ahead of us. "It may only be desert, but we love it," he said with a smile as broad as the distant horizon. With the other arm he reached down to the car floor, steadying the four rocket-propelled grenades (RPGs) which bounced and clanked alarmingly beneath his feet each time the car plunged down into a dry river bed. The second land was Darfur. Behind us we had just left eastern Chad, a similar country of hardship, sand and insurrection. I was riding towards the closest thing to a frontline in the war for Darfur.

Rebels from the Justice and Equality Movement (JEM) had been as good as their word. After a series of satellite telephone calls to commanders deep in the desert and a courtesy call on their representative in the Chadian capital of N'Djamena, a rebel car – smeared with mud as camouflage and an RPG launcher dangling from a wing mirror – picked me up in the Chadian border town of Bahai, a scorched flyblown sort of place built, apparently, on a rubbish dump. There had only been one moment when it looked as if our crossing might come unstuck. As we left for the frontier our vehicle was flagged down by Chadian police. It proved a farcical stop, a moment of meaningless muscle flexing. They pored over my travel papers before warning me in broken French that I had no right to stop in any of the towns around Bahai. Then they waved us on towards the border and our illegal journey. They paid no heed at all to the RPGs or the AK-47 wrapped in the seatbelt to my side. This may have been Chad but it was still clearly Darfur rebel territory. The border itself was meaningless. The same Zaghawa tribe lived on either side, crossing at will to visit relatives, or to find water or grazing for their bony cattle and camels.

Clear of the wadis, our young driver, Yahia, put his foot down, sending up a plume of dust. Our car scattered a herd of what must have been more than one hundred donkeys, nosing around in a clump of thorn trees. They were nibbling at thin patches of yellow grass. Others stood stock still in whatever shade they could find. It was several miles back to Bahai and it was rare to see donkeys so far from human habitation. I had heard stories of vast herds roaming wild through Darfur. As villages were razed and villagers fled for the safety of camps, their animals were left to fend for themselves. None of the aid workers or peacekeepers I knew had ever been able to confirm the stories, but as we drove on into North Darfur I couldn't help wondering whether this was one of the mythical feral herds.

We left the animals behind as Yahia swung the vehicle this way and that along the dirt tracks that criss-crossed the land. A hot hairdryer wind whipped sand into the air as we raced along. Yahia had only a few clear inches of windscreen to peer through – the rest was smeared in a thick layer of dry, grey mud to stop the glass reflecting – but he seemed to know exactly where he was heading through a country devoid of landmarks, bar the odd bleached bone or acacia tree. A yellowing sheep's fleece covered the dashboard, catching dust and insects. Every so often the strong smell of apple tobacco wafted through the car from storage boxes piled in the back, making the cabin smell like a Khartoum shisha den.

This journey into Darfur was my chance to meet some of the men who led the rebellion against Khartoum, to uncover their philosophy and motivation. After my trip to the Jebel Mara with the much fragmented SLA, JEM had emerged as the strongest of the rebel armies. They were positioning themselves as the only armed movement worth the name. But I knew too that their leader, Khalil Ibrahim, had once been close to Hassan al-Turabi, Khartoum's ideological kingpin and strategist. The movement was often described as Islamist and the hand of Turabi was detected in its founding manifesto. And they had a programme that stretched far beyond redressing Darfur's marginal status in Sudan: they were fighting to overthrow Bashir's government altogether.

Our Toyota Land Cruiser bumped to a stop. Yahia was peering frantically through his tiny clearing in the windscreen. Next to him the fourth passenger, Bongo, whom everyone called "the judge", was talking excitedly in Arabic and pointing to the sky. This was bad. Bongo had spoken only fitfully, weighing carefully each word of Arabic that passed his lips. His babbling was unnerving. Then we were off again, jolting our way into a sparse copse of thorn trees. Yahia pulled up close to a trunk, branches spread across the roof. High in the sky, the reason for our sudden stop became clear. One of Sudan's Antonov cargo planes was describing tiny, tight circles above us high in the sky. The Antonovs were ageing and unreliable, built by the old Soviet Union as one of its workhorses. The Sudanese had found another use, turning them into bombers. They were crude and inaccurate – as likely to kill donkeys as villagers, or fall harmlessly in the sand – but their main weapon was fear. We are in control, was the message beamed out by the tiny speck above, and you cannot hide. The crew must have spotted the plume of choking brown dust kicked up as we raced from the border. Now it was almost hovering, trying to home in on our position. I had read about these planes bombing villages many times. Maybe one had flown directly overhead during my trip on a donkey with the SLA – but it was not really until I was squatting in the shade of an acacia's thorny branches, peering at the sky, that I realised quite how fearsome their droning engines could be. It was easy to imagine a team of spotters with binoculars on board trying to seek out targets.

Gradually its course straightened and the Antonov seemed to finish its surveillance of our shelter. We were off again, this time doubling back towards the border and another ragged clump of trees. We jumped back and forth for the rest of the afternoon, hopping from one hiding place to the next. The Antonov was never far away. Every time it seemed to straighten it was not long before it banked once again into a circling, searching pattern.

Night came suddenly, the sun dropping fast below the horizon. It was clear we were well short of the main rebel column and would spend the night alone beneath the stars. My hosts began unloading their gear from the roof of the car. Each had a blanket and groundsheet which they spread side-by-side in the dust. As they arranged their boots and AK-47s for the night, we heard the Antonov finally unloading its brutal payload. Somewhere to the north, back towards the border with Chad, a series of explosions crashed through the still desert air. Maybe they had found another dust trail or rebel village, or maybe they were simply unloading their bombs so they could begin their return to El Fasher airport.

Tommy had unfurled a second groundsheet and blanket. Painstakingly, he brushed it free of sand before gesturing that it was for me. "Don't worry, I'll be right beside you with this," he said, laying down his semi-automatic rifle next to my bed for the night.

The rebels obeyed strict light discipline. With Antonovs patrolling the skies it was far too dangerous for a cooking fire after dark. Dinner would be a simple affair. My three companions took it in turns to hold a shallow metal bowl up to their mouths, each taking a deep draught in turn. The bowl was passed to me and I hesitated for a moment. The light had faded fast and there was no way to tell what exactly was in the dish. "This is our special water," said Tommy. "You should drink it."

I took a cautious mouthful, before gulping down the invisible liquid. It had been a long, thirsty day and I'd been trying to preserve my own meagre supplies of drinking water, uncertain how long I'd be staying with the rebels. The mixture was thick and sweet, and not entirely unpleasant. With a drop of honey or fruit it might even have tasted like a smoothie. Tommy explained that the drink was their secret weapon, an energy-boosting concoction made up only of sugar, flour and water, which was nicknamed the "curse of Darfur", for reasons he struggled to explain.

"The government says we take drugs to fight," said Tommy, lounging on his groundsheet beside me. "We don't. This is all we need."

My blanket was thick and warm. Its man-made fibres crackled and popped as I wriggled around to get comfortable. In the darkness I could see static electricity sparking around my legs. Next to me Tommy began to explain how he had joined Darfur's armed opposition. Just like General Rokero of the SLA, whom I had met in the Jebel Mara, Tommy was about my age, just a couple of years older. He was educated too. The son of a schoolteacher, he had left Darfur to study in Omdurman, where he obtained a degree in information management. From there he had taken a job in West Kordofan at a university library. Then war had closed in on his family's home of Abu Gamra in North Darfur – not so very far away from where we were stretched out beneath a dark sky speckled with stars. Abu Gamra was a typical Zaghawa village. Even in the harsh, undeveloped, arid land of Darfur, it had a school and a clinic. Villagers grew sorghum and peanuts, and some kept goats and a few camels. That was until the Janjaweed arrived with orders to empty the village.

"They destroyed it completely – mosques, the schools. It was genocide. In this time I lost most of family. My uncles, aunts, grandfather and many friends were killed by the Janjaweed. The rest left for Chad," he said, stretching his arm back in the direction we had come from. "I could have stayed working at the university, but that is not the way to help our country. So it was my duty to come back."

Now he said he was fighting so that his three children, Mohammed, Sajeed and one-year-old Muhand, could return to the village where their father grew up, tending the family's goats. He began to explain the names of his children, how Sajeed was the name of the dust mark on the foreheads of the pious, where they have touched their skin to the ground, and that Muhand was the name of a deadly blade.

"This is not a knife. It's a long sword, like you use to cut off the head of Bashir and other dictators," he said, throwing back his head and laughing hard.

With the Antonov gone, the night was silent. The stars spread out above us like a Pollock painting with no black spaces between them, just a never ending speckled ceiling. With the villages around us emptied it felt like we were the only living things in the desert. There were no humming generators or crackling radios. Anywhere else in Darfur the night would have been punctuated by braying donkeys or maybe the clatter of women rinsing pots. Here there was not even the buzz of insects. Two shooting stars raced across the sky. They would have been invisible back home in Nairobi, where there was enough light pollution to obscure their trails. Perhaps I should have made a wish, hoped that Tommy would one day bring his wife, children and parents back from Chad to live here again in peace. But superstitions are not really my thing. And anyway, doesn't everyone wish for peace? The problem is always deciding what sort of peace it is you are wishing for. Who is in charge? Who gets a hand on power? Are the spoils shared? No, wishing on stars was not for me. It seemed enough to watch the pair arc through the shining night and simply be reminded of the vast scale of Darfur's emptiness.

*   *   *

Dawn arrives early for those whose watches are set to Darfur time. Tommy, Bongo and Yahia had rolled up their blankets and were supping at their bowl of sugary water by the time I had cleared my eyes of a night's accumulated dust. My watch said 5.00am, yet it was already broad daylight. The sun in this part of Darfur had risen an hour earlier than I had wanted from the warmth of my borrowed blankets. The reason was simple: JEM had set up its own time zone, one hour behind the rest of Sudan, bringing dawn forward. The clock change was a symbol of their rejection of Omar al-Bashir's 1989 coup, when he had underlined his Islamist credentials by altering Sudan's time to put it in the same zone as Mecca. Whatever the time, I felt like I needed more sleep, but with yesterday's brush with the Antonov still fresh in the memory everyone was keen to move on before it returned for its morning sweep.

It turned out we had been close to the main body all along. Within thirty minutes of setting off, our groundsheets were pulled back off the roof-rack and spread in the shade of thorn trees once again. This time we were not alone. Here and there clusters of men sat sipping tea next to technicals armed with heavy machine guns. Some sat on smart red woven carpets; others on the bare dirt. One or two were praying, bending and kneeling in unison. In all there must have been about one hundred vehicles strung out through a sparse copse that ran the length of a narrow shallow hollow that may or may not have turned into a thin river during the rains. Goat droppings marked out the best patches of shade and even though the sun was still low in the sky, its burning heat was obvious.

Tommy had disappeared off, but soon returned with a thermos jug which he used to fill a tiny glass with hot, well-sugared tea. He handed it to me using his body to shield it from the sand which was carried through the air by a sharp desert wind. "Don't worry, the sand is our friend. It hides us from the Antonovs," he smiled.

That afternoon I saw the crude damage inflicted by the makeshift bombers in Kornoi. JEM had taken control of the abandoned town a few days earlier from a government garrison and they were keen for me to see their prize. It lay no more than thirty minutes drive from our holing up spot. Kornoi was not much to look at – a sad collection of huts that had been battered and prised apart by the wind. Rubbish was strewn everywhere. Plastic bags were caught on dilapidated fences and the whole place had a melancholy air. Its residents had fled to Chad in the early days of the war. And on the edge of town, not far from a watering hole, was the twisted shrapnel left behind by an Antonov bombing run as it searched for the victorious rebels. The blast had left a three-foot deep crater, edged by scorch marks. It was surrounded by steel cables – the finger-thick wires that would normally be used to reinforce

71

concrete. Now, though, they were bent out of shape; the result of being packed into an oil drum with explosives and then dropped from several thousand metres. It would have been a crude and unsophisticated way of killing anyone, relying as much on luck as judgment.

The town had been captured after a brief fire fight. The guerrillas had struck in classic fashion. They had mustered as much firepower as they could manage just outside town – more than one hundred vehicles, including several with Kartyusha rocket tubes – before unloading everything they had on the neat collection of mudbrick homes, defended by a network of shallow trenches that marked the army barracks. Many of the government soldiers had simply turned and run. They had left pretty much everything behind, from five army trucks parked in an open-air workshop to combat jackets hanging on doornails. Coffee mugs and bowls lay upturned among the debris. The thick stench of rotting flesh emanated from one of the defensive trenches where a body was decomposing in the sun. Three bombs lay in the centre of the compound, next to a concrete bunker, where they would have been stored for the helicopter gunships that flew in and out of a landing pad.

My hosts were moving from hut to hut, searching for anything they could carry away. A bed sprung with plastic twine, a chair and a wide metal platter were piled on to the back of one of our pickups. A lot of the loot had already been taken away. I kept my distance, remembering a training course run by former Royal Marine commandos that taught journalists how to survive in hostile environments. They had explained that checkpoints, bases or towns recently taken by one side or the other were prime sites for booby traps left by retreating forces. That did not seem to bother the JEM fighters, who treated the base like a supply depot, upturning beds, rummaging in a grain store and picking through room after room. As I stayed out of range, I noticed a row of small red flags pinned to one row of houses at the edge of the camp, the edge nearest the town itself.

"This is to tell us the battle is coming, that they are on their way to terrorise us," said Majdi Adbulrahman Idriss, one of the commanders who had fought in the conflict. He carried his rank on his face, in the form of the goatee beard favoured by officers. Most of his face was obscured by a turban wrapped around his head and looped under his chin. It was perfect for keeping the sun off the head and dust from the eyes, and I took to wearing one myself.

When the rebel assault had come, few of the government soldiers had any stomach for a fight, and the whole thing was over within a couple of hours. Inside Kornoi's mosque it was easy to see why. A grand brick building, easily big enough to accommodate all the town's men, it was one of the few buildings that was still standing, but it also bore the scars of war. Its steps were crumbling and the government soldiers had left graffiti on its inside walls. "Who imprisons us in this place what is so called Kornoi," one soldier had written. Others had declared their loyalty to the rebels of the SPLA. These soldiers were Southern Sudanese, with little loyalty to Khartoum. They were far from home, tasked with waging a war they had little interest fighting.

I saw some of the captured soldiers later. JEM commanders had told me they'd seized more than one hundred. I counted about forty – still a sizeable haul. Some were sitting atop empty wooden ammunition crates aboard a captured government truck; others in a circle being debriefed in the shade of a thorn tree. Their eyes betrayed no fear, more a combination of exhaustion and relief that their war was over. Many had the long limbs and facial scarring of the Southern tribes. Just like the soldiers who had left their graffiti in the mosque, they came from people who had spent two decades fighting the government and may have had more sympathy with the rebels than Khartoum. Plenty of analysts had told me the government had a problem with its army, dominated as it was by Darfuris. Khartoum was reluctant to trust the loyalty of senior commanders ordered to wage war against their own people. Just as in the Southern civil war, Bashir had relied on local militias whose temporary loyalty could be bought and he was now importing soldiers from across his empire to do the dirty work of war.

We could not stay long in Kornoi. The window between Antonov sorties lasted only a couple of hours. They were not searching randomly through the dust of Darfur, but were concentrating on the area around the town in pursuit of the rebels. Best to hide up in the shallow dip beneath what little scrub we could find for cover. By the time we arrived among the main column it was time for a late breakfast. A big steel platter was laid on the ground, with what looked like a large mound of camel dung at its centre. It had the colour of the sand around us and the surface texture of an ill-digested plate of roughage. In fact, it was a Darfur staple known as assida – a thick, dry porridge made from millet – surrounded by a gloopy green sauce made from okra. On previous trips to Darfur I had managed to make my excuses and avoid this particular delicacy, knowing that the next meal of roast goat or pizza at an NGO guest house was not far away. This time I had no choice. I dug my fingers into the pile, scooped out a bite-size piece, then dunked it into the sauce. The taste was not so bad. The okra was sweet and salty and imparted enough flavour to mask the blandness of the millet porridge. It was the texture that was problematic. In ideal conditions it would have had the consistency of soft clay; in the desert, though, it had the consistency of soft clay mixed with sand.

After breakfast, the day dragged on lazily. The sun was too strong to do anything but sit in the shade, drink tea and talk. I had been promised an interview with Dr Khalil Ibrahim, the leader and founder of JEM, but was happy to wait soaking up the life of the rebels around me, eating their food and hearing their stories. In between, I flicked through the pages of a document downloaded from the internet that set out JEM's founding manifesto.

At first no-one knew the identities of the authors. They signed themselves merely as the "Seekers of Truth and Justice" but their manifesto, printed on twenty-five sheets of A4 paper stapled together and distributed outside mosques in Khartoum, quickly raised a stink. It was not so much their conclusions – that a small, unrepresentative northern elite had dominated power and wealth since Sudan's independence – that shocked or surprised. For many Sudanese, used to a northern president and cabinet posts dominated by his associates, that was already an obvious truth. It was more the fact that in the year 2000 a group of dissidents could be so bold as to actually publish and distribute their conclusions. With strict control of the media and dissent rarely tolerated, the Black Book was an overnight sensation. Some 1600 copies were distributed, a number that multiplied within days as readers thronged photo-copying booths. The Black Book: Imbalance of Power and Wealth even appeared mysteriously in ministers' offices, slipped in by their officials. Legend has it that Omar al-Bashir himself returned from prayers to find the simple document placed on his desk.

"Al kitab al aswad", as it was known in Arabic, laid bare the nepotistic workings of the Sudanese state. In a series of tables inter-spersed with indignant rhetoric, the anonymous authors dissected the anatomy of the ruling class to show how little more than five percent of the population had dominated power. Table after table described the regional make-up of cabinets, state governorships and government committees since independence. In short, it provided an explanation for the unrest that had dogged Sudan ever since the British left: the neglect of Sudan's regions by a northern ruling elite based around the Nile.

"We called it internal colonisation," said Dr Khalil, one of the Black Book's authors, when I met him the following day. "This domination of resources led to instability and fragmentation. Everyone is trying to find their own way out of poverty. This is a big country with a lot of diversity of languages, tribes, religions, backgrounds. So any unity is difficult. We think that if there's no justice then Sudan cannot function as one country."

Dr Khalil had not always been a thorn in Khartoum's side. He was once a keen supporter of Bashir and Turabi's 1989 coup. He had served as a volunteer medic with the Popular Defence Forces, a Jihadist cadre set up as the shock troops of the new Islam-ist state, as the regime put together its own military wing. Gradually he climbed through the ranks of the National Islamic Front under the wing of his sponsor, Turabi himself. He had a stint as state education minister in Darfur during the early 1990s, and served in other regional governments, before becoming an adviser to the government of Southern Sudan. Then came his loss of faith in a government that had continued the rule of the northern tribes and perpetrated the grievances set out in the Black Book. The man in front of me was dressed in the combat fatigues and loose yellow turban of a Darfur guerrilla. He wore spectacles – often a symbol of education in Africa – but his feet were bare against a thick, scarlet carpet. While the SLA's leader, Abdul Wahid Mohammed al-Nur, preferred to live in Paris, Dr Khalil had stayed with his men in Darfur. From time to time he would flit across the border into Chad – just as he had a week earlier to meet Barack Obama's special envoy – before returning to his troops in the bush. We were only a few miles from the captured town of Kornoi, and the threat from the Antonovs was never far away, as Dr Khalil laid out his plans. Fighting to topple the government, he said, was the only way to stop the break-up of Sudan and its disparate regions.

"What we want is collective self-determination with all regions sitting down together. This leads to consensus between all regions to live together," he said. "The regions should have equal rights. For sixty years all the presidents are from the one region. Now we want presidents from south, east, west, central, as well as north Sudan."

Better representation from all the regions, and the replacing of the northern riverine elite in power, was needed. A new country – the United Regions of Sudan – would be the result, he added, emphasising the federal structure which he believed would be the only way for the vast empire of sand to hang together. Seeing the regime from close quarters had helped him identify its short-comings. At first he had attempted to agitate from within, gently trying to nudge the ruling National Islamic Front (NIF) in the right direction. He formed a secret cell in El Fasher to begin exactly such a process, but gradually frustration set in, and Khalil resigned from his regional post in 1999. The Black Book was the result of his years of studying the NIF from the inside, along with a secret committee of twenty-five. It was supposed to be the spark the government needed to realise its mistakes and begin a process of reform, but its authors were denounced as regionalists and its arguments dismissed.

Instead of triggering an internal review it laid the political framework for a rebel movement.

"Then the government started burning villages and displaced many people, particularly in Masalit areas," said Dr Khalil. "The resistance started. Principally it started as non-political resistance. We supported that."

The non-Arabised tribes of Darfur, the ones who still counted their traditional languages as their mother tongues, had been defending their land and animals against Arab raiders throughout the 1990s. The Fur, Zaghawa and Masalit communities each had their own militias for defence and these became increasingly active and organised as the threat increased. The Zaghawa, for example, had been buffeted by drought in the 1980s, bringing them into conflict with the Arab herders who crossed their land, moving northwards in search of water. Then failed rains in Northern Darfur forced the Zaghawa south, pitting them once again against Arab militias. The Fur too had been organising in the 1990s, bringing together its dispersed network of defensive units to take on the government, rather than simply see off other hostile tribes. It was these armed resistance groups that eventually coalesced into the Darfur Liberation Front, which announced itself with an attack on the provincial town of Golo in February 2003. A month later they had captured the town and announced a new name: the Sudan Liberation Army. For this strand of the rebellion, the politics came second to survival. The militias had been formed to defend families and farms from rivals, but had now been recruited for a bigger struggle.

Meanwhile, the other strand of the rebellion, Dr Khalil's search for justice and equality, had begun with the politics of the Black Book, before taking the struggle to the bush. It produced a movement more politically sophisticated than that of the other rebel groups, with senior commanders from inside the NIF government. It was fighting to take Khartoum and rebuild Sudan on federal lines – a much more ambitious programme than seeking greater autonomy and a bigger slice of the pie for Darfur, as the other rebels were advocating. But it also raised difficult questions.

77

Dr Khalil had been close to Hassan al-Turabi: was JEM part of Turabi's latest masterplan to regain power; his latest reincarnation as Darfur freedom fighter? The Sudanese government has often made the claim, and even Turabi himself had told me he identified with Darfur's oppressed and had offered advice to rebel leaders. The Black Book is based on the sort of Islamist analysis he would endorse. It sets out five principles of good Islamic governance, before judging Bashir's government and finding it wanting.

The authors point out that Justice is one of the ninety-nine names of Allah, before continuing its assessment: "Justice and equality are our demand. Remaining within Islamic slogans which this government claim to raise, we indicate that justice and equality are essential to full realisation of Islamic rule. That can only be realised if we are prepared to speak out for justice. Prophet Mohammed once said: "Support your brother whether he is just or otherwise." In so saying, he does not mean standing with injustice. Rather, what he meant is that you take your unjust brother by the hand, and direct him to where justice lies. This is our approach to our brothers in the Northern Region."

In other words, the Khartoum regime has failed because it did not use Islam as the guiding light it claimed. By concentrating power and wealth in the hands of a small minority, depriving its southern, western and eastern regions of investment, it failed to fulfil Islamic principles of justice. Having used religious rhetoric to seize and retain power, in many ways the Islamist coup of Bashir had not been Islamic enough.

Dr Khalil shifted to his knees, jabbing his finger at the geometric design on the carpet beneath him, as he took pains to distance his movement from its roots in Turabi's NIF. He had no interest in ruling by Sharia law, he insisted. Instead, a conference of the regions followed by a constitutional conference would be set up to work out how to organise the new United Regions of Sudan.

"So when we come we don't want to impose Sharia on anyone. There are Christians and there are other religions. This will be a question for the conference. We want to generate religious and personal freedom. To keep people united, then, we have to respect people's rights, otherwise everyone will fight."

Unity, though, has often been in short supply among the rebel movements themselves. Almost as soon as it had formed, tribal fissures developed within the SLA. Minni Arkoy Minawi, a Zaghawa, and Abdul Wahid Mohammed al-Nur, a Fur, squabbled over power, eventually each claiming to be leader and taking their tribemates with them. The split was formalised in 2006 when the two took rival positions at peace talks in Abuja. Minawi signed a deal with the government, which Abdul Wahid refused. The result was a rapid fragmentation of the rebel movements. Suddenly every commander wanted to head his own splinter group and win a seat at the table. Groups merged and split in the blink of an eye. SLA-Classic, SLA-Unity and SLA-Free Will emerged in a bewildering array of acronyms. Nineteen commanders dissatisfied with the outcome of the talks formed G-19. No sooner had a new lexicon of groups appeared then they started disappearing in a mist of coalitions and amalgamations. The National Redemption Front (NRF) brought together an SLA faction, JEM and an older opposition group, the Sudan Federal Democratic Alliance, all hosted by the Horn of Africa's arch meddlers – Eritrea. The NRF lasted about a month, before it too split, giving birth to the United Front for Liberation and Development. This time JEM was not included, replaced by the National Movement for Reform and Development, which had broken away from Dr Khalil's grouping in 2004. At times, there were more than twenty different rebel factions at work on the ground.

A friend in Khartoum had helpfully given me a family tree of Darfur's rebel groupings. It showed JEM and the SLA in big, bold letters at the start of the conflict, before quickly disappearing into a spider's web of connections and annotations. A cloud of arrows linked one group to the next, identifying splits and mergers. Here and there it described the tribal makeup of different groups, showing how tribe and clan were key drivers of reorganisations – for example, the Zaghawa commanders of the G-19 who had split from the Fur leadership of Abdul Wahid. They, in turn, were from a different Zaghawa sub-tribe, the Wogi based in the arid lands stretching from Kornoi, where I was sitting, to the North Darfur capital of El Fasher, to the Kobe of Dr Khalil, which were concentrated in Chad and the borderlands. As a map of Darfur's competing factions, the spaghetti soup of acronyms and arrows was next to useless; as an illustration of the dense, confusing morass of rebel movements, their internal conflicts and the ethnic dividing lines, it was invaluable. I still wasn't sure who was who, but it helped show how the fragmented rebels were often more interested in their own power struggle; policy seemed less important than clan. And the sheer complexity of the chart – a tangle of hieroglyphics – showed that disunity was a big part of Darfur's problem. How could anyone decide who was to get a seat at the table with so many different groups competing for space? One leader would claim to have the biggest military presence, while another would trumpet the loyalty of camp populations. Without a single, unified position it seemed that Khartoum could play one group off against the other, and keep Darfur in a state of chaos. And each faction needed cars, cash and sat-phones for the war effort.

As I sat talking with Dr Khalil, I could count maybe a dozen or more Toyota pickups, all camouflaged with mud and all crammed with guns, RPGs and ammunition. There must have been a hundred or so parked among the thorn trees. Yet there couldn't be a car showroom within 1000 kilometres.

It reminded me of the men I had met in Nyala a few months earlier, men like Ismail, a driver with one of the dozens of aid agencies operating in Darfur, and each a victim of the rebels' desperate need for vehicles.

* * *

The first man gripped a grenade in his hand. Two others held pistols and a fourth carried an AK-47. They had come for Ismail's car, a smart Toyota Land Cruiser and the vehicle of choice for rebels, Janjaweed and bandits.

The man with the grenade flung open the driver's door and shoved Ismail into the passenger seat, screaming, "Where are the keys, where are the keys?"

His face was hidden by sunglasses and a green scarf wrapped in a turban as he started up the 4x4. The three accomplices piled into the back. Ismail had just dropped two nurses at a clinic outside the state capital, Nyala. As a driver in Darfur he knew the risks. It was his turn to be carjacked, just like his brother who worked for an aid agency, and half his colleagues in South Darfur.

The driver gunned the engine and turned the 4x4 towards the road out of the government controlled town. Ismail pushed himself as far into the seat as he could, trying to make himself invisible. He knew what was coming. Movement up ahead marked the boundary of the town, where Janjaweed militiamen manned a roadblock. The car was through even as they rambled for their weapons. They managed to fire off a few ill-aimed shots but the car was long gone, the bandits whooping as they heard the crack of Kalasnikovs behind them.

The man with the grenade kept up his speed as the car bumped and lurched along a sandy track. It took six hours to reach their destination, the town of Deribat. Now Ismail knew the identity of the gunmen, for the town was held by rebels of Abdul Wahid's SLA. A crowd of khaki-clad guerrillas soon gathered around the prize. In a war where the government could call in airstrikes or send the highly mobile Janjaweed to do its dirty work, the Japanese 4x4s were highly coveted by the growing band of rebel groups. Many still relied on donkeys or travelled on foot.

"They took it in turns to test it out," said Ismail, once he was safely home in Nyala. "They drove it around and around in tiny, tight circles sort of showing off with it."

He looked older than his twenty-six years. His crooked teeth were stained brown with tea and cigarettes. His hair was thin and wispy, his gaunt face serious as he continued his tale.

Ismail knew he was in deep trouble. He worked for a government health agency, making him the enemy as far as the SLA was concerned. He was a long way from home and knew that many drivers never returned from being carjacked.

The man with the grenade allowed Ismail to telephone his family to say that he was well, before locking him in a cell at the town's police station – long since abandoned by the government. It wasn't long before another rebel stinking of booze wandered in with a stick, grabbing Ismail before beating him around the back until one of his comrades dragged him away from the cowering driver.

"They thought I was a government agent and wanted me to confess everything. I kept telling them I was just a driver, but I expected them to come and get me and to kill me one day."

Ismail was moved to the town of Jawa, where the SLA had taken over an old government prison. He was dumped in a cell with fifteen other men, and countless cockroaches and rats. The beatings stopped only when he fell sick, wheezing and coughing with asthma. After forty-five days he was turned over to doctors with Médicins Sans Frontières in Faina, the little mountain town where I had hired donkeys and a guide a year earlier. The rebels finally said he could go home when he swore on the Koran that he would not tell the government about his treatment.

"The SLA are very bad people because many of them are drunkards. They were rough with me, beat me. I still have pain from their beatings," said Ismail, in a matter of fact tone, twisting his shoulder to show the part of his back that still keeps him awake at night. "When it's cold I have problems breathing from what they did to me."

We met in his family compound on the edge of Nyala. It lay at the end of a tree-lined street in what passed for a smarter neighbourhood. Ismail sat with his brother, who had been abducted by bandits six months earlier. Both were still working as drivers. It carried risks, but their neat home – a collection of huts made from wooden frames, complete with new beds, and a Chinese-built motorbike parked in the corner – marked them out as a reasonably well-to-do family. Both smoked, which was rare in Sudan where few could afford such luxuries. They reckoned their salaries with aid agencies outweighed the threat. Yet each year the chances of being snatched were growing. In 2007 some 137 humanitarian vehicles were hijacked. A year later the figure had risen to 277, along with 218 personnel, according to statistics collected by the UN.[4]

It was often impossible to tell who was responsible. Many vehicles disappeared off to the West and crossed the border into Chad's growing car market. Some of the carjackers were bandits pure and simple, selling the spoils for cash. But the rebel movements were probably responsible for the majority, stealing aid supplies for their soldiers and using the cars and Thuraya sat-phones to equip their commanders. UN officials often thought they could detect a spike in attacks ahead of peace talks, as rival movements vied for power and influence on the ground: the more cars, the better the chance of a seat at the talks. Sometimes it was impossible to tell the difference between bandits and rebels – both wanted cars and both made it more difficult to deliver food and medicine.

*   *   *

That was the old days, said Dr Khalil confidently, as the sun dipped towards the distant horizon. A dust-filled sky set the dusk air alive with reds and oranges as he tried to explain that his JEM was now the only rebel movement with influence. During the previous days I had been introduced to commanders who had joined his band in the weeks before I arrived. There was Mansour Arbab Younis, a former secretary general of the G-19 who later formed SLA-Mainstream, before bringing his 320 soldiers to JEM in January 2009. Adam Ali Shogar had likewise made his way through a similar chain of groups, ending up in SLA Field Command, before joining JEM in March 2009. There was a commander from southern Sudan, from Kordofan and from the east of Sudan – all from way beyond the borders of Darfur. Gradually, I was told, the fragments and factions were reuniting under Dr Khalil's leadership into a national movement, a new JEM. They each mentioned the same

---

4 – *Darfur Humanitarian Profile No. 34, published by the Office of UN Deputy Special Representative of the UN Secretary-General for Sudan UN Resident and Humanitarian Co-ordinator, January 1, 2009*

reason, a spectacular attack a year earlier by a fast-moving column of pickups that had driven across the desert right into Omdurman, the historic capital of Sudan, and had come close to breaching Khartoum itself. The shifting array of rebel movements could be influenced by one important factor – the prospect of power; just like the Somali militias or the guerrillas in the Congo who seemed to switch alliances with the wind.

The attack had been a tremendous publicity coup, exposing Khartoum's military fragility and helping JEM leapfrog up the rebel pecking order. It had been easy to suppose that Sudan's war machine had turned the capital into an impregnable fortress. Yet 151 technicals had simply driven out of Darfur and into the heart of the governing regime. My young driver, Yahia, had been at the trigger of a Dushka anti-aircraft gun aboard one of the technicals that covered more than 1000km in five days, speeding through the dust. They started from three bases, forming up into a single strike force only as they converged on the capital. Several times they were spotted by the Sudanese air force, he said, and had to hole up to avoid the attentions of Antonovs and the more deadly Migs. It was early afternoon when he reached the tarmac roads and higgledy-piggledy sprawl of Omdurman. Yahia's unit was tasked with hitting Wadi Saidna, an air force base near Khartoum, where they destroyed three aircraft, before moving on to Radio Omdurman. There things began to come unstuck

"When we got there we couldn't work the equipment," said Yahia.

Instead of broadcasting a message of victory across the country, they found themselves fighting their way through the city trying to link up with the two other columns, who were closing on the bridges that linked Omdurman to Khartoum. As darkness fell, though, they realised that the Sudanese military was listening in to their radios and sending false orders. Switching off their communications put an end to the disinformation, but threw the entire operation into confusion.

The audacious assault ended as rapidly as it had begun. The rebels had failed in their objective of taking Khartoum. In fact, they were beaten back just short of the bridges across the Blue Nile. Skirmishes continued for several days but the Blitzkrieg attack had run out of steam in sight of its objective.

"The idea was not to take Khartoum but to send a message that this government is not strong," said Tommy, who joined the rebels in the months after the attack, but had already developed a nice line in spin

More than 200 people were killed as helicopter gunships and tanks were deployed across Omdurman. The government captured dozens of rebels, who were sentenced to death a year later. And despite what Tommy said to me a year later there seemed little doubt that wresting power from President Bashir had been the ultimate aim. Yet he was right – the attack had been a huge shock to the capital. Suddenly Darfur was no longer a distant war. It had arrived on the doorstep of the Northern tribes that JEM held responsible for Sudan's inequalities. It had come to the smart new coffee shops springing up across the city – air-conditioned joints where I had once spent $20 on a mug of Jamaican Blue Mountain. Ministers would find it more difficult to assure the army of Gulf sheikhs with oil dollars to invest that Darfur was not an issue. Roadblocks became part of everyday life. There were rumours of a giant trench being dug around Omdurman and extra tanks were stationed on the bridges. Residents said the city felt like it was under siege. The attack lifted JEM above the fog of rebel movements, allowing it to claim itself the dominant force in Darfur.

But the attack also exposed a less favourable side to Dr Khalil's rebel army. Among the soldiers captured in the attack were children, some as young as eleven, who had been pressed into fighting. Rather than fight, though, some simply laid down their weapons as quickly as possible. In all, eighty-nine children were picked up by the Sudanese military and moved to a special facility outside Khartoum, where UN officials were allowed to visit them.[5] Many had been plucked from refugee camps on the Chadian side of the

---

5 – See, for example, Unicef welcomes access to children held after Justice and Equality Movement attack on Omdurman, press release, May 31, 2008

border. There were few facilities for children once they were too old for primary school, making them ripe for recruiting. Teachers in the camps along the north-eastern border of Chad, deep in Zaghawa territory, were also part of the sensitisation process, pointing out to young boys that the refugees were mainly women and children: men were needed across the border as part of the struggle. JEM commanders and vehicles were regular sights in camps around Iriba and Bahai, where I had been picked up by rebels. Often the NGOs would leave camp by 3.00pm, to be replaced by rebels who then had free rein to entice youngsters into their ranks.

A Unicef official in Chad had even told me that recruitment had accelerated in the weeks and months after the Omdurman attack as fresh fighters were needed to plug gaps left by the dead or captured. "They are being more cautious in terms of recruitment. It is becoming more difficult to see, particularly in terms of abductions, and the sensitisation has become more difficult to see because of our investigation, but it has simply gone underground," he said.

The fighters around me in the presidential column in Darfur were young, but not that young. Once or twice my hosts had gotten jumpy as I tried to stroll alone around our camp, and they preferred me to stay close to the shade where they lolled drinking tea. One boy in a yellow kadoumoal, or turban, had looked babyishly young. When I asked how old he was I was told thirteen, no fifteen, and that commanders had tried to send him home but that he kept returning. For his part, Dr Khalil insisted that JEM did not resort to underage fighters.

"JEM is not recruiting children," he said, jabbing his index finger at the carpet once again. This time he was not just emphasising a point; he was losing his temper, starting to shout. "We don't have any forced recruitment for adults. We don't have recruitment from camps. In Omdurman what happened was that enemies of JEM tried to find evidence that could take us to the International Criminal Court. They collected street children and they indoctrinated them, telling them what to say, intimidated them to say 'We came from Chad with Jem.' I do not accept it. They have no proof. This is a clean movement."

The United Nations observers who had visited the captured prisoners said differently. Officials had also quietly told me that hospitals across the border in Chad were currently treating young boys injured while fighting for JEM. Yet this seemed to be a side of the rebels that was frequently overlooked, along with the fact that at times they had been the main barrier to aid deliveries. Of course they were fighting an oppressive regime in Khartoum; a regime that had mobilised thuggish militias to do their dirty work across Darfur. And my hosts had been courteous and treated me as an honoured guest. They had said the right things, explained their agenda and allowed me to see for myself the damage and fear wrought by the sinister Antonovs. But it was important to remember that this was all part of their media operation, a slick PR machine that operated from one of their Land Cruisers. Smeared with mud, it looked like any of the other cars. But with little more than a satellite phone, a couple of laptops and a generator they were updating the JEM website and uploading videos to YouTube. Criticism by Khartoum, the United Nations or NGOs was swiftly followed by rebuttals from the field. It was an impressive operation – not least for the cramped and difficult conditions the small team operated in.

The result was a glowing media profile. Reports tended to focus on tales of courage, heroic injuries and rebel accounts of government atrocities. Abdul Wahid, leader of the SLA, was frequently interviewed in his Parisian home or a salon de thé. He would display his scars as if they were medals, but rarely had to explain why he had been away from Darfur so long or answer allegations that his troops too were using child soldiers. One of my own colleagues had spent time with JEM, and wrote a series of glowing articles for *The Times* about how their call for "justice and equality" had attracted an "impressive array of doctors and lawyers and a sophisticated agenda that extends to redistributing power among Sudan's oppressed and marginalised peoples."[6] No 'embed' on the government side would have been so soft. A double standard

---

6 – *Black Book's call for equality drew intellectuals and exiles to struggle*, The Times *(London), March 20, 2009 by Anthony Loyd*

seemed to be at work. It was partly the willingness of the rebels to host journalists – both General Rokero in the Jebel Mara and my JEM guides in North Darfur had shown an instinctive knack for providing me with the stories I needed. And possibly it was the result of journalists tending to view rebels as the good guys, wherever they were fighting around the globe. It was difficult not to sympathise with their cause, of course, but that should not be enough to mask their weaknesses. Few African wars had been so neatly divided into good versus bad, black and white. And, up close, these rebels were rather grubbier than they seemed from a distance.

It was twilight by the time Dr Khalil and I finished talking. The Antonov was back, invisible in the gloom, but its steady hum filling the air with menace. Seeing my startled face, Dr Khalil chuckled and tried to offer words of reassurance. "When the Antonov flies in a straight line then there's no need to worry," he said. "When it circles then you know it has found you."

It reminded me of one of the traditional expressions so loved across Africa: "When the elephants fight, the grass gets trampled," or some such. Together we listened to the engines drone off towards the North. As I strolled back through the camp towards my mat and blanket, silent flashes lit up the dark sky – rather like lightning dancing across the horizon.

5. IN SEARCH OF THE ARABS

It was an almost identical tale to the ones told throughout Darfur. Whether among the smouldering ruins of destroyed villages or amid the higgledy-piggledy life in the aid camps, Sheikh Hassan Mohammed Mahmoud's story seemed desperately familiar. It was shortly after dawn when the gunmen struck from the west. They had left their pickups far from Marla, the sheikh's town, and arrived on foot to increase the element of surprise in their deadly raid. The inhabitants had just finished their first prayers of the morning. The women had their cooking fires burning. Men were sipping tea or preparing to check their cattle. The day's life was just getting going when the killing started. Those first sounds came from close to the well, where women and children were fetching water.

As the sound of gunfire moved closer, Hassan did not wait to find out what misery was unfolding. This was not "good shooting". He gathered up as many of his twenty children as he could manage and started hurrying them away from the danger. Sanctuary lay in the forests about two hours' hike from the town. The shooting was louder now and he could hear shouting as he made a last check of his mudbrick home, making sure no-one had been forgotten. Then a searing pain ripped through his thigh. He had been shot. His white jalabiya was turning red as blood soaked through the fabric.

His journey to safety passed in a blur. The sheikh's helpless body was bundled on to a donkey cart by two of his sons and he closed his eyes as he clutched a rag to his wound, gritting his teeth against the agony.

There was little left of Marla by the time they returned two days later from their hiding place in the hills. There were only dead bodies, charred homes and smashed pottery. Sheikh Hassan found the corpses of two of his sons. A third would die in hospital. Some twenty-five cows, thirty-five goats and a horse – Sheikh Hassan's wealth – had been stolen. There was no longer any way to ignore the war, and the people of Marla began the long trudge to safety.

"We found the village was burned," he said. "There was nothing left. War had come so we came here."

Here was Al Sereif camp, home to 13,000 people just outside Nyala, the capital of South Darfur. Thousands of villages have been emptied in the same way. Millions of people forced into camps; two thirds of Darfur's population made reliant on aid. My notebooks are crammed with the same stories from North, South and West Darfur – each of the three administrative regions. Villages burned, homes looted, sons dead, daughters raped.

This, though, is where Sheikh Hassan's story started to depart from the rest, for he was from one of the tribes rarely cast as a victim of Darfur's war. Ask who was responsible and the story of Darfur is turned upside down.

"Harakat," is his one word answer – the Arabic word for "movement" or rebels.

Sheikh Hassan is a leader among the Beni Halba tribe. He calls himself an Arab, from a tribe that has furnished Janjaweed commanders and offered some of the stiffest resistance to the rebel movements. Even before the Darfur conflict began, Beni Halba militias known as fursan were notorious for burning Fur villages and killing civilians after defeating a Southern rebel commander who had tried to drag the western province into the civil war. Yet Sheikh Hassan and his village never took up arms. Like many Arab tribes or branches or sub-tribes they stayed out of things. Instead of being the persecutors of war they found themselves the victims of a conflict they had done their best to avoid when rebels loyal to Minni Minawi came calling. While the world focuses attention and aid on the settled farming tribes – or black, African tribes in the confusing argot of Darfur campaigners – there are other victims. Many of the Arab tribes have stayed outside the camps, preferring to try to hang on to what is left of their herds and centuries-old lifestyle. But hostile tribes to the north have closed their traditional migration routes to Libya, Chad and Egypt, and the livestock markets are gone, closed by the war. Inside the camps, said Sheikh Hassan, everyone was a victim. Suddenly the distinctions between African and Arab, farmer and nomad, are meaningless.

"I don't talk about the Arabs or the Africans. Me, I am one of the heads of all the tribes in the camp here," he said, explaining that he was a representative working for everyone. "But if you ask me how am I an Arab it is because I don't speak in any local language. I speak in Arabic only."

Hassan Mohammed Mahmoud looked like any of the other sheikhs in Darfur's camps for the displaced. He had lost his home and his village but was doing his best to keep his people together among the dust-blown shacks and lean-tos. He still had his cane, a symbol of his authority, and a brilliant white scarf around his neck. The jalabiya he wore was grubby and his leather slippers dusty and scuffed, but his serious dark face edged with a neat white beard still carried the authority of his fifty-three years. This was a man used to leading.

I met him with half a dozen other sheikhs in the shade of a roof woven from reeds. Some sat on a splintery wooden bench, others on mats. All had lost their villages. Some represented Arab tribes, others so-called African. As I scanned from face to face it was impossible to distinguish which was which. Hassan's wrinkled skin was the colour of coal. Another Arab sheikh, also from the Beni Halba, had still darker skin. A member of the Fur was sitting with them, from one of the supposed black, African tribes that rose against the government. Suddenly it seemed silly to call him black or African. Arab and non-Arab, they were all black and African.

"There is no conflict between Arabs and Africans," said Sheikh Hassan with a growing hint of anger. "It's between government and rebels. In our area there were soldiers and police and that's who the rebels were attacking."

He was getting sick of my questions about Arab identity. With a flash the mood of the meeting changed. Gone were the jokes about using magic to help me become as fertile as a sheikh. The men stalked off for a conflab, returning to inform me I could interview anyone else I liked but that there would be no photographs. With that they were gone, muttering something about being very busy. Asking about tribes and identity seemed to have re-opened old wounds. Maybe they thought I was just another reporter looking for the Janjaweed. Or perhaps my questions seemed irrelevant, a reminder of artificial distinctions that had no real meaning. If I couldn't tell the difference between the Africans and Arabs while sitting in front of them, what did it matter?

Further into the camp, past a dusty football pitch, through the stacks of firewood waiting to be burned and further on beyond the donkeys eating from nosebags, there was a woman who explained what the question was all about.

Mariam Mohammed Bagar reckoned she was about sixty – although her creased face and three teeth poking between her lips when she smiled suggested she was much, much older. Around her neck she wore a single orange bead on a thin string, marking her out as a member of the Fur. She had left her home in Umm Qasr, a two-hour truck ride north of Nyala, after a Janjaweed attack in 2004. For years, though, her village had lived in harmony with the nomads that roamed past. As she poured boiling water from a blackened kettle through a strainer filled with tealeaves and cinnamon into a glass already an inch deep with sugar, she explained what life had once been like.

"Before, they lived with us peacefully. They lived outside and we would live in the village. Arabs came into our market and would sell us meat and milk. They would buy dura, simsim and onions that I had grown myself," she said, using the local words for sorghum and sesame. She passed me the scalding glass before looking up, her clear eyes obviously seeing a more innocent time. "I don't know what changed."

Understanding what changed is at the heart of understanding the conflict in Darfur.

* * *

My driver was nervous as we bumped across the sun-scorched dirt backstreets of Nyala towards the animal market. This was the place to meet Arab herdsmen. They would bring their camels here from the grazing land close in around Nyala or on their return from pastures further north. There was news to swap and animals to be sold, tea to be drunk. It seemed the right place to get under the skin of the nomadic tribes who call themselves Arabs. For many of the locals though Arabs meant trouble.

"These are Janjaweed," whispered my driver as we pulled up before a small tea stall, where a couple of men in jalabiyas eyed my white skin. "You must be very careful here. They will wonder what you want."

In front of us, dozens of camels sat hobbled in the dust. Bored-looking herders stood in the sun waiting for business. A pickup truck in camouflage colours was parked at the edge of the market. It was waiting for two men in military fatigues who seemed to be haggling over a particularly large beast. The ground's thin soil was covered in goat and camel dung. The place stank of animals.

I wandered over to one of the herdsmen and asked how much he was selling his camels for. The price was 1500 Sudanese pounds – or about £350. This was big money when traders regularly brought as many as 200 animals to sell. The camel man thwacked one of his charges on the rump, forcing it up to its feet the better to admire its physique. It looked dirty, its coat matted and grey from the dust. One leg was bound at the knee and the animal stumbled back to the ground as I nodded my head in what I hoped was the correct manner to appreciate a smelly ungulate. By now we had gathered a crowd who were wondering why a khawaja had turned up at the market. Someone shouted at my driver, who was by now shifting his weight from foot to foot in anxiety.

"They are saying, 'This man is not welcome here. He will be in trouble if he stays,'" he whispered to me.

"Explain to them that I am looking for someone called Ahmed Ismail,"[7] I said back.

---

7 – *Not his real name*

A mutual acquaintance had set up a meeting for me the evening before, but Ahmed, whom I knew only as a tribal leader, had not appeared at my hotel as arranged. The mobile telephone network was even more sluggish than usual, so the only option had been to pitch up at the animal market and ask around. In Sudan everyone seems to know everyone and within a few minutes we were back in the little taxi with a young boy who had promised to take us to Ahmed's house.

His was a prosperous home. A whitewashed brick wall enclosed a courtyard with palms laden with dates. We waited inside a cool sitting room, sipping more cups of sweet tea with enough sugar to coat the teeth for the rest of the day. Two men in jalabiyas arrived first – Ahmed's brothers I was told – before finally Ahmed himself, dressed in a green safari suit. As so often in this part of the world, I still wasn't entirely sure who he was or why a meeting with him was so important. After the usual pleasantries, we started to talk about his Mahariya tribe, one of the landless camel-herding tribes – or Abbala. With no land of their own, it was these tribes that provided the backbone of the Janjaweed in return for promises of a homeland of their own.

"Ten years ago life was very easy," he said. "We lived as we had always done, but for the past five or six years we are suffering more."

Drought, he said, had made grazing in the north of Darfur more difficult to find. Wells had dried up and his people were forced to spend more time in the south, in areas they would normally have passed through rather than lingered. His words, I knew, were backed by United Nations estimates that the Sahara had drifted south by 50–200 kilometres since records began in the 1930s. Although the research was far from conclusive that this was a permanent and continuing transformation, there was no doubt that it was an additional stress on the lives of the herders who found their pastures more difficult to reach each year.

"The problem is that people from the outside misunderstand," he said, now developing his argument. "They think all Arab tribes are bad. And because we have camels people think we have wealth.

The rebels want people to believe they are the only ones with problems so they will get support. The black people are given aid and we are not. In our tradition we cannot go to the camps so people cannot find us."

As he talked, two powerful themes were emerging. There were echoes of my conversation in Al Sireif camp. One was a notion of victimhood. The Arabs in Darfur were suffering. They were losing their animals and their traditional migration routes in the war. Only no-one was listening to them. They were in pain but voiceless, having to watch as the world poured food and money into camps which catered for the other side of the conflict.

And then there was the question of Arab identity, of Arab pride. Arabs would never want to move to the camps as it meant giving up their way of life. It seemed that taking charity and settling down in one place meant losing face; going hungry out of sight at least meant that their sense of self was intact. They were still nomads upholding a noble way of life. Never mind that they were dirt poor and watching that way of life disappear in the face of drought and war – the one thing they had left was their identity. The notion of Arabhood and the differences between Arab tribes and non-Arab tribes was proving elusive, but inevitably that made the perceived difference all the more vital. No-one had managed to explain exactly what it meant to be Arab, but it was something that people were clinging to. So who were they?

Darfur's Arab tribes had begun arriving as early as the ninth century, drawn by the region's fertile plains. A second wave from northern Africa and the Nile Valley came in the fourteenth century. There were other migrations and people arrived in dribs and drabs, at a time when Darfur was the crossroads between the North and South, the African and Arab worlds. The Darb al-Arba'in or Forty Days Road linking Sudan to Egypt meant traders, slavers and herders were constantly passing through. The sultanate was long a melting pot of different peoples, and so it seemed the Arab groups had just as much claim to be Darfuri as any one of the other ethnic mixtures and political amalgamations that make up what we call tribes.

Nowadays if some spoke Arabic as their only language then maybe they were Arabs. If they pursued a nomadic lifestyle, like their ancestors, then maybe they too could be called Arabs. But the more I looked for any real ethnic basis, the more elusive it proved. The boundaries between tribes were fluid and shifting, but that didn't stop Ahmed feeling them all the same.

He needed someone to blame for a disappearing life and he didn't have to look very far. He detailed attack after attack on camel trains around Wadi Hower, in North Darfur, en route to the livestock markets of Libya, carried out by rebels. In all, he reckoned 3700 camels had been taken from his tribe since 2003. He had lost 350 of his own in a single attack. More than fifty men had been killed, he added. Similar numbers were detailed in reports by Human Rights Watch.[8]

Against a backdrop of a proud people humbled by rebel attacks, he made the emergence of Janjaweed militias seem like a rational response to the war. A way of life was under threat. Livelihoods were disappearing. New ways to live were needed.[9]

"The nature of Darfur is that everyone has guns to defend their walls and themselves," he said. "If you have no guns then you can't defend yourself."

Suddenly our meeting was over. Ahmed said he needed to get to another appointment. We made our farewells and arranged to meet again at the market later in the afternoon. He wanted to introduce me to women who had lost their husbands to Zaghawa attacks and explain some of his tribe's traditions and livestock rearing skills. Outside, my driver was waiting in his little blue Taiwanese taxi. The engine was already running and the door was open. We were bumping along the street towards the town centre before I had even closed it.

"That man is Janjaweed," said the driver.

---

8 – *"If We Return, We Will Be Killed" Consolidation of Ethnic Cleansing in Darfur, Sudan, Human Rights Watch, November 14, 2004*
9 – *A full description of Darfur's Arabs, their plight and misrepresentation is offered in Livelihoods, Power and Choice: The Vulnerability of the Northern Rizaygat, Darfur, Sudan by Helen Young et al, Tufts University, January 2009*

"How do you know? Why didn't you tell me before I went in?"

"I thought you must know him," he replied quickly. "While you were in there a truck pulled up filled with soldiers. They waited for one of them to go inside, then when he returned they left again."

It was impossible to know. I'd started to learn that people in Nyala and throughout Darfur used many different definitions of Janjaweed. The more historical use seemed to be to refer to bandits. Anyone with a gun on a horse might be described as "a devil on horseback". Others used Janjaweed and Arab interchangeably. My driver seemed to view everyone at the animal market as a potential threat, as if every Arab was Janjaweed. And then there was the real thing, the tribal militias armed and directed by the Sudanese government against rebel-supporting tribes. I hoped Ahmed Ismail would provide some answers later in the afternoon. If Ahmed Ismail was indeed a leader of the Mahariya then it seemed only natural that he would be in close contact with the tribe's traditional militia, used to defend livestock and pastures.

We pottered back to the market later in the afternoon. The camels were still there and a few goats wandered aimlessly looking for something to chew. But there was no sign of Ahmed. We asked around. No-one knew where he was. My driver was still anxious and keen to leave as quickly as possible, but I managed to persuade him to hang on for a few minutes. He was talking to some of the herders while I wandered off, slipping my camera out of its case and – after getting permission from their owners – snapping some shots of the camels.

It only took three photographs to get into trouble. A small man with dark glasses came racing up to me waving his hands. He was rude and aggressive but it was the glasses that gave him away: large, brown, plastic frames with a dark tint. I'd seen them worn by countless government officials before – this man was from National Security. My driver was convinced I'd been set up. I wasn't so sure, but either way my encounter with Nyala's Arab camel herders was over. A camera in a public place invariably risks a run-in with the legions of security officers or informers that roam every street and market in Sudan. I climbed reluctantly back into the taxi with the spook who by now was clutching my press card as if it was exhibit A. He would be disappointed when he phoned his boss only to be told that no, the man he had detained in the market was not a spy, but a bona fide journalist with the correct accreditation and every right to be in Nyala. But that would be two hours away. First we would have to drive back to my hotel, rummage through my paperwork, and then endure a pointless round of questioning during which I'd apologise profusely for taking a photograph of a smelly camel.

* * *

"Honey is very good. This is the best medicine."

Al Siir had dragged me from corner shop to corner shop and supermarket to supermarket until we had found what he was looking for. The five kilogram tin of honey was now perched on my lap, soaking my trousers in sweat, as we hared over the bridge from Khartoum into Omdurman. Al Siir had devised a plan that we both hoped would land an interview with the man who could tell us everything we needed to know about the Janjaweed. Netting the scoop, though, required an introduction from a closely related tribal leader. It was someone Al Siir knew well and I had met once before. The only problem was that he was laid low with dysentery. Hence the honey. Al Siir had great faith in the giant tin pressing into my thighs. "This is very good for the stomach, no?"

We pulled up at another of Omdurman's sizeable villas. Chairs had been drawn up beneath a canvas awning in a courtyard for a meeting of tribal sheikhs that was due to start shortly, and we were ushered into a bare waiting room. The tin of honey was passed to the sister of the sheikh we had come to see, with our best wishes for a speedy recovery. After suitable cooing at the size of the gift, she promised he would be in touch as soon as he was well enough.

By then though I had left the country. Time and time again I tried and failed to secure an introduction, but it never happened. The man I was trying to find was Musa Hilal, head of the Mahamid tribe and the closest thing to a Janjaweed commander-in-chief. This was not the sort of man to meet people he did not know. Particularly khawajas. So for two years Al Siir and I sped around the city following leads, being offered introductions and having meetings cancelled. During this time, Hilal was made a government adviser, and there were frequent trips to wait at his office in front of a smiling but ineffectual secretary.

"Al Siir, this secretary must be able to arrange a meeting for us," I would say, under my breath, as we waited.

"No, no, no Mr Rob," Al Siir would hiss back. "This is just his secretary. He will know nothing."

Some aspects of Sudan would remain opaque no matter how many times I tried to understand the workings of society.

I followed Hilal to Nyala, only to learn he had just returned to Khartoum. Another time, Al Siir arrived breathlessly at my hotel restaurant to tell me to run, we had a meeting in thirty minutes. We raced to his office only to be told Mr Hilal was ill, and would be unable to see us. And it was not as if he did not give any interviews: I had helped a Greek TV crew secure a meeting and several journalists had been granted access. It was just that as a man synonymous with the slaughter by Arab militias, he was sensitive to when he could speak and when it was best to keep his mouth shut. He would disappear for weeks to his North Darfur base in Misteriya, shutting off his mobile phone before returning to his government responsibilities in Khartoum.

The charges against him were simple: that he had organised, recruited and led Janjaweed militias in Darfur. Dozens of witnesses reported his involvement in attacks. His Mahamid tribesmen have been a key component of the Janjaweed, although Hilal himself has always denied a commanding role. "It is a lie. Janjaweed is a thief. A criminal. I am a tribal leader, with men and women and children who follow me. How can they all be thieves and bandits? It is not possible," he told *The New York Times* in 2006.[10]

---

10 – *Over Tea, Sheik Denies Stirring Darfur's Torment*, by Lydia Polgreen, June 12, 2006

The force he led may well have been based on the tribal loyalty he commanded as leader of the Mahamid. And his militias – rather like the rebels – may have been based on traditional tribal armies, established for self-defence, but they were being deployed in a very new capacity. A communiqué from his Misteriya headquarters, obtained by the Sudan scholar Alex de Waal, spelled out their sinister mission: "You are informed that directives have been issued . . . to change the demography of Darfur and empty it of African tribes" through the burning, looting and killing "of intellectuals and youths who may join the rebels in fighting."[11]

Like any extreme movement, the Janjaweed had its roots in hardship and victimhood. Desertification and a series of devastating droughts throughout the 1980s may have intensified pressure on land, closed off pasture and increased tribal tensions. But it needed one last ingredient to transform it into a vicious killing machine: a notion of Arab supremacy. Musa Hilal brought that, along with his several thousand-strong militia – and it came not from the Arabs in power in Khartoum, but from across the Sahara.

At its centre was Colonel Gaddafi of Libya, who had long viewed Darfur as the backdoor to Chad and the best way of realising his grand vision of a pan-Arab kingdom stretching across the Sahara. His government hosted Chadian opposition elements during the 1970s, a movement that gradually became known as the Arab Gathering. Eventually he got his hands on Darfur when he struck a deal with the government that replaced Nimeiri in 1985. In return for oil and weapons, Khartoum turned a blind eye to recruitment of Darfuri tribesmen into his Islamic Legion. Chadian dissidents were also rearmed and launched on cross-border raids. With the arms and trainers came an Arab ideology that quickly won favour. Fur leaders appeared to be in the ascendant after a reorganisation of local government, so leaflets listing how the rights of Arabs had been ignored by an African government in Chad and black

---

11 – A New History of a Long War *by Alex de Waal and Julie Flint, Zed Books, which also offers a comprehensive account of the origins of the Janjaweed, the rebels and the conflict*

dominance in Darfur found a ready audience. They called for an end of rule by the zurgha – or blacks. It was time for the Arabs to have their turn. For the first time, AK-47s and RPGs were in plentiful supply, but the key change, the one that would come back to haunt Sudan two decades later, was the emergence of a racist ideology. Every other ill – drought, political representation, land, migration – was now being expressed in terms of blacks and Arabs. The distinctions had always been there. They were part of people's lineage, their history. Now they had become matters of life and death. Musa Hilal was at its centre; a member of the Arab Gathering.

Visitors to his training camps at the start of the conflict described how recruits were indoctrinated with stories that Darfur had been stolen from the Arabs by black tribes. Racial hatred was stoked constantly. Africans were parodied in songs, leaving the militiamen in no doubt about the identity of their enemy. At the same time, Musa Hilal himself was delivering public warnings designed to frighten and intimidate his enemies.

A witness at a 2003 speech in Misteriya's market place told State Department investigators that the Janjaweed leader had addressed a mixed crowd of Arabs and Africans.

"Musa Hilal said he was sent by the government of Sudan, and he told the people that we are going to kill all blacks in this area, and that if you kill people, nobody will be prosecuted. Also if you burn, nobody will prosecute or question you. Animals you find are yours," said the witness, who added that Hilal ended with a final call to arms for his chosen followers. "I have come to give the Arab people freedom," he said.[12]

* * *

Mariam, the elderly Fur woman who made me tea, had wondered what had upset the centuries-old tribal balance. This is what had changed. Where once the tribes had rubbed along together,

---

12 – Darfur and the Crime of Genocide, *John Hagan and Wenona Rymond-Richmond, Cambridge University Press*

intermarrying at will and resolving conflicts through old traditions of dialogue and diya, or blood money, now outside forces had disrupted relations. The multiple identities of the region's people – Sudanese, Darfuri, Arab, tribe, clan – were giving way to a single label. Combined with the carefully fostered sense of victimhood, the conditions were set for the emergence of armed militias ready to forge a new way of life that replaced livestock with weapons as the main source of income. Armed with a divisive ideology and plentiful AK-47s, there was no shortage of gunmen ready to do the government's bidding. Yet while Musa Hilal bought into the new way of doing things, there were plenty who did not.

* * *

To the government soldiers they probably looked like any other nomads. The armed men on camels and horses could have been herders; their guns used to defend their animals from raiders. Or maybe they were Janjaweed. Either way the Arabs were nothing to fear. They were harmless desert wanderers or they were members of a militia allied to the government. But as they rode down the hills towards the army camp near En Siro, the riders unslung their weapons and began firing at the government forces. The fighting didn't last long. It was a typical short, sharp guerrilla attack. There was no attempt to take any territory. The objective was simply to inflict casualties and loot arms. The attackers left with two pickups, but lost one of their own vehicles. It was over in minutes. The difference was that the assault was carried out by Arab rebels of the Sudanese Revolutionary Front (SRF), drawn from a tribe notorious for its role in the Janjaweed.

The fighters were led by a young man from the Mahamid tribe, Anwar Adam Khater, who should have become an engineer in Sudan's oil industry. His father sold several camels in Libyan markets to ensure the boy an education in Khartoum and a future far from the arid plains where the family made a reasonable living from their animals. High school and university had qualified the young man as a computer engineer but he never went on to work in the country's booming petrol sector. He never finished the training. By now it was 2004 and Darfur was in flames. His father, along with other members of the Abbala tribes, was prevented from travelling to the lucrative markets of Libya and Egypt. Zaghawa militias, allied to Darfur's rebel movements, had closed the routes Anwar's ancestors had used for centuries.

"One time my father tried to send female camels to Egypt and the government said female camels could not leave the country so security forces took them," said Anwar, in halting English. "Twice Zaghawa took the camels on their way to the North. Three times he lost everything. My father did not ask me to come back because my brothers were there, but I felt my father was suffering and I should find a way to help him."

Anwar's father was one of the big men of Zalingei, one of West Darfur's dust-blown towns. By any measure he was wealthy and successful. He had enough camels to send 300 or so plodding along the ancient routes to Egyptian and Libyan bazaars every few months. Then there were his children – thirty-nine by five different mothers. One wife had been divorced so that Anwar's father could stick to the four allowed by Islam. This was the sort of powerful man the locals would go to with their disputes. He was once an adviser to the late Hilal Abdalla, sheikh of the Mahamid whose exalted reign is remembered with fondness – unlike that of his son, Musa Hilal. The war changed all that. Anwar's father was still a wealthy man, but the repeated raids reduced his camels to about one hundred, making it difficult to produce enough to send to market and keep thirty-nine children provided for (not to mention four wives and an ex). Other sons may have tried to get a job. Anwar tried to win the war that was costing his father so dear.

He went back to his Mahamid people around his birthplace in Zalingei and convinced a few hundred tribemates to join his SRF. It was one of a handful of small Arab groupings that grew out of a sense of injustice at government neglect and its inaction over the camel raids. They included the Popular Forces Army and the short-lived National Movement for the Elimination of Marginalisation, adding to the messy, complex picture of rebel factions.

For much of his rebel career, Anwar lived in fear of his life. The government put a bounty on his head, informers riddled his small outfit and relatives were rounded up and threatened. Twice he was forced to flee to areas where he was not known. He was desperately dangerous to a regime that relied on Anwar's tribe for its counter-insurgency.

Few foreigners had ever met him. Those that had spoke of his unease with strangers, which would turn gradually to charisma once he was sure of his audience. Al Siir and I tracked him down to a small office on the outskirts of Omdurman. He greeted us warmly with glasses of freshly-squeezed lime juice before ushering us into an office. The room was bare. A hole in the wall showed where an air-conditioner would one day be placed. Or maybe it had been recently removed. The only furniture was an empty desk and a blender sitting on the floor. A year earlier the thirty-three-year-old with a neat goatee beard had been forced into an accommodation with the government. He had tried and failed to reach an alliance with the other rebel groups, who thought his Arab fighters should turn over their arms and serve under existing commanders, while Anwar wanted a more formal recognition that his SRF be considered part of a pan-Darfur rebellion. There was no longer a price on his head, but he said he had not given up the struggle.

"The Mahamid have been exploited by the government," he said, stirring two heaped tablespoons of sugar into his lime juice. "Musa Hilal is a leader of Mahamid and now he is a part of the government. We have a saying in Sudan that, 'If you have a lot of food in your mouth you cannot cry.'"

Musa Hilal was the young man's uncle. His contempt was clear as he explained how taking the government's dollars had estranged his uncle from the needs of his people, needs that could be far better met by working with other tribes alienated by Khartoum. For Anwar, part of the problem was a false division. He picked his words with care, avoiding the labels of black or African for the non-Arab tribes.

"We are Africans and we are Arabs. I am against these definitions as separate groups. We must co-exist not as Masalit, Fur or Arabs but as Darfuris. It is wrong to think that the Arabs are outsiders. In the beginning the Janjaweed groups attacked non-Arabs. This got a lot of publicity. This made the international world support Darfur and the non-Arabs. Arabs were the bad guys."

It was not difficult to see why groups like the Fur, Zaghawa and Masalit had been portrayed as victims of Darfur's Arab tribes: they *were* the victims of Arab raiders. But the story got skewed to the point where they were cast as the only victims in a war where the Arabs were the aggressors. Thousands from what were called "African tribes" had crossed the border into Chad at the start of the conflict, fleeing government Antonovs and devils on horseback. There they were filmed, photographed and interviewed by journalists who couldn't obtain a visa for Sudan. Once travel into Darfur became possible, the focus remained on the non-Arab tribes. The Arabs – most of whom had no role in the killing and who were watching their ancient trading routes and markets disappear – went largely un-vox popped. They lived far from the three main cities of Darfur, making them difficult to reach. Like so many nomads in so many other countries they lived on the edge of things. They were less organised and less educated than the settled, farming tribes. When trouble hit they were less likely to make for the aid camps springing up around Darfur's towns, so they remained out of sight of the aid workers, human rights monitors and journalists who began arriving.

Anwar went to his uncle to urge him to take on the government, using the combined strength of the Arab tribes to bolster the rebel-supporting Fur, Zaghawa and Masalit. He found the growing divide between African and Arab meant he was always viewed as an outsider.

"I said we have nothing. Why are we sitting [doing nothing] when the government does not bring us schools, hospitals. Unless we fight we will get nothing. The Fur, they supported me. Khalil supported me. There were some weapons, Thuraya phones, food, but they did not put me in their hearts – we were friends but separate. The rebels never quite completely accepted us." he said.

"I told him we have nothing. More than the Fur we should fight against the government. We are one of the biggest tribes in Darfur.

Our population, politics, economics, we are in front of them – we are strong and can lead. What are we waiting for?"

* * *

I never met Musa Hilal. Nor did I ever see Ahmed Ismail again. I wanted to get inside the minds of the Arab tribes and try to find out why some had taken up Khartoum's call to arms. Few journalists had ever bothered, and I was disappointed not to have gained more of an insight. Those that I did meet as I criss-crossed Sudan in search of Hilal had helped clarify a few ideas though. It was clear that many of the people who called themselves Arabs were victims of a conflict they never signed up to, and they felt neglected and ignored by a world that sided with the rebels. All the people of Darfur, regardless of their tribe, were living on the periphery – both geographically and economically – of Sudan. Anwar Adam Khater's short-lived rebel grouping recognised that. His uncle had followed a different path, using Khartoum's cash and weaponry to carve a new lifestyle in Darfur's dehydrated environment. I didn't get the chance to ask him, but it seemed to me that just like the government proxies in South Sudan, the decision to take on the rebels was an economic as much as ideological choice. The same factors had driven uncle and nephew in opposite directions. The key difference was that one had bought into Gaddafi's notion of Arab supremacy, while the other defined himself as Darfuri, seeking common cause with the rebels.

These were stories that were too rarely told. They were complex and fell outside the accepted narrative of popular understanding. Pitching these kinds of stories to editors was not easy. I've never heard anyone's eyes glaze over, but that's how I interpreted the long silence that would follow my enthusiastic proposal. "Hmm, it's a bit 'Inside Baseball' isn't it," would be the inevitable pithy reply, suggesting it was the sort of esoteric detail of interest only to Darfur aficionados. Stories of the latest Janjaweed massacre, on the other hand, were lapped up. How much sexier to read about "days and nights filled with the dread of 'evil horsemen' called Janjaweed".

With this sort of coverage, it was hardly surprising that few Arabs wanted to talk to me. They were no doubt highly suspicious of the Western media and a world that seemed to be arranged against them. But that led only to a vicious circle, with the rebels able to dominate the news agenda. General Rokero in the Jebel Mara had spent two days with me discussing the aims and ambitions of his faction of the Sudan Liberation Army. He introduced me to rape victims, organised a demonstration of women and children calling for UN peacekeepers and continued to call me with details of the latest bombing raids in his area. So too JEM with its mobile media unit, website and small army of supporters in the diaspora. Rebel commanders passing through Nairobi would call me up on my mobile to invite me for tea. In contrast, the Arabs I met were nervous. Living in government areas, they may well have been scared of saying the wrong thing. But the end result was that their story was not being told. Their people were far from the aid camps, where journalists were able at least to get fleeting access. It all led inexorably towards one side of an artificial division where they were being labelled perpetrators and the other victims.

None of this is to deny the terrible abuses committed by Janjaweed militias in Darfur. They were responsible for atrocity after atrocity, committed against civilian populations at the bidding of Sudan's rulers. But to deny context, to forget the economic hardships that all Darfuris faced, and to ignore the Arab victims, was to grossly oversimplify the conflict. Most Arabs had avoided the conflict altogether. Relegating history, geography and identity to footnotes may make for a better headline, but fails to help our understanding. Ignoring the meddling hand of Gaddafi and branding the Janjaweed as "evil horsemen" helped no-one. Delving into context showed that rational actors were at work, defending the interests of both sides. Journalists like me had contributed, of course. I had searched for fresh Janjaweed atrocities, knowing they made the best stories. Editors had inserted phrases such as "black, African" into my intros and it was only after a couple of years covering the conflict that I began to object, pointing out that everyone in Darfur was black and African. I made little headway.

There was only one narrative at work. As long as there was an extremist, Islamist government in Khartoum, a president who had once hosted Bin Laden and whose capital had been bombed by Bill Clinton, shades of grey were not needed. When one side was an international pariah you did not have to look far for villains. It took one of the most bizarre and exhilarating stories of my career to offer an alternative understanding of how the Sudanese government worked. And even then it was tempting to slip into cliché and stereotype.

6. A TEDDY BEAR NAMED MOHAMMED

Thwack, thwack, thwack. It was the sound that first caught the attention. A dull, rhythmic beat. Deep in the throng of journalists, security officers and curious members of the public it was difficult to see what was happening. The crowd shifted one way and then another. Sweat was trickling down the back of my linen shirt despite the ceiling fans. But there it came again: a steady, walloping sound, rather like a carpet being beaten. As the mass of bodies swayed once again the source of the noise became clear. It was the sound of Sudanese law in action. A man was being whipped in the hall of Khartoum's courthouse.

Half a dozen policemen in blue uniforms swarmed around the convict. They had spread-eagled him against a wall while another officer – his sleeves rolled to the elbows – wielded a brutal-looking length of red rubber tubing. The operation was clinical. Hefting the metre-long hose at one end for maximum leverage, the officer swung time and again. The beatee's loose t-shirt rode up his back. I counted nineteen thwacks. There were no screams of pain. No shows of emotion. Just a cold, clinical punishment for a man convicted of murder. He was to spend the rest of his life in prison and the lashing had been added for good measure. It was the sort of justice meted out every day under Sudan's odd marriage of colonial British law and Sharia punishment.

The British consul, Russell Phillips, was sitting a couple of yards away on a bench. He looked every inch the diplomat in his smart blue suit, tie knotted neatly, side parting in place. He clearly wanted to be anywhere but watching a flogging. He fiddled with his mobile phone, pretending not to notice.

109

The beating was a sideshow. Neither he nor I was there to watch a murderer being punished. We were there to follow the case of the teddy bear teacher, a British woman arrested for allowing her class to name a cuddly toy "Mohammed". As we waited for her to appear in private, the lashing was an illustration of what she might face. If guilty, the punishment was forty strokes, up to six months in prison or a fine.

My phone rang. It was *Sky News*. Producers were calling me on the hour every hour for updates that were leading their bulletins. A Turkish TV crew was outside waiting to interview me for *ITN*. I still had to file for *The Times*, *The Irish Times*, *The Scotsman* and *The Daily Mail*. For the past four days I'd been running on four hours sleep a night and as much illicit gin as I could find. The international press pack was stuck in Nairobi or London unable to obtain visas and I was one of three British reporters already in the city when we broke the news. One or two of the other international correspondents looked down their noses at the tale. Why focus on a teddy bear, they said, when Darfur is in flames and Southern Sudan is on the brink of war? For me, though, it was always the perfect story. Sure, there was a Brit and a teddy bear but it was also a remarkable tale of cultural misunderstanding. It shone a light on the workings of the Sudanese government and diplomatic manoeuvres and, more than anything else, it offered an insight into what makes Khartoum tick. But best of all, I was in the middle of it – the right place at the right time.

* * *

Amber Henshaw was just clearing away our dinner plates, while her husband, Andrew Heavens, checked the wires for stories one last time one Sunday evening. I had met Amber, a reporter with the *BBC World Service*, earlier that year. We had spent a week together in a grubby hotel in Northern Ethiopia as we roamed the fiery Danakil Depression, searching for a party of British diplomats kidnapped in the desert. We shared a taste for red wine and gossip, so when she moved to Khartoum their spacious villa became my base. In return for deliveries of Kenyan coffee, packs of bacon and as much Cheddar cheese as I could carry they would let me crash in their spare room. As usual I was cooling my heels waiting for travel permits and scratching around for story ideas.

It was November and the fierce desert heat of summer had passed. Yet even after dark it was still too hot to sit indoors. The slabs of the garden terrace warmed my feet, releasing the energy absorbed from the sun through the day. We had spent evening after evening like this, listening to the roar of the jets taking off from the airport nearby and wondering where our next story would come from.

"I really don't know what's going on. There's just nothing around at the moment. I've never known it this quiet," said Amber, plonking herself back down at the wrought iron dinner table.

It had been the theme of the week. My plan was to drive down into the oil fields of southern Kordofan to report on an audacious move by Darfuri rebels to widen the war. Their new targets were Chinese oil companies and the huge revenues paid to Khartoum. Choking off the flow of oil and cash might help even out Darfur's lopsided battlefield. Once again I was waiting in the capital for a travel permit to materialise. Only this time there were precious few feature ideas to fill the days. Or so we thought. At exactly the moment Amber and I were bemoaning the quiet week we had just endured, Andrew stuck his head around the door.

"Erm Rob," he began, "There's something here that might interest you."

The story on the Sudanese Media Centre website was garbled – no doubt the result of an automated Arabic to English translation – but the salient points were clear enough. A British teacher had been arrested. She had named a teddy bear Mohammed and fallen foul of Sudanese laws designed to protect against blasphemy. The school's name, the brief report claimed, was Disunited School. And that was it. The name was clearly some sort of mistake.

"I think I know where that might be," said Andrew.

* * *

111

We drove into the city centre the next morning, looking for the narrow doorway in a tall brick wall decorated with Arab arches that signalled the entrance to Unity School. A police car was parked outside amid the usual jumble of taxis, tea stalls and hawkers. We were ushered straight through the entrance lobby, past a playground where teachers and parents were huddled in tight circles, to the director's officer. Robert Boulos was at his desk, speaking to a government minister on the telephone. He was speaking little, his silvered jaw set firm as he listened impassively. The surroundings reminded me of my own Victorian-built grammar school. The impressive parquet floor was rather scuffed and dusty, and the walls were covered in sepia photographs of the school first XI hockey teams dating back to colonial times. This was the sort of place where Sudan's elite chose to educate their children. There were more expensive schools for the UN families and diplomats but this one, with its mix of Sudanese and European teachers, was the one chosen by government officials and a growing middle class.

As we waited for Mr Boulos, Bishop Ezikiel Kondo wandered into the office and introduced himself as the chairman of the school council. He was dressed in black clerical robes, a silver cross dangling from his neck. I did a double take as he settled into a chair, not expecting to run into a bishop in this most Muslim of cities.

"The thing may be very simple but they just want to make it bigger," he told us when we explained we had heard about a problem with a teddy bear. "It's a kind of blackmail."

Andrew and I looked at each other. That was easy. We had the right school. As Mr Boulos finished the latest in a series of crisis calls to the Sudanese authorities, he turned his attention to us and began to explain exactly how one of his teachers had been arrested over a teddy bear.

The whole thing probably seemed a very good idea to a teacher only recently arrived in Sudan – the sort of thing she might have done at her old school in Liverpool. Gillian Gibbons was getting over a divorce and had arrived in August ready for a new life overseas and the start of term in September. She was in charge of a class of six and seven-year-olds and had come up with the idea of class teddy, the sort of thing the children could dress up and look after as a way of learning about bears and their habitats. She asked the class what they would like to call the bear and several names, including Abdullah and Hassan, were put forward. Mohammed was chosen after a ballot, winning twenty out of twenty-three votes, apparently in honour of the class's most popular boy. A letter was typed up and sent home introducing the new classmate.

My dear parents,
    We have a teddy bear in our classroom. His name is
Mohammed and he wants to visit your families and write
his observations about his experience in a diary. So if you
want to have a family party or you would like to organise
a trip or any other special occasion then we hope you
will give us the honour of taking our bear with you.
We would be particularly pleased if you took photographs
too.
    I have completed a page myself to show how it might be
done. So if you would like to borrow our bear then please
write to me as soon as possible.
    Miss Gillian, class teacher

For two months nothing happened. Mohammed was loaned out for weekends and parties and always came back with the journal filled with his latest exploits. No parents or teachers complained, said Mr Boulos with an air of gentle exasperation. He had known the name was sensitive, but there seemed to be no problem. That was up until November. The day before Andrew and I sat in the director's old-fashioned office, armed police had arrived asking for Miss Gibbons, who lived in a flat at the school.

"We tried to reason with them but we failed," said Mr Boulos. "There was a strong presence from the Islamic court. There were men with beards asking where she was and saying they wanted to kill her."

The school was closed on the Monday for fear of reprisals. The police outside were an extra precaution. Children had been turned

113

away at the door and the school's courtyards were filled only with parents or staff trying to find out the latest. No-one knew what could yet happen in a city that had once hosted Osama bin Laden and with a government still keen to prove its Islamic credentials. Cartoons of the Prophet Mohammed in a Danish newspaper had provoked massive demonstrations and outpourings of anger a year earlier.

"We have lost one of our best teachers," said Mr Boulous, in his impeccable English. "She took it just a little naively, innocently. She had no idea what the problems might be."

Outside, among the teachers and parents who knew her, the feeling was the same. No-one believed the new member of staff to be guilty of a deliberate snub.

"We didn't complain because it didn't really seem anything wrong. She didn't mean Mohammed the Prophet, so what's the problem," said one mother, her hair and shoulders hidden beneath a bright, floral scarf of the sort favoured by Sudanese women. One hand rested on the head of her seven-year-old son, also named Mohammed.

Another mother, who had hosted the bear for a weekend, said: "Our Prophet Mohammed tells us to be forgiving. So she should be released. She didn't mean any of this at all."

Al Siir was waiting for us outside. As Andrew crammed his tall frame into the back seat, a wave of elation swept over my body. I might have come to Khartoum to research a worthy piece on the Darfur conflict, but nothing made me happier than a good, old-fashioned foot-in-the-door kind of story. This was going to be a heck of a week and a lucrative one too, if I played it right.

"Andrew," I asked, "any chance you could file this a bit late in the day, there's a good chap?"

As a *Reuters* correspondent his copy would appear in every news-room on every continent minutes after he hit send on his computer. Delaying its arrival to later in the afternoon would allow me to steal a bigger march on my rivals. I knew that *The Telegraph*, *The Sun* and every other Fleet Street paper would have correspondents queuing for visas at the Sudanese embassy in London as soon as they saw the story. Stringers in Liverpool would be knocking on doors looking for relatives. Snappers would be deployed to the schools were she had worked. But if they didn't see the story until late in the day, my guys from *The Times* and *The Daily Mail* could have a run at it first. Andrew told me to forget it. I couldn't blame him; it was his story after all.

My day one piece was ready to be filed by lunchtime, complete with quotes from colleagues and parents and a comment from the British Embassy. It would also go to *The Irish Times* and *The Scotsman*, guaranteeing a pretty decent day's pay. Naturally I didn't send it until later, just to emphasise how hard I was working.

The rest of the afternoon was spent in the study of Ghazi Suleiman, one of my old friends in Sudan. Al Siir had taken me to visit the veteran opposition politician on my first ever visit, when I really wasn't sure of the value of meeting this rather eccentric looking man. His dishevelled mop of fuzzy white hair and oversized braces that slipped down over his shoulders always put me in mind of a clown. But the more time spent in his company, poring over colonial-era law books or discussing his role within the Sudan People's Liberation Movement, the more I warmed to this slightly off-the-wall character. He had an endearing habit of quoting famous figures from British colonial history and frequently looked crest-fallen as I failed to spot the reference. Just the day before, he had invited me for Sunday lunch. He made sure to offer me the choicest bits of grilled lamb and piled my plate high with stuffed peppers and all manner of Sudanese fare, while quoting Churchill at me. Today, though, it was his legal expertise I needed. The Sudanese Media Centre was reporting that prosecutors were preparing to charge Miss Gibbons under Article 125 of Sudanese criminal law, on suspicion of insulting faith and religion. I wanted to know what punishment she faced.

"Now, let me see," he said, running a finger down a page of one of the thick books that surrounded his desk. "Here we go. The punishment is forty lashes, six months in prison or a fine."

This sounded barbaric – but the story was getting better. Now we were into the territory of mad Muslims beating a middle-aged divorcee, all because of an innocent mistake over a teddy bear. I asked Ghazi whether this was Sharia law in action.

"Well that's the interesting thing," he said, returning his braces to his shoulders for the umpteenth time and peering at me over his reading glasses. "The law itself is British but the punishments are Islamic. A lot of Sudanese criminal law is based on British colonial law and these are probably quite similar to your blasphemy laws, but the punishments are . . . um, how shall I put it? Sudanese."

Glasses of sweet tea and bottles of ice-cold water arrived as we sat mulling over what would come next. The story that would appear in the press tomorrow would be one of a clash of civilisations, of a religion stuck in the dark ages that saw fit to whip teachers. My own copy already described a society governed by Islamic principles, where women were beaten if they failed to cover their heads and where alcohol and pork were banned. It portrayed Sudanese justice as brutal. And it was. Yet Miss Gibbons had fallen foul of a law drawn up not by Sudan's Islamist rulers but by its old colonial masters, the British. In 1983, the imposition of Sharia law had brought a new raft of punishments. But many of the underlying crimes remained the ones defined by British law. We chuckled at the irony.

Ghazi, no great fan of the government, also pointed out that at a time when Khartoum was already risking pariah status over its actions in Darfur, this was probably the last thing it needed.

"This is an embarrassment for the government but now it seems that it's in the hands of the legal system. The sensible thing would be to let her go because it doesn't sound intentional, but that would look wrong, as if the law is being ignored. Al Bashir is now probably the only one who can do something."

* * *

The story was an immediate sensation. My copy made page three of *The Times* with a picture of Miss Gibbons on the front. Then all hell broke loose. The morning of day two brought an avalanche of phone calls from news desks across Britain and the US as newspapers, TV and radio stations played catch up. Some wanted to interview me. Others asked for advice on how to get their journalists into the country. Only a couple of weeks ago I had been trying to interest my editors in a story on how Sudan's Comprehensive Peace Agreement – the deal that ended civil war in the South – was on the brink of collapse. No-one cared. Now an innocent misunderstanding with a teddy bear was turning into a media haboob.

Al Siir and I set off early that morning to find Miss Gibbons. If she was locked away somewhere in the city then we wanted to seek out her cell. Al Siir was in a good mood, as he always was when set a special task. He reckoned a cousin of his in the police force would help us locate the police station where she was being held.

"I find myself when I work with you," he told me over and over again as we raced through Khartoum's bewildering road grid as fast as his dilapidated taxi could carry us.

It was a gruelling day but Al Siir seemed to be in his element, finding his calling. We went backwards and forwards over the Blue Nile, then the White Nile, from suburb to suburb. I was never quite sure where we were until once again the muddy waters appeared and I could regain a tenuous hold on my bearings. Sometimes Al Siir would leave me sweltering in the car while he went to find a cousin or another of his contacts. Other times I went with him into police stations, as if to provide proof that Al Siir was working for a "very important person", as he always called me. Eventually he returned to the car, beaming.

"I know where she is," he said proudly and we set off back towards the Blue Nile, and the area of the city known as Khartoum North.

Al Siir pulled up in an anonymous side street. It was dusty and edged with sand where the pavement should have been. Two-storey family homes lined the road, only their roofs showing behind outer walls bleached white by the sun. Most well-to-do families lived their lives like that, behind tall walls where the courtyards could be used as an extra room – somewhere for the women to cook, and the men to lounge. It was like a million other roads in the city. No landmarks or points of interest. Just endless walls hiding Sudanese life. I was astonished we had found the right place at all. Three or four blue-uniformed policemen were loafing on broken plastic chairs in the shade of a palm tree. A woman covered in a peach-coloured wrap was serving them tea, her jars of cinnamon, ginger and cardamom arranged in a row on a tin box. Behind them, a sign above a wobbly wooden door read "Criminal Exploration Bureau". Al Siir stepped forward to help me ask if we had the right place.

"She is sitting all by herself. No-one has talked to her. No-one has been in to see her today and she looks very sad," said one of the guards in Arabic, translated by Al Siir.

"She has also had no food yet."

That was easily put right. We had passed a kebab shop on the main road just around the corner. I ordered up a beef kebab and a chicken schwarma, then nipped next door to a general store for packets of biscuits, crisps, apples and bottles of water. Puffing out my chest and relieved that I was wearing a freshly ironed shirt, I marched into the little waiting room demanding that the provisions be delivered to the foreign prisoner. Now, I would never try to pass myself off as a lawyer or diplomat. But if people jumped to the wrong conclusions, well that was hardly my fault was it? It had worked for me in Ghana earlier that year but Sudan was a very different place. Here everyone was a spy or an informer or someone scared of being informed upon. My bag of provisions was taken without comment, but there was no way in for me.

That left nothing else to do but wait. I had my story. Having written up the arrest yesterday, today's piece would be about the conditions in which she was being kept. The questioning was continuing, it seemed, although she still had not been charged, leaving a small chance that she could be released and sent straight home. Al Siir and I headed back for a kebab each and then settled down next to the tea seller to see what would happen next. Donkeys pulling tanks of water lumbered past and taxis beeped their horns impatiently. Eventually a smart, white 4x4 pulled up with three members of staff from the British Embassy. They got no further than I did and were clearly embarrassed that I was there to watch.

"We have not been given access this time but we are providing full consular assistance to Miss Gibbons. We have already seen her and delivered food and water," said one.

Things were frantic back at the house. Amber had set up a camera and satellite link in the back garden, and was busy feeding the beast of rolling TV news. In between hourly bulletins, she was also doing radio for the *BBC World Service*. Not for the first time I was glad I had only one deadline a day. Amber couldn't travel far from her satellite feed, yet was still expected to be gathering news. Andrew was equally busy. Between us we had divvied up pretty much all the British media outlets and a few others besides. So while he was talking to *CNN* from a quiet room inside the house, I was talking to *Sky News* from the garden, hoping I wasn't getting in Amber's way. His copy was going to *The Guardian* as well as *Reuters*, while mine was going to my regular strings. The three of us had the story sewn up. We swapped tips and numbers and kept each other abreast of who was doing what. It was one of those moments when I was glad to be far from the Fleet Street rat race, where everyone is trying to get the jump on each other. Working as a foreign correspondent in an unfamiliar city, in a country where you don't speak the language, means you can work far more effectively as a team.

There was just one problem. We were frazzled. Each long, pressurised day was making sleep more difficult.

That night, we went for a dinner at a diplomat's house. It was one of the places where the host would be able to offer a glass of wine or a can of Heineken. I drank until my head stopped spinning – in a reversal of the usual order of things – and I knew I'd be able to sleep. Dinner was interrupted twice to record a two-way for the *ITN* evening bulletin and for *Sky News*, who by now were calling me every hour on the hour.

* * *

The Hilton Hotel, on the banks of the Nile, was by now the hub of the media operation. A reporter from *AP* and a couple of journalists from the French news agency *AFP* were staying there, in town by chance as they began setting up a Khartoum bureau. The hotel had long ceased to be part of the global chain. From the outside, it looked like another gloomy government building, all beige stonework and dark windows. The depressing tone continued inside; its rooms were well in need of an update, the pool was filled with water dirtier than the Nile and the juice bar in the lobby was filled with tired sofas. But it was still a reasonable place to hang out each morning, grab a coffee and compare notes for the day ahead.

It was there that I bumped into an American freelance reporter who was on his way to Darfur.

"I don't know why everyone is getting so excited by this teddy bear," he sniffed. "It's not a real story."

I knew American journalists took a different view of the job from us Brits. While we all aspired to be like the hard-nosed reporters we had grown up with on local and regional papers – in my case the Glaswegian compositors and typesetters who became writers at *The Herald* – they considered themselves intellectuals. Journalism was my trade; it was their profession. We had totally different outlooks on our role and influence. I was doing a job; he was answering a calling. I'd had the argument before with friends in Nairobi. I couldn't resist.

"I think you are talking bollocks," I said, knowing that the profanity would shock and momentarily confuse him. "This is a bloody great story."

I was deadly serious. Each day so far we had a fresh line without trying too hard. The story was developing day by day from arrest, to the cells, and eventually to the court and Miss Gibbons' conviction (although we didn't know that then). It had a teddy bear, immediately offering the reader an attention grabbing headline. And, if you smuggled in the serious stuff lower down, you had an audience reading about political Islam, the nature of Sudanese government and how to resolve diplomatic spats so that no-one lost face. How much better to sneak 300 words of that beneath a headline about "grizzly conditions" into *The Daily Mail* or *The*

News of the World, read by millions of people who had never heard of the Darfur Peace Agreement or the National Congress Party, than a worthy 2000-word analysis piece on the inner machinations of the Khartoum government in *The New York Times*? I always found it more rewarding to develop a fluffy story with a deadly serious underside.

Anyway, I reckon I had the last laugh. By the following Monday the snooty American reporter was doing live two-ways with an American TV network.

That day's news line came late in the day. All along, British diplomats had been hoping Miss Gibbons would not be charged but simply released and sent home. That option disappeared in the evening when she was formally charged with insulting religion, inciting religious hatred and contempt of religious beliefs. She would be due in court the following day. It was our first chance to lay eyes on the woman at the centre of our story.

* * *

We arrived early. As usual my phone had been ringing as I got out of the shower at 7.00am. It was *Sky News* calling for the first of the regular updates. After a breakfast of hot, strong coffee and toast Al Siir drove Amber, Andrew and I to the courthouse for a long day of waiting. Security was intense. Pickups crammed with squads of riot police armed with long batons and shields parked outside. It took an age to argue our way inside to join the hubbub of journalists, diplomats and curious Sudanese people who crowded into the first floor hallway. Then we waited. And waited. It was not until lunchtime that a surge in the crowd suggested something was about to happen.

After writing about the teddy bear teacher for four days, it was a shock to finally come face to face with her. Surrounded by a phalanx of police officers wielding their rattan canes, she was being marched to the courtroom. She looked shaken and very pale. Her wavy, auburn hair was in need of a wash. It hung limply on the collar of her black blazer.

"Miss Gibbons, I'm a reporter with *The Times*. Just wondered how you are, erm, you know, coping?"

She looked at me as if I was from outer space then turned her gaze to the floor, before being wheeled away. It was a close call but I had managed to stop myself asking how she was "bearing up".

The rest of the afternoon turned into a circus. Three cameramen were arrested somewhere in the melee. Amber spent hours trying to negotiate the release of the freelancer she had hired for the day. Then came the thwack, thwack, thwack of a flogging for a murderer punished in the hallway. And all the while I was getting calls for updates with little in the way of fresh information coming out of the courtroom. The session had apparently been adjourned while the judge waited to hear from the person who originally made a complaint.

It was, at least, a chance to find out more from people close to the case. Isam Abu Hasabu, chairman of the school's Parent Teacher Association, helped explain why an innocent teddy bear could have caused offence.

"The whole matter boils down to a cultural misunderstanding," he said patiently. "In our culture we don't have the bear as a cuddly symbol of mercy. So people assume naming it Mohammed has a different connotation."

In Britain calling someone a donkey, say, might cause offence. Take away the notion that a bear can be a children's plaything and suddenly a teddy could be a similar problem. He added that it seemed that the teacher had been a pawn used by a member of staff with a grievance. Sarah Khawad, a secretary, had emerged in the courtroom as the main accuser. She had been fired by the school and had apparently made good on a threat that she would try to shut the place down. Accusing teachers of un-Islamic teachings was the ultimate payback. No-one else, it seemed, had been that upset by the bear, but once the authorities had been informed it seemed that common sense would have to take a back seat.

With deadlines looming, it wasn't until 8.00pm that we learned her fate. One of her defence lawyers, Ali Mohammed Ajab, appeared on the dark steps outside the courthouse. Gillian Gibbons had given a full apology to the court he said, but had been convicted and sentenced to serve fifteen days in prison.

It was a frantic rush to file my copy and keep up my various broadcast commitments. Everything was done by 11.30pm but my head was swimming yet again; my body exhausted but my mind still racing with the events of the day. This time there was no booze in the house and no chance to unwind before bed. The last time I looked at my watch it said 4.30am.

* * *

The case was done. After the mayhem of the previous four days, Friday felt like a day to relax. Far from it. The Sunday papers were now calling, desperate for any fresh angle. The story was now the prison. How was she being treated? What were the toilet facilities? How many rats lived in her cell?

Friday was also the day for demonstrations. Islam's holy day was generally spent in prayer and with family. That made it the perfect day for mobilising people on their day off from work. At times of political crisis, imams would whip their followers into a feverish state of mind ahead of government-sponsored rallies at the end of the morning.

That would come later, which meant Al Siir and I had time for our own Friday tradition – fried fish in Omdurman. On every visit we would trundle across the bridge to the old capital of Sudan to breakfast on steaming plates of fish and bread. The restaurant was next to a sandy canal that only filled when the Nile was in flood. It was reputed to have the freshest fish, although no-one could ever tell me exactly which species. It didn't matter much. This was Al Siir's treat and we always made sure to get there early when the huge cauldrons of bubbling oil were still clean. The heat from the cooking fires was intense and I'd watch from a plastic chair as Al Siir wandered around the kitchen – a bare room in what looked like a bombed-out brick building – picking out the best looking fish for me. It would arrive crisp on the outside and juicy inside.

He always tried to lead me into one of the restaurant's windowless rooms. There fans whirred against the stifling heat while a TV blared Sudanese pop music – much better to eat outside with the regulars. There were no women to be seen. The only customers were men, some with young sons. We would squeeze tiny limes over the plate and then eat the flesh with hunks of bread dripped in a fiery chilli sauce until the grease ran down our arms.

"This is the most tasteable fish in all of Omdurman," Al Siir would tell me. "Very good for you. You must have more."

Another plate filled with bony Nile perch, or maybe tilapia, would arrive. Invariably, we would get chatting to the people around us. Proud fathers would push their boys towards me so they could practise their English as we rounded off the meal with thick, bitter coffee flavoured with cardamom.

This Friday, though, we didn't have much time to talk. We finished up our breakfast and clambered back into the little yellow taxi for a tour of the city, trying to spot demonstrations and get a sense of the mood. Things were quiet. The mosques were still full and the streets empty. It must have been about midday before I got a tip: people had begun congregating near the presidential palace, on the banks of the Nile.

We pulled up close to Martyrs' Square, often the focus of rallies, leaving the car a couple of blocks away and setting out on foot. The anger was obvious from a distance. There were maybe 1000 people crammed close together beneath green banners of a Sufi sect. The glint of ceremonial swords caught my eye as they were waved in the air. A flash of flame and a placard went up in smoke. Many of the protesters wore green or red headbands and the cries of "Allahu akbar," – God is great – were clearly audible. There was another chant: "Kill her, Kill her, Kill her," in Arabic.

"Are you sure it's safe?" I asked Al Siir, who was trotting enthusiastically towards the obelisk at the centre of the square.

"Oh yes. This is no problem," he reassured me.

It soon became clear that there was a problem. We had taken up a position close to a police truck for protection, about forty metres from the demonstration itself. From there, I jotted down a few impressions of the protest: angry, noisy, flags fluttering, swords, fists, pictures of the teacher being burned. As I looked up it was clear we had been spotted. One or two young men strolling towards the rally were shouting at us. "Go away," was Al Siir's interpretation. Things got rapidly worse. Within sixty seconds we had been surrounded by a crowd of angry youths. They were shouting words I didn't want to hang around to hear.

"Al Siir," I whispered urgently, "I don't think we should be here any longer."

My trusty fixer had other ideas. With me stranded in the middle of a mob, he had decided the best strategy was to argue our way out of it. He was now haranguing the young men, who had clearly taken exception to Al Siir's role in bringing me so close. The row had caught the attention of a police commander who now moved in. This would only make matters worse, as Al Siir now began arguing with him. Being arrested was not part of the plan. Time to go. I turned around and simply headed for the car, walking as briskly as seemed safe.

My departure was spotted. One man, thick set and menacing, drew a finger across his bearded throat. Half a dozen people broke off from the crowd and began shadowing me towards the car. This was not good. How far was the car? And anyway, Al Siir had the keys.

"There's no problem, Mr Rob."

Al Siir was back at my side. Even better, he had brought the police commander with him. Gradually our shadows dropped back. The car was where we had left it and we were soon beetling back towards the hotel, breathing easily for the first time in a while. It had been a hairy moment, although a heavy police presence probably meant it was never going to get out of hand.

That demo made it on to the front pages of some of the British papers. Beneath pictures of swords being waved, there were descriptions of "protesters spitting with fury". Editorials fulminated against hardliners and fanatics who tarnished the reputation of Islam, and the thousands of Sudanese victims of intolerance. The burning pictures and calls for execution fitted perfectly with the outside world's view of Sudan. This was a dangerous Islamic government that had supported terrorists, and now its people were demanding the death of Miss Gillian, the hapless victim of a murderous regime. Its people were barbaric.

Yet that wasn't quite how things looked from Khartoum itself. I'd spent all week trying and failing to find mobs. The story was not dominating the local media in the same way it had captured the public imagination back home. Sure, one or two of the harder line newspapers had gone to town. *Akhir Lahza* – Last Moment – had printed an angry op-ed piece demanding that Bin Laden's old chum, Hassan al-Turabi, be called in to make a ruling – preferably one that involved a firing squad. And there were angry leaflets doing the rounds. One propaganda sheet called on a million people to take to the streets on Friday. "What has been done by this infidel lady is considered a matter of contempt and an insult to Muslims' feelings and also the pollution of children's mentality as an attempt to wipe their identity," it said.

But by and large, the mainstream news outlets had maintained a rather embarrassed quiet on the subject, keeping coverage to a minimum. It took four days for them to pick up the story. There had been a few demonstrations as well, but they were small, rather lacklustre affairs. It was often pretty clear that the protesters were government workers bussed in for the occasion. My tours of the university campuses and the more radical mosques had yielded precious little, too. On one occasion my questions provoked baffled expressions and a series of questions – who was this woman, why was she in Sudan, what is a teddy bear? – before a student declared his outrage. There would be a demonstration within thirty minutes, he promised. His colleagues took it in turns to brandish my copy of a daily paper bearing Miss Gibbons blurred picture, while he sat quietly writing a statement for me. I seemed to be creating fury, not finding it.

There was some anger in the people I spoke to – but there was confusion also. Why on earth would anyone name a teddy bear? The overriding reaction was bewilderment. Yet it seemed to suit the government to keep a few demonstrators festering. They were needed in case the British Foreign Office got tough and Khartoum needed to show it was at the mercy of public opinion. And there were enough radical groups to play ball.

Back at the Hilton, I bumped into the chubby, red-faced figure of David Hoile. He was an interesting character, someone who had supported almost every unfashionable rightwing cause since his student days in the 1980s. He famously had once worn a "Hang Mandela" sticker on his tie, an episode brought up frequently in *The Guardian* diary column. Now he expected payment for his loyalty. He ran the European Sudanese Public Affairs Council from his base in the UK, essentially a lobby group paid by Khartoum to manage its image overseas. He was a prolific letter writer and publisher of pamphlets with titles such as *The Darfur Rebels, War Crimes and Human Rights Abuses* and *An Assessment of Allegations of Genocide in Darfur*. He may have been an apologist for the regime, but he also had the ear of its leadership, which always made him worth listening to. He generally spoke with a slight stammer. Now, in the middle of a high-stakes story, this made him sound as if excitement was getting in the way of his words.

"I've got an exclusive for you," he said.

Two unlikely saviours were on their way to Khartoum on a mission to secure the freedom of Miss Gibbons, he told me. Two Muslim members of the House of Lords – Conservative Baroness Sayeeda Warsi and Baron Nazir Ahmed of Labour – were due to arrive in the early hours of the following morning. They were coming as private individuals, rather than British representatives, and had a series of meetings lined up with key Sudanese officials.

"I think she'll be pardoned in the course of tomorrow," added Hoile for good measure.

If David Hoile was involved, with his close connections to the regime, it seemed her release may well be a fait accompli. Such a deal had been in the wind all week. Once arrested, it seemed impossible for Miss Gibbons to end up anywhere other than court. Hardliners within the regime would have objected to justice being avoided for a foreigner. The Friday demonstrations were also a signal that there would be more anger if she was released early. Yet the case was acutely embarrassing for the government. It faced international opprobrium for its actions in Darfur. There seemed no need to pick another fight with the West.

Earlier in the week Professor Al Tayeb Haj Attiya, director of Khartoum University's Peace Research Institute, had guided me through the president's dilemma. Professor Al Tayeb's cluttered office was another regular stop for me in Khartoum. Amid models of nineteenth century sailing rigs and piles of dull-looking books, he would listen patiently to my latest naïve analysis of Sudan's politics before helping me to a better understanding. This time he explained how the rise of political Islam was key to interpreting the government's reaction to the teddy.

"There is a sort of 'who's the best Muslim?' competition to this whole thing which makes it difficult for the government to be seen to back down," he said.

President Bashir needed to save face. Giving in to Western opposition would have angered many within his own administration and suggested his grip on power was weak. He was a military man accustomed to getting his own way. He was unlikely to bow to outside pressure. Things might be different, however, if he could sit down and drink tea with two fellow Muslims. They could discuss things in the Sudanese way and come to an arrangement. A pardon, far from being a sign of weakness, could be spun as an act of compassion.

The two Muslim peers arrived on Saturday morning and disappeared off to meetings with government officials and clerics immediately. It wasn't until late in the afternoon that they arrived back at the Hilton Hotel for a toasted sandwich and a tall glass of pink grapefruit juice. Baroness Warsi looked glamorous in a sequinned black scarf. She slipped her shoes off and lay down on one of the deep sofas in the lobby. She had managed two hours sleep in the previous two days. Lord Ahmed loosened his stripy pink tie and fiddled with his portcullis cufflinks as he gave an impromptu press conference. He had a reputation for a chirpy demeanour and a joke for every occasion, but a day negotiating with Khartoum's ruling elite had left him looking punch drunk and exhausted.

"There are a lot of positive signs but the Sudanese government is under extreme pressure from those who demonstrated in the streets yesterday and those religious people who delivered strong sermons yesterday, where they said they should rescind the fifteen days and take her back to court . . . let alone even think about her release," he told us, looking as if he'd been promised a done deal only to find out there was still quite a bit of doing to be done.

The two had paid for the trip out of their own pocket. David Miliband, the British Foreign Secretary, had initially objected to the mission, arguing that the government would be unable to bail them out if they ran into trouble. He also told them it was inappropriate for a Tory peer to be involved. Eventually he lifted his objections, but told them they would only receive limited help from the embassy in Khartoum.

They were on their own, which was probably an advantage. Travelling independently meant they came without the baggage of a Western government that had once ruled Sudan and had troops in Iraq. Still, they were picking up different signals in different meetings. There was a deep sense of embarrassment from the ministers and presidential advisers, the ones who had initially suggested they would be open to discussions with the British Muslims. The politicians seemed to recognise that this was not a battle Sudan needed to fight: a quick solution would be in everyone's interests. The problem was selling a compromise to the clerics. Why should Sudan reconsider the verdict on Miss Gibbons, tried in a courtroom, when Britain was holding terrorist suspects without trial and Muslims were still locked up in Guantanamo Bay? the country's religious leaders argued. She was not going to be released over the weekend, it seemed, or at least not until the clerics had been brought round.

* * *

Everyone had got word that the meeting would be at about 10.30am on Monday. Except, it seemed, the man from the British Embassy. He had to telephone reporters to find out what was happening and arrived late, running across the well-watered lawns of the Republican Palace. Once again the Brits were being kept out of the loop, just as they had been all week. He arrived breathless on the steps of the president's residence, close to the spot were General Gordon was reputedly killed as he tried to defend the city from spear-wielding dervishes in the nineteenth century.

The two British peers were already meeting with Bashir himself. White-gloved servants glided back and forth carrying trays laden with glasses of hot tea or iced Karkadeh juice, made from hibiscus flowers. It was cool in the open lobby despite the number of journalists. Most were local but a few internationals had trickled in from London and Nairobi. For forty-five minutes we waited outside, amusing ourselves by trying to guess which step Gordon had died on and whether Bashir was deliberately making us wait in a place where Britain's adventure in Sudan took a bloody turn. A local journalist eventually pointed out that the palace had been rebuilt long ago and, anyway, no-one really knew how or where the Victorian hero had died, rather spoiling the fun.

Eventually the two peers appeared for a press scrum. By this stage, with Bashir giving face time to two visitors, there was no way a deal was going to fall through. Lord Ahmed announced that Gillian had been freed, while Baroness Warsi read an apology from the teacher.

"I have been in Sudan for only four months but I have enjoyed myself immensely. I have encountered nothing but kindness and generosity from the Sudanese people," she read. "I have great respect for the Islamic religion and would not knowingly offend anyone. I am sorry if I caused any distress."

The story was into its final phase and I couldn't help feeling a tinge of regret. From the moment Andrew had emerged on the terrace this had been our yarn. Now it was all ending in a dull press conference with a bunch of strangers.

Still, the main thing was that Gillian Gibbons was free. She was already on her way to the British Embassy. A hot shower and meal of spaghetti bolognese awaited. (I have always been rather disappointed by the meals on offer to released prisoners at British Embassies. The Brits kidnapped in Ethiopia earlier the same year had been given bangers and mash before flying home. I would have wanted something rather grander.)

My stories were filed by the middle of the afternoon. Things might change, but the words could easily be updated later. In this part of the world, and in the midst of a breaking story, one of my rules was always to file when you had the chance. Later you might find yourself far from an internet connection, with a dead computer battery, or stuck in a police cell.

The *BBC* team – Amber, plus a producer, journalist and cameraman who arrived from Nairobi a few days earlier – had set up camp on the Acropole Hotel's first floor balcony. Amber was doing radio while Adam Mynott was stuck in front of a camera for television. There was only one thing left to do: try to find out which flight Gillian Gibbons would be on. There weren't many options. Lufthansa flew to London via Frankfurt at 1:45am, BMI went via Beirut later the following morning and there was an Emirates flight to Dubai at about 8.00pm that night.

For the rest of the afternoon I sat with Nawaz, the *BBC* producer from Nairobi, in the BMI office. It was just around the corner from the Acropole, off one of Khartoum's shady, colonnaded pavements. *The Times'* travel agent in Manchester was already making me a reservation for the Emirates flight. Sitting in the BMI office, making the booking directly, had an advantage. Every time the attractive sales assistant left her computer, Nawaz and I twisted the monitor around so we could pore over the list of names with a booking. It took a while but eventually we found the right names. Ahmed and Warsi both had bookings on the flight. We left with tickets in our hands and pottered back around to the Acropole, ready for a cold Coke and a spot of dinner.

My phone rang as I reached the hotel's first floor. It was Opheera McDoom, the perfectly named *Reuters* bureau chief in Khartoum.

She was breathless. A friend at the airport had told her Gillian Gibbons was on the Emirates flight. It left in an hour. Adam was just preparing for another live, but I shouted the news.

"We're screwed," I said. "They're on the Emirates flight."

I slumped into a plastic chair and watched him talking to a producer in London. The adrenaline was seeping out of my body and exhaustion starting to take over. It was all done. Although I had a reservation on the Emirates flight it was no use. The ticket office was closed now and in Khartoum I would need a paper ticket to travel. A reservation was not enough. We'd all gambled on flying the following day. We were all wrong. I'd been here for the start of the story. I'd had a good run. What did it matter to miss the final instalment?

It mattered a lot.

"Fuck it," I shouted to a startled *BBC* East Africa Correspondent. "I'm going to give it a go. Anyone coming?"

My stories were already in the hands of editors in London, Dublin and Edinburgh. There was nothing to lose by racing to the airport. I had come this far. Why not go the extra mile? I was carrying my passport, a laptop case and notebook – everything I needed. Without waiting for an answer, I headed down the stairs, phoning Al Siir as I went. He was ready, engine running, as I came hurtling through the doors and across the street towards him. For once the traffic had eased and we made good time as I tried to explain to Al Siir what was racing through my mind. We pulled up at the international terminal about forty-five minutes before the departure time. Dusk was falling as I shot through the doors towards a deserted check-in desk.

"Am I too late for the Emirates flight?"

The woman behind the counter looked up: "Do you have a ticket?"

"No, but I have a reservation."

I cursed. Electronic ticketing had yet to reach Khartoum. My credit card and booking number were worthless here. Without a piece of paper in my hand there was no way of getting on the flight. My heart began to sink. Pretty much anything is possible in

Africa. Countless "no, that's not possible"'s can be converted into "certainly, sir, whenever you like" – rules were frequently overlooked for a white man, particularly one with dollars. But that took time. The one thing I didn't have.

"Is there anything else I can do? Anything at all?" I asked, aware that my tone was edging towards desperate.

"Perhaps you could try the Sudan Airways office, sir. They can sell you a ticket and with that you can travel. You just need a ticket. Any ticket. Get back here fast though, we're just about to close the flight."

Without waiting to find out how it worked, I ran straight out of the nicely air-conditioned terminal to the airline offices just outside, almost sending Al Siir flying as he tried to catch up. There, a ticket to Dubai was going to cost $400. I'd worry about getting to London later. My wallet held $100, a £20 note, 20 euros, 60 crumpled and torn Sudanese pounds plus a few thousand Kenyan shillings – way short.

"Al Siir, how much money do you have?"

He had been making $150 a day for the past ten days. He was the best known and best paid driver in the whole city. He was famous for not spending any of that money on his beat-up car. Now was not a moment for me to be too proud to ask for a small favour. Al Siir, however, looked unsure.

"It's OK. I have money," I told him. "It's in my bag at Amber and Andrew's. Just go there this evening and you can pick it up."

In the end, the ticket office accepted Al Siir's identity card and a promise that he would return the following morning with my cash. I wanted to kiss the little fellow. Once again he had saved the day, but this was no time to congratulate each other. It was straight back to the check-in counter, where my ticket was accepted with a smile. But what if Opheera had it wrong? What if I was about to board the wrong flight and everyone else had it right?

"Oh, just one other thing," I said to the woman at the counter. "Has my friend Gillian Gibbons checked in yet?"

She ran a finger down a printed list. Bingo. The names Gibbons, Ahmed, Warsi and a couple of British officials had all been written on by hand at the bottom. I was ushered straight through to the departure lounge, and on to a waiting bus.

As we boarded, I still couldn't get a look at Gillian herself. The Brits were up front in business class. Al Siir's identity card was only good for a coach ticket and a surly Australian stewardess made sure no-one could "accidentally" turn left instead of right.

It was two hours before I managed to sneak forward and see for myself. Gillian was chatting to the British Embassy's security officer, her eyes shining with a mixture of elation and exhaustion. The whole party was chatting loudly, keeping some of the other passengers awake. The mood, it seemed, was one of celebration. Lord Ahmed kept cracking jokes. At one stage he started on a joke about Muslims named Mohammed, only to be shushed rapidly by Gillian herself.

She didn't really want to speak to me. No doubt the deal to free her had involved a promise not to say too much or criticise the Sudanese authorities who had imprisoned her. She simply said she was glad to be halfway home.

"I just want to relax, I don't want to say any more," she added. "I'm too tired."

* * *

That was enough for me. The story was phoned through by satellite telephone from my seat. It made the front of *The Times* the next morning. Best of all, it was datelined Flight EK 0007.

The rest of the trip was spent chatting with Baroness Warsi and Lord Ahmed, getting the behind-the-scenes story. As I listened to the details of their meetings with clerics and ministers, there seemed to be a clear message. Two Muslims had been able to sort out a spat which had left the Foreign and Commonwealth Office floundering. Sitting down with President Bashir over a cup of tea had produced a result. There had been no sanctions, no lectures – just an appeal to common sense. It seemed that there were pragmatists in the government who knew which hands were worth folding. A compromise had to be reached which allowed the

Sudanese president to save face. The teddy bear story might have seemed a frivolous waste of time to some journalists, but it had given me a much deeper understanding of Khartoum's workings. Whatever the inner rivalries and ideology of the government, one of their key instincts was the collective survival of the regime. And perhaps it offered an example of how to engage with the country over Darfur. Threatening no-fly zones, military intervention and sanctions had all increased pressure on Khartoum to end the war. At the same time, though, they had backed President Bashir into a corner. Khartoum's grip on the country was not as strong as I had once believed, and threatening the country's sovereignty seemed to close down the chance of negotiation. In short, the rather shrill approach of the Save Darfur coalition failed to offer a face-saving way out. End the war or else, it seemed to say.

Of course, that's not to suggest that President Bashir was not responsible for a lot of the bloodshed. He was. But that isn't the point. The point is to end the bloodshed, not to force the country's military ruler into a position from which he can not back down.

We changed planes in Dubai. A business class ticket was waiting for me, and I slept most of the way back to London.

The cold caught me by surprise when I stepped off the plane. The sweat of a long day in Sudan's desert capital and a long night on two flights had soaked through my thin, cotton shirt. My trousers were made from light, breathable fibres more suited to the African heat than the English winter. I stank. The pilot had told us the temperature outside was 1°C. I looked down at my laptop bag. It threw up clouds of Khartoum's dust each time I touched it. I gritted my teeth to stop them chattering and imagined collapsing into a hot bath and a warm bed. My phone was already ringing. It wasn't quite over yet.

7. HUMANITARIAN EMERGENCY

The silence of the sleeping camp was broken at four in the morning. Under cover of darkness, 1000 soldiers, police officers and security agents formed a ring around Kalma, one of Darfur's biggest aid settlements. A densely packed city built from sticks, plastic sheets and thatch, it had gained a wretched reputation as a hotbed of criminal and rebel activity. More than sixty vehicles – pickups crammed with troops or technicals bristling with weaponry – had moved into position to the south of the camp, just beyond a railway line. Their revving engines and the shouts of commanders jolted residents awake. The government had come to act on a warrant to search Kalma for drugs, weapons and criminals. But as they tried to move north their way was blocked by a gathering crowd, intent on keeping out the intruders. Many of the people living in the camp were from the Fur tribe – loyal to the SLA – and had arrived in Kalma after losing their homes to government and Janjaweed attacks. Now some of the same forces lined up in front of them. An angry stand-off developed between up to 6000 camp residents on one side of the railway and uniformed security forces ten metres or so back on the other side. Both sides lobbed insults across the divide.

Some witnesses later told UN investigators that they heard soldiers shouting: "Let us in or we will destroy you."

The shooting began just after 8.00am. At first the soldiers fired harmlessly into the air. Then the bullets were directed at the crowd, now convulsed with panic. As people ran one way then the other, rocket propelled grenades and heavy machine guns mounted on the backs of pickups joined the barrage. The open space became a killing field.

"There were people running everywhere," one of the survivors told me by telephone in the days after the attack. "It was terrifying. We heard bullets whizzing around. There were people in the crowd throwing stones and some had sticks and spears, but we didn't have the guns like the soldiers.

"I tried to get back to shelter but everyone was getting in each other's way. I tripped and fell and was lucky to get away. I saw other people covered in blood. I don't know if they escaped."

Plenty did not. As the shooting continued, more and more people fell and didn't get back to their feet. The sandy soil turned red.

"My friends and I had sticks to try and defend us against the soldiers. But then they started shooting, and we ran for our lives," said Jamal Ibrahim, a young man of twenty-four whose eyewitness account was collected by one of the aid agencies that arrived in the bloody aftermath. "A woman was running in front of me and I saw a bullet hit her back and head. She fell right in front of me. I stopped to help her but she was already dead. We had to keep running, so I had to leave her body there. I will never forget that moment. Later, after the shooting stopped, we went back to collect the bodies and bury them. There were so many. Even young children were shot. Too many people died that day. They came to kill us in our villages – now they have killed us in the camps too."

It was all over in twenty minutes, but by the time the bodies were counted thirty-three people had died. They included ten women and nine children. Some of the bodies were found sheltering behind walls built from nothing more than reeds. One was an old woman who drowned in a pool of water as she tried to escape the slaughter. The rest died from gunshot wounds. Five more would die from their injuries as the days wore on. Another 108 people were injured. Some had their skin and flesh shredded by shrapnel. Two nurses at a clinic run by the Dutch branch of Médicines Sans Frontières battled to keep sixty-five patients alive in a facility with only ten beds.

Outside the camp, aid workers in Nyala were desperately trying to organise a relief convoy to rescue the injured. First they had to arrange for an armed escort from the United Nations to accompany their ambulances. Then they had to negotiate their way through a government checkpoint where they were kept waiting for two hours.

It was after 4.00pm by the time Lydia Geirsdottir, MSF Holland's project manager, arrived. She found a scene of devastation.

"There was blood, lost shoes in the mud and thousands of people screaming, 'We are all dead, we are all dead.'"

Hundreds of people had crammed themselves in and around the MSF clinic, seeking shelter or help with their injuries. Most of the wounded were simply lying on the floor.

"The injuries were just horrific," she said. "I don't know what ammunition they were using but we saw the shells afterwards – some the size of a hand. Every gunshot wound came with fractures and broken bones. The majority were women and children."

One pregnant woman had lost the baby she had been carrying for six months, but the injuries to her abdomen were so severe there was no way to remove the unborn child. A single bullet had killed another pregnant woman, along with the child strapped on her back and the baby she was carrying inside her.

"There was a ten-year-old boy who had been shot through the hips. The same bullet had gone in one side and out the other. There was nothing left to put back together. We couldn't even amputate his legs because there was so much damage to his hips."

But such was the fear of the government that many people did not come forward for treatment. Weeks afterwards they were still being found in their little huts, lying on the bare ground or rickety beds strung with unforgiving rope. They would rather suffer in secret, they said, than risk being transferred to the city of Nyala where the government would arrest them.

In the end, the security forces never made it into the camp to execute their warrant. A handful of technicals and officers lingered outside for another forty-eight hours keeping the camp in a steady state of anxiety, but eventually they gave up and went home. In the days that followed, residents dug trenches across the camp's main roads and dragged tree trunks into strategic positions as defence against future invasions.

The raid on Kalma was a mess, carried out in breach of international humanitarian law, but it illustrated a fact that was becoming all too obvious in the camps of Darfur through 2007 and 2008. Places like Kalma, Gereida – the biggest of the camps with 130,000 people – and Abu Shouk were becoming lawless cities and no-go areas for aid workers and security forces alike.

I saw the impact for myself in the camps around El Fasher in September 2007, when aid agencies were warned to scale back their operations in Zam Zam, Abu Shouk and Al Salaam. UN security officials had declared the three camps to be tinderboxes: tensions between tribes and hostility towards the government had created a febrile atmosphere. The NGOs were warned to keep international staff out for fear they may be targeted by leaders with a point to prove. That was all very well for the charities but what about the people living there? People like Fatima Adam Yaoub, who had been living in Abu Shouk for four years by the time I drank sweetened tea with her, sitting cross-legged on a straw mat. She lived in a thatched shack and had done her best to turn it into a home. It was surrounded by a reed fence that closed off a tiny patch of the camp for the children to play in. Each morning she would sweep the sand with her pathetic broom, bent double, clutching nothing more than a handful of twigs bound with twigs, swishing back and forth. She could brush away the goat droppings and shredded plastic bags that blew in on the breeze, but never the unease.

"We live in fear because there is no security. In the evening – after eight – no-one will be outside their house. It is too dangerous," said the fifty-two-year-old mother, grimacing nervously to reveal a gap-toothed smile. She was wreathed in a bright red wrap decorated with Arabic script. It was voluminous enough that her hair and shoulders were hidden and the rest of the thin fabric covered what looked like a well-fed body. There was enough maize, sorghum and vegetable oil, she said, to keep her ten children from hunger. Food and water were not the issue; crime was the problem here.

I knew this camp well. Just a mile or so outside El Fasher, a busy town with daily flights to Khartoum and a big peacekeeping presence, it was a regular stop-off for VIPs on whistlestop tours

139

of Darfur. They could arrive in the morning, stroll between the stick fences that marked out family enclosures, feeling the sand scrunch beneath their feet, and be back in their air-conditioned Khartoum hotel by dinner time. Cynics called it humanitarian tourism. On one trip, with the then Irish foreign minister Dermot Ahern, we had met some of Abu Shouk's 47,000 IDPs, lunched with Irish aid workers and been sipping cold beer on Ireland's government jet on our way back to Khartoum before six. It was also on George Clooney's itinerary when he made a forty-eight-hour trip to Darfur. Ban Ki-Moon, Secretary General of the United Nations, had stopped off a couple of weeks before I sat with Fatima outside her shelter built from sticks and interwoven with plastic bags. She said there was sometimes a sinister twist to the VIP visits. She knew two women who had been raped while Ban had been in the camp.

"It happens," she said. "There are lots of security people around making sure things are in order. Lots of strange faces. It is a frightening time."

It was the guns, though, that really brought fear and a rising tide of crime, she said. Gunshots provided a soundtrack to nights in the camp, a menacing sort of background muzak to life in Darfur. No-one believed their simple shelters, with walls of mudbricks for the lucky, would stop a bullet. But at least staying inside meant being out of sight of the gunmen. UN officials told me of several violent incidents in the run-up to my trip. An aid vehicle had been hijacked on its way into the camp by gunmen who pulled AK-47s from a hay cart. A few days earlier two men from the Fur tribe had been shot by unknown men inside the camp. Incidents of homes being torched were also on the increase.

Rebels, with many sympathisers inside the camps, had long been known to use the rambling shanty towns to hide arms caches. At night they could slip in and out unseen to collect weapons and ammunition. Food was passed on by relatives. The camps were not prisons, after all, and had no fences to keep residents in or outsiders out.

Fatima added that both sides were adding to the instability.

"The government is providing guns to two tribes here and causes many problems," she said. "The government says it's a tribal problem but they are the ones causing it."

Her account was confirmed by a contact at the UN. He told me that the government was indeed supplying arms to two tribes: the Gimir and the Kinnen. Both were fiercely pro-government. Both describe themselves as Arab and many Gimir in particular have fought with government counter-insurgency forces. The reason, he told me, was the same explanation that would lead to the attack on Kalma. El Fasher's three big camps were essentially seen as vast, lawless reservoirs of anti-government feeling. About 150,000 were camped around the regional capital after being forced to flee their homes by government allied forces. Here, they could nurse their grievances egged on by rebel elements which used the camps as recruiting grounds and arms dumps. All of this was going on around the three capitals of Darfur, each a government garrison town. In short, the camps were a huge problem for the government.

"So they are strengthening the old tribal divisions that already exist, trying to cause division and tension within the camps, and to force people to go home," he said.

The latest tactic was even more menacing. Local radio stations had begun broadcasting lists of names, asking them to leave the humanitarian camps and return home. Tribal leaders said their people felt under constant pressure to return home, even though the war was far from over.

I met Salar Bakhour outside the camp, at a juice bar favoured by peacekeepers and aid workers where he could avoid the prying eyes and ears of government informers. As an umda or tribal leader he should have been one of the powers in Abu Shouk. In his village he would have been a big man, running affairs. People would come to this tall figure, dressed in his brilliant white jalabiya and muslim skull cap, for advice, protection and guidance. As we sipped Cokes at a plastic table in the shade he explained how his new life in the camp was very different. It was one of those moments, like watching the orchestrated demonstration in the Jebel Mara rebel stronghold, when things suddenly shifted into focus. Then I had felt only despair as the old woman grabbed at my arm and asked me for help. This time, Salar's sad eyes seemed to reflect his predicament. He knew things were hopeless as he explained the daily threats.

"They tell us that they want us to leave by October and they are giving guns to the other tribes. Shootings are happening every day and every night. I cannot protect my people any more," he said simply, resigned to the fact.

The women were still women. They collected water and provided for their children in the camps. They were scared and faced daily dangers but they were still mothers, carers and helpers, just as they had always been. Salar may have been an umda in title, but he knew the aid agencies and government security officers ruled the camp. He could go to them with his problems and make sure his people got their fair share of the handouts, but he was barely a leader any more. If he could no longer protect his community, his role had gone.

The camps had been set up to provide a refuge for Darfur's IDPs. There was some semblance of security: government police manned checkpoints at the main entrances and the African Union had also set up police posts at some of the camps. But the truth was the people who had sought refuge here were trapped. They could not return home as the war rumbled on with no end in sight. Women feared leaving even for an afternoon to collect firewood. And even the camp itself seemed to offer no respite from the violence. Worse than that, they were destroying an entire social order.

"No. I do not deal with journalists," said the thick-set man wearing a tie and dark glasses. The tie looked unfamiliar. Most Sudanese men wore their shirts open at the neck. Al Siir was the only other person I'd seen knotting a tie. The dark glasses, on the other hand, I knew about. These marked him out as a government official. "Go away. All you do is come here and write lies and I get into trouble with my boss. Go away."

"Oooh dear, erm, ooh," I dithered, trying to sound as innocuous as possible. "I really think I'm supposed to register with you so that I can go and visit the camps. Might that, erm, you know, be . . ."

"Go to National Security! Don't speak to me!"

He was shouting, almost screaming, by now with rage. This was not a good start. Once again I had arrived in El Fasher ready to report on Darfur's humanitarian predicament. And once again things were not turning out as I had expected. Ibrahim, the Humanitarian Aid Commissioner, was in a bad mood and in no state to facilitate my trip. I needed his stamp on my travel permit to stay in the town and his signature to allow me into the camps. Driving up the hill out of the market to the offices of National Security did not help much either. Their place was notably smarter – a small crowd was watching a football match on a television in the reception hallway – but the attitude was the same. After being led into a spacious study, arranged Sudanese style with sofas along the wall facing in towards one of the largest desks I have seen, another thickset man, this time wearing a khaki safari suit with his dark glasses, entered the room.

"Who do you work for?"

"*The Irish Times* and *The London Times*."

"No. This is not the case. They don't pay you. Who do you really work for? Who pays you?"

"That's who I really work for. I'm a freelance journalist."

"You are not a journalist. Tell me what you really are doing here."

"I'm not quite sure what you mean."

"You are a spy aren't you?"

The conversation went on for maybe thirty minutes and got no further than a series of accusations followed by a series of denials. In the end I promised to return with a selection of cuttings to prove that my work had been published. That took the rest of the morning as I scrambled around the town looking for a working internet connection and a printer.

The man at National Security looked as if he had forgotten who I was by the time I pressed the folder of stories into his hand. He didn't even pretend to look at them.

"Now you must go to HAC," was all he said.

My heart sank. The last thing I needed was another to and fro with a commissioner who had already said he wanted nothing to do with me. I was in luck. By the time I returned to the low buildings in the middle of the market he had left for the day. There was nothing for it but to return to the NGO compound where my bags were waiting and crash out. Darfur days could pass easily in a blur of activity before grinding to a halt. Waiting was a skill every bit as important as reporting.

The next morning found me back at the HAC compound. There was no sign of the commissioner in his office, which was a relief. Instead I was led to a broken-down caravan where his staff spent their days stamping and folding forms. One took my travel permit and studied it hard.

"You want to do what?" he asked in halting English.

"To visit some of the camps and go on patrol with the peacekeepers," I replied.

And that was that. He scrawled something on the corner of my permit, scrabbled around on his desk for an impressive-looking stamp – all eagles and flags – and, with everything apparently in order, handed back the by now scruffy, fingerprint-covered piece of paper

"Everything is tamam?"

It was one of my few words of Arabic and generally seemed to mean "fine".

"No, you must leave immediately for Khartoum."

There was nothing wrong with my papers but the man from HAC took great delight in finding a series of apparent problems. First of all it seemed that I had failed to register on the day of arrival. Pointing out that I had been turned away by his boss only seemed to make matters worse. Then it seemed that my problem was spending the night at an aid agency guest house, without notifying the correct authorities. Finally, he settled on my plan to spend time with the UN peacekeepers in town without having asked for permission from the press accreditation people in Khartoum – something I knew was unnecessary. Arguing was pointless. The stamp and Arabic scrawls in the corner of my permit meant it would be useless for El Fasher. My trip was crumbling, even though I had followed the same protocol as every previous visit. The man from HAC was clearly determined to make a point and was not going to change his mind. (I later found out that I had arrived at the worst possible time. At 11.00am he would have been wanting to take his breakfast – not deal with a new journalist in town.)

Another man dressed in regulation safari suit arrived on a motorbike. His eyes were hidden by sunglasses. He took my passport and said it would be returned when I boarded a flight out of town.

In the end I managed to salvage something when they finally relented and allowed me to another part of Darfur, but not before a second meeting with the grumpy commissioner was brought to a rapid end by Janjaweed storming the market outside. For me it was all an inconvenience. But these were the same people who held sway over the world's biggest humanitarian operation. I had lost time and money to a small-minded bureaucrat, and for aid agencies time and money meant lives. The same delays and obfuscation could bring aid programmes to a halt in a place where HAC officials needed to approve every application to travel into Darfur, clear flight manifests and give licences to transport cash around.

Every aid worker and UN official seemed to have their own story. One friend had turned up for a flight to travel into the field only to be told the stamp on his travel permit was too big. By the time he returned from the office in town with a smaller stamp, the plane had left. With flights to remote clinics and towns few and far between, that could be enough to put back a work programme several weeks.

Local Sudanese staff might go for weeks unpaid because officials had not got around to approving requests to ship large amounts of cash from the three regional capitals to the field. International staff often resorted to smuggling huge bundles of Sudanese notes on to flights, bundled up with clothes in rucksacks or hidden in laptop bags.

Getting equipment and supplies into Sudan was a desperately time-consuming business. Vital communications equipment, such as Thuraya satellite phones, would be delayed for weeks on end.

Customs officials were capable of holding up vital consignments of food aid for months. In 2008, government authorities kept 5000 tonnes of sugar at Port Sudan for four months before starting to allow shipments to leave.

The authorities were particularly keen to restrict the flow of fuel into Kalma, a camp they had long suspected of being a rebel stronghold. In 2008, officials started to quibble over permits needed by NGOs to ship diesel into the site for water pumps. By the time the permit was granted HAC had invariably struck a couple of barrels worth of diesel from the allowed shipment. Not to be outdone, National Security would then strike a couple more from the paperwork. The government knew Oxfam needed seven barrels per week. The figure had been agreed with officials. But often the camp would receive only half the fuel it needed to keep borehole generators running. Some weeks only one barrel would reach its destination. By the end of each week labour-intensive hand pumps were often the only way to draw water from the ground.

This was the way the authorities seemed to operate. There were often good reasons for the bureaucracy. The threat from the rebels was real. And what country wouldn't put some sort of regulation in place when the aid industry numbered about 16,000 workers at the start of 2009. There was a war going on and restrictions on fuel, cash and movement could be justified in terms of protecting aid workers themselves. Yet at the same time, the rules provided a framework that could be used to bully and intimidate foreigners and local staff. Exit visas could be denied to people desperate to go on holiday after long weeks in the field. Bureaucratic wrangling was a constant problem, a time-consuming distraction for aid workers. Few would talk about it publicly for fear of bringing further disruption, but some voiced their frustration privately.

"It was a classic example of the chess games that the government was playing – they were always two moves ahead. The focus on visas and permits distracted attention from causes of the humanitarian crisis, occupying everyone – diplomats, NGOs, UN officials – in discussions about important details but missing the bigger picture," said one.

Beside the steady strangulation of programmes with red tape, there were more sinister episodes of intimidation, smears and expulsions. Things seemed to escalate in 2008 when HAC officials – some drafted in from Khartoum and accompanied by agents from National Security – arrived unannounced at offices in South Darfur to interrogate staff.

"Usually in Sudan people always say a polite hello, even if they're about to cause you problems. But it was clear from the start that they were not interested in being remotely polite," said an aid worker after eight government officers turned up late one morning.

They asked to speak to all the international staff and a few local employees. One by one they questioned the workers. Two officials did the asking, while the others stood around looking menacing. They demanded to see CVs and personal documents and asked for computer passwords. Refusing to comply brought an increasingly hostile reaction.

"He was shouting in my face at this point," said the worker, whose account was recorded in a confidential charity report. "He said that he controlled all of our movement and if I ever wanted to get permission to leave the country – whether for good or on holiday – I should give him everything he needed. I refused to hand over my emails, but I know a few other people did. It was extremely intimidating – like an interrogation – although it never got violent."

The same thing was being repeated at several different NGO premises. The officials focused on staff who worked on security and protection. Sensitive files, including details of rape cases, were copied and taken away.

"By the time they had spoken to everyone, they had taken all kinds of documents and information. They asked for our bank details, our assets lists," said the worker. "They demanded to know which local suppliers we used, and details of all our donors and money transfers into and within Sudan."

The interrogations were simply another example of the government's ability to intimidate foreigners. Charities offering lifesaving services were left in a constant state of siege, wondering when staff might be kicked out or their entire programme closed. No-one knew when the next visit might come.

A security officer with the aid agency Care was expelled after being accused of spying. She was called in for questioning to be confronted with one of her own confidential emails. It contained a security report of the type all NGOs use in conflict areas. It set out a series of possible violent scenarios and the response Care would adopt to protect its staff. The officials at National Security saw it differently. They said security was not a matter for humanitarian outfits. They took one look at her Jewish surname and expelled her, accusing her of being a spy with Israeli intelligence agency Mossad for good measure. Four months later her country director was also kicked out, accused by government officials of "fabricating reports on the security situation in Darfur".

The email had probably been passed on by a Sudanese member of staff. They may have been a spy, in the pay of the government, or more likely just a regular Sudanese employee whose position with an NGO had brought heavy pressure from intelligence agents to begin informing. It was just one of the everyday problems with which agencies working in Darfur had to contend.

"It's very unpleasant to have to assume that you are employing informers but there's nothing much more you can do about it," said one aid worker with whom I discussed the issue.

Then there were the general media smears; public attacks in government-linked newspapers often quoting unnamed officials designed to damage reputations. Many repeated accusations that the agencies were riddled with Western spies or were part of a conspiracy against Khartoum. Even the Pope was accused of using the humanitarian operation to find converts to Catholicism in Darfur. The clumsy rhetoric gave the stories a comical air, until you remembered the aid workers were operating in a region riddled with guns and where attacks on cars and charity compounds were reported weekly, almost daily.

A story in *Sudan Vision* in September 2008 was typical. It quoted Abdallah Masar, a presidential adviser and one-time leader of the Arab Gathering, who accused the international NGOs of "aggravating the conflict" in the region. "Masar stated that the said organizations are many and most of them are intelligence arms for international forces taking the humanitarian aspect as a cover for its activities," it continued.

My favourite, though, was an interview with Ali Mahmoud, the Wali or governor of South Darfur, published in *Al Intibaha*. As well as accusing international NGOs (INGOs) of preaching Christianity, wasting money on luxury cars and distributing rotten food, he turned his fire on the calibre of staff. "INGOs, my brother, have not come to serve us and whoever believes that is stupid!! See the quality of their workers who are educational wastage, and are menial, coming from Europe for they do not have jobs!!"

*   *   *

The water pumps on the hill overlooked a dry wadi, a grey riverbed of sand and rocks that ran like a scar through the land. All around the parched ground suggested this part of West Darfur was not the sort of place to sustain life – any kind of life, much less the tens of thousands of displaced people living around El Geneina for safety. There could be no water here for many metres underground. The pumps were new and not yet working, but they were the latest in life-saving technology. They relied on a gleaming new solar panel to convert the rays of the burning African sun into electricity which, in turn, could be used to draw the precious liquid from the depths of the earth.

"These are more expensive and more difficult to maintain," said the man from Save the Children who was showing me around the camps, "but they are the best technology available."

For all the insecurity, the tribal rivalries and the armed movements that frequently turned the shanties into war zones; for all the government harassment, bureaucracy and smears, Darfur's humanitarian operation was something of a success story. The statistics alone were staggering. Of an estimated population of about six million, more than four million people had been touched by the conflict and needed aid of some sort. More than two and a half million had been displaced from their homes, with most ending in one of the camps. Fighting often made roads impassable and put villages and town beyond the reach of help, yet the United Nations reckoned that more than eighty percent of the population remained reachable for much of the conflict, dropping back to around two thirds by the end of 2008. On average, through 2008, 3.4m people each month received rations of maize meal, bags of beans, salt and a blend of corn and soya flour for the children along with a tin of cooking oil. Somehow, amid this arid land at the heart of Africa, the water kept flowing from the wells and boreholes.

There were often problems – food rations would have to be reduced if trucks were being hijacked and the diesel-powered water pumps frequently ran out of fuel – yet many of the key indicators kept moving in the right direction.

Overall mortality had fallen from 0.72 (measured as the number of deaths per 10,000 people per day) at the start of the conflict to 0.29 by the end of 2007. Rates of severe malnutrition in children under five had halved from 3.9% to 1.9% in four years. More than three quarters of the population now had access to clean water, compared with less than two thirds in 2004, according to UN.[13]

And it had all been done in one of the world's most inhospitable regions, in the middle of a war, in a country whose government viewed the aid agencies with suspicion.

The presence of NGOs was obvious in every camp. Each would have an international aid agency as camp manager, overseeing its day-to-day running. Its office would be signalled by a flag fluttering high above the one-storey homes clustered all around. The British charity Oxfam ran water pumps and maintained latrines. Solidarités was another charity that had water engineers skilled in drilling boreholes. Others specialised in delivering food. The International Rescue Committee ran health clinics. In all, some eighty-five international NGOs were at work providing life-saving services alongside 120 of their Sudanese counterparts.

---

13 – *Food Security and Nutrition Assessment of the conflict-affected population in Darfur, Sudan 2007, Unicef and the World Food Programme, June 2008*

In Krinding, on the edge of El Geneina, the new solar-powered pumps stood close to more old-fashioned diesel-driven water pumps. Women and children clutching jerry cans and empty vegetable oil bottles queued to use the six taps that were left running, their cold, clear water gushing in a steady stream.

One young woman, who said she was nineteen but whose big brown eyes and braided hair made her look much, much younger, had a sleeping baby tied to her back, slung in a wrap that ran over one shoulder. She had a cylindrical container which meant she could roll it home – a trick used by many of the young girls.

"There are many problems here with Janjaweed," she said, using the term as shorthand for bandit. "We fear robbing at night. There are good things, too, like this water and the schools."

Since 2004, the camps had begun to take on an air of permanence. The first shelters, little more than frames of sticks covered with plastic sheeting, were being replaced by homes built from mud bricks. Trenches at the edge showed where the earth had been excavated before being pressed into blocks and dried in the sun. Each of the camps had a market, where tomatoes, onions and bad tempered goats always seemed to be on sale. Small children ran kiosks selling matches and sweets. Once I even saw a television aerial poking from the roof of a house. Even in the most miserable of wars there were ways of coping and making life a little more bearable.

There were even opportunities on offer. Inside a thatched workshop, Hayat Clement was overseeing a sewing class. A skilled tailor was at an old-fashioned Singer sewing machine, pumping its pedal as his class of a dozen or so women watched him hem a pair of trousers. Children's dresses in primary colours hung all around the room.

"They get problems when they go outside to get firewood," explained Hayat, who ran the women's centre which offered alternative ways to make money, ways that meant the women did not have to risk wandering into a war zone outside. "We train them in activities such as tailoring or other income generating activities like breadmaking."

I suppressed a smile. The term "income generating activities" always grated. It was aid agency-speak of the worst kind. It seemed training people with the skills they might need to start a small business had to be described in politically correct terms. The camp residents were picking up the same language. No matter. The centre was busy with activity. As well as the budding seamstresses, others were building fuel efficient ovens; simple wood or charcoal burners that meant they could collect wood less often and produced less smoke than an open fire.

The tour ended at a school. It was closed for the weekend and its tidy yard was empty. Again it had been built by an NGO, although it was run by the government. It was made from bricks and had a corrugated iron roof. There were windows. It was unlike any other school I had seen in Darfur. The children still had to pay to attend, but at least they had a school and one that seemed to look like a school, not a bombed-out shell or the shade of a tree. Somehow, against the odds, bits of life in the camp just about worked, thanks to the efforts of the massive aid operation which brought millions of pounds every week into Darfur. The money was keeping alive a displaced population. It was also transforming the entire region, providing opportunities for canny entrepreneurs.

* * *

The piles of dates and bowls of fragrant ginger and cumin at the entrance gave a traditional Sudanese feel to Mohammed Osman Babkir's dusty general store. But step inside and the unwary customer is transported to a trendy European foodhall. Bottles of olive oil from Spain, balsamic vinegar from Italy and jars of preserved cherries are stacked neatly on shelves like an old-time grocery store. For all the suffering in Darfur's humanitarian camps, the emptied villages and the scorched earth, the conflict made good business for some. Land prices around the main towns have all rocketed and the vast influx of aid workers, peacekeepers and United Nations officials has brought a new market with per diems to spend.

"This is all for the expatriates and some for the rich Sudanese," said Mohammed, waving his hand at jars of Nutella, tins of Ovaltine and bottles of red wine vinegar (labelled "grape vinegar") that have survived the journey along rutted roads from Khartoum. He sported the large belly of a prosperous man beneath his shop-keeper's apron. Business was obviously good.

"There's high demand ever since the African Union and the aid agencies came here."

Every visit I made to Nyala and El Fasher, in particular, the more it looked like Darfur's war economy was booming with the influx of aid cash. Where once the little wooden stalls held a few cheap Chinese watches or radios that would break within weeks, the latest in consumer goods were now on display. Every time I returned there would be more and more mobile phones for sale. By 2008 the phones were being replaced by iPods. And in the centre of it all, Darfur's tallest buildings – two six-storey blocks of shops, offices and a hotel – were rising from the market. Their skeletons had already nosed past the city's tallest structure, a minaret. One block had already leased all fourteen of its shops and office units way ahead of completion. I watched the city change with each passing year of the war.

The shops at the edge of the market were all the same. Their dingy interiors – with no windows so as to protect from the burning heat of the African sun – hid all manner of French cheeses, luxury butter and other tasty treats. It felt like a little bit of home, a little bit of normality in the middle of the Sudanese desert. And it made me smile. In Khartoum a friend working for the UN in South Sudan asked me what Darfur was like. "Is there anything other than aid camps?" she had said. There was a lot more than tents and burnt villages. The truth was that there was a bustling economy. Outside, tiny blue Daewoo and Hyundai taxis scooted through the streets like dodgem cars, overtaking donkey carts and weaving their way around army technicals. One of the town's traditional grill-houses had begun serving pizza and construction sites were springing up everywhere, bringing more piles of sand and dust into the city. Most of the construction was based around the razor wire fence of the African Union head-quarters in the city. Anyone with land was putting up houses for officers. And even before their ranks were swollen with officers of an expanded force, due to be deployed in 2008, simple four-bedroom houses, with outside toilets and showers, were fetching $2000 a month.

Driving through the sandy back alleys of the city, it wasn't long before we found one of El Fasher's new breed of entrepreneur. Tajel al-Din Dissa did not look a rich man. His skinny frame was draped in a jalabiya and he was sitting on a half-built perimeter wall in the shade of a thorn tree, supervising a small army of builders, all residents of one of the aid camps. He had time on his hands and seemed pleased to have company. He already had one house rented to an AU officer for $500 a month. This second one, he reckoned, would push his earnings above the salary he earned as an economics lecturer at the city's university. Eventually he hoped to rely solely on property rentals for his income. He smiled as he admitted to profiting from misery, like many others in El Fasher.

"The per capita income has increased because many people are finding work with the NGOs and the African Union or the United Nations, and then there is a knock-on effect of more purchases in the market," he said. "But in the field of peace nothing has improved."

El Fasher University lies at the end of a bumpy dirt track that runs through a broken-down barbed wire fence and in and out of yellow fields of scorched grass. In places, the dirt road merges with the sand to disappear altogether. From his cramped office, with only a broken-down fan to cool the room, Abduljabbar Abdellah Fadul had watched with incredulity as plots of land had risen from $1000 to $15,000 in the past four years.

"Five years ago you would not see Cornflakes in El Fasher. It's there today," said the economist who ran a consultancy from his simple office at the university. "Where people are really making the money, though, is building homes. The demand is there for nice places so there's a lot of investment right now."

Some of the people in the camps had found work on building sites. The fruit juice bars and pizza parlour looked to be making good money from the number of white 4x4s parked outside. El Fasher seemed to be running on aid money.

*   *   *

In Nyala there was a similar boom. New government buildings were going up beside the smooth tarmac road that ran into the city from the airport. A smart hospital was under construction. And although the old market was still a smelly, muddy backstreet choked with motor rickshaws and donkey carts, there were grand plans to transform the rest of the city.

The ideas were to be found inside inside the smart office of Adam Mofaddal, where small bowls of dates held down sheafs of papers against the cool breeze of the airconditioning system. With a deft click of his mouse, the man in charge of South Darfur's reconstruction concluded his PowerPoint presentation with a transport map of his region: not as I had seen it outside – a mess of rutted tracks through the sand – but as it will be in five years time. A ring road encircled the state capital, linking provincial towns, and a railway stretched away towards the Central African Republic.

This was the Darfur the government wanted journalists to see. Not the war-torn expanse of desert and rock, where burned villages had emptied and squalid aid camps had filled, but an imaginary land of smart new roads, power stations and peace. The six-year, $8bn vision was all thanks to the Darfur Peace Agreement, explained Mofaddal, South Darfur's commissioner for redevelopment and reconstruction. It had been signed in 2006 and a year later it was still being used by the government to justify its denial of what was happening all around. The deal allowed Khartoum to insist that no-one need stay in the camps. There was a peace deal and it was time to go home.

Mofaddal admitted his plans were ambitious, but said the deal made everything achievable.

"We have more money and more power to make this work," he said, passing around plates of dates and boiled sweets in his smart office, filled with leather sofas.

"The DPA has created stability for people to go home and for investors to come here."

This was the government version of Darfur and it was pie in the sky. Never mind that the camps all around town were still growing every day as trucks arrived with dozens of families fleeing violence; never mind that the peace deal had prompted a surge in aggression as the rebel movements fragmented; Khartoum wanted the world to believe that Darfur was not the war-riddled mess I had seen. It did that by harassing aid agencies – the people who knew better than anyone about the human misery and suffering – into silence, and by preventing access to areas under attack, as I was to see for myself.

* * *

The man from HAC could not have been friendlier this time. I was back in El Fasher yet again and hoping to fly on a UN chopper into two areas held by rebels of the SLA. The plan was to travel with an aid agency to see for myself the lack of clinics, schools, wells and other facilities in areas where there was little access for charities. It was generally difficult to travel outside government-held towns and this was a perfect chance to see another part of Darfur's story. Birmarza would be particularly interesting as it was a base for one of the new rebel factions. Abdul Aziz was courteous and polite as he checked our travel request in the little caravan.

"Yes, there is no problem with flying to Kutum and to En Siro but you cannot go to Birmaza," he said, before adding as an afterthought, "not this week."

Abdul Aziz was one of the more reasonable of an unreasonable bunch, always ready with a smile and a helpful word of advice. Yet his response seemed odd.

"Why not? What's happening this week?"

Abdul Aziz gave a chuckle. I swear he almost winked as he looked up from the sheaf of papers on his desk.

"Not this week," he repeated.

Something funny was going on, but it was not until later that evening that the truth became clear. I had returned to the aid agency's guest house – a sprawling villa with half a dozen rooms used by staff as they travelled to and from the field – to drink tea and chat to the head of office about the restrictions she faced working in Darfur. It was gradually turning dark and the cook had arrived to begin preparing dinner. I was hoping it wasn't the same chewy beef we had had the night before.

The head of office disappeared off to take a sat-phone call from one of her people in the field. I swatted flies that had evaded a net set up around the dining table and waited for her to return.

"So that's why they won't let us go to Birmaza," she said conspiratorially, settling back down at the table. "Their Antonovs are bombing the place."

The HAC office had clearly known what was going on and didn't want us anywhere near. Perhaps they were acting out of concern for our safety. Just as likely, they didn't want any witnesses to the killing.

"And after tonight," continued my hostess, avoiding my eye, "I'm afraid you can't stay here any more."

With Antonovs in the air over North Darfur and bombs falling not far from the aid agency's areas of operation, a journalist had suddenly become a security risk. It was not the first time this had happened. With so much harassment from HAC and the security apparatus, few NGOs were prepared to talk to me, much less put me up in a guest house. If charity workers were being expelled for apparently overstepping their humanitarian boundaries with security reports, then talking to journalists would also seem to be off-limits. Anywhere else in the world, these same charities would fall over themselves to offer rides in 4x4s to refugee camps, on-the-record briefings and guided tours of newly dug latrines – anything to get a bit of publicity. Darfur was different. This was another of the place's many inconveniences. But I couldn't really blame my hostess for putting her programme of clinics and feeding centres ahead of my sleeping arrangements.

Then again this was about more than my personal comfort. There was a bigger issue at stake. Many organisations had diverted resources into hugely successful advocacy arms, which lobbied politicians and mobilised public opinion on aid and development. Rather than acting merely as an emergency service, delivering help to the dying, displaced and vulnerable, the trend was to agitate for change and find solutions to the root cause of conflict or hunger. Plenty of NGOs were noisy when it came to issues like aid, fair trade and debt relief. Press officers bombarded me with emails on drought in the Horn of Africa, plans to tackle malaria or the scourge of corruption. They were desperate to get their message into the paper as they pushed for change. This powerful voice was missing from the coverage of Darfur.

It had been different closer to the start of the conflict, but loud public statements soon became a sure-fire way of attracting the worst kind of attention from the government. Oxfam GB had accused the UN Security Council of "dithering" over Darfur only to face extra harassment from Khartoum. Save The Children reported a bombing raid over the town of Tawilla in a press release, and was immediately threatened with expulsion.

In 2006, an American agency, the International Rescue Committee (IRC), had published a report on the incidence of rape around Kalma camp. Researchers reported 200 rapes around the camp in just five weeks. In interviews, IRC officials said the statistics were a reflection of the downward spiral of violence and called for peacekeepers to step-up firewood patrols, protecting women as they left the camp. It was a dramatic story which offered an insight into life in the camps, and it gained coverage all around the world. It was a story Khartoum did not want anyone to hear. During the next couple of years the IRC was frequently singled out for public smears and private harassment. More than many of the other agencies, staff found their visa applications simply disappeared and travel permits were not forthcoming.

"Their programmes were just strangled," said an aid worker with a different agency.

After that the charities began to play safe. The agencies put into play a cost-benefit analysis to determine when it was worth speaking out. Every public statement had to bring a clear positive. Anything that might undermine the safety of staff in the field or compromise their ability to get to people in need was ruled out. There were still fundraising appeals but they would focus strictly on issues of food, water or medicine, rather than voicing concerns about the security of people living in the camps or the wider conflict. Protection issues, as the NGOs called them, were simply too political. As far as Khartoum was concerned they would be overstepping their humanitarian mandate.

Press releases, reports and public statements were not the only way to make a difference. There were other ways to make a case and NGOs gradually switched to lobbying privately, relying on meetings with government ministers, donors or celebrities keen to get involved. These allowed opinion formers and decision makers to keep abreast of what was happening without the risk that public lobbying carried. Information was also being passed on to campaign groups outside Sudan. They were free to publicise injustices, bombings and abuses without having to worry about the security of staff on the ground or maintaining access to programmes.

Of course neutrality has long been one of the tools of the aid movement, particularly in conflict. How else to deliver help to both rebel-held territory and camps clustered around government towns than to avoid taking sides? A non-partisan approach is crucial to maintaining credibility with all parties. And in Darfur staying out of the political arena, at least in public statements, was the best way of maintaining access on the ground. For visiting journalists, it often seemed as if neutrality was being interpreted as silence.

In other conflicts – in Somalia, the Democratic Republic of Congo, Uganda – aid workers and journalists were often thrown together in difficult circumstances. The usual pattern was to find a bar, get drunk and talk shop. Tips would be exchanged and rumours embellished. For journalists parachuting into a story, the

NGO staff would be an invaluable source of information. They would know where the latest fighting was, which commanders were up to what and where to go to get the story. In exchange for another bottle of Ethiopian gin or Congolese beer they might have a telephone number or the name of a driver who could help.

Darfur was different. There were actually places to get a drink in Darfur. If you knew the right people there were invitations to drink-sodden parties. Guests would arrive with illicit bottles of the local date brew – nicknamed Janjajuice – to be poured into vast buckets, mixed with Coke and fruit juice. The heady mixture was optimistically declared a "cocktail" and thrown back with gusto. But there was less talk of shop. Letting people know you were a reporter was like announcing you had a spot of leprosy. Conversation became stilted and drinking companions became nervous. There were fewer tips or nuggets of information on offer here.

Over time I managed to build up contacts. There were aid officials who were more confident than others in knowing how far to push the boundaries. Documents were sometimes leaked or quotations offered without attribution.

But it was still frustrating. These were the people operating day in day out in difficult circumstances. They knew what was happening on the ground. They understood Darfur and its conflicts. They knew what the government was doing. As they criss-crossed the desert and hills they also saw what the rebels were up to, and how the splintering of factions had made the conflict worse. Their staff were being carjacked, beaten, or worse, by numerous armed elements. They talked to Arab leaders about their needs or the Janjaweed commanders who controlled roads or water holes. They saw the Antonovs taking off in the morning and returning in the afternoon, the convoys of technicals heading out of town on the latest government offensives. They dealt with the minutia of the war every day, as they negotiated access to faraway villages or talked to sheikhs in the camp. They understood the complexity. In short, they knew Darfur.

It was their presence on the ground that gave them such an exceptional understanding of the place, its problems and its needs.

Their public silence was understandable as they sought to maintain that presence. But it left a hole in the coverage of the conflict and a vacuum in the debate on how best to save Darfur. It was a vacuum that other voices were happy to fill.

8. SAVING DARFUR

It started with a rumble somewhere in the distance, growing steadily to a roar. It wasn't until the Fantan warplane was directly over the table where my omelette was cooling that the source of the noise became clear. By then the sound of its engines had risen to an ear-splitting scream. It passed by no more than ten metres overhead. The palm trees in the hotel courtyard swayed in the wash from its engines. For a few seconds the noise died to a bearable howl as the Chinese-built ground attack jet disappeared over the corrugated iron rooftops of Nyala, tracing a brutal arc. Then it was back. Almost low enough to touch its swept wings. My cup and saucer shook with the vibration. Then it was gone, leaving nothing but ringing ears and rattled minds in its wake.

While the rest of the world was taking to the streets to mark a global Day for Darfur, the Sudanese military was putting on a show of strength in the skies overhead. In the minutes after the roar of the jet died away, a helicopter gunship carved figures of eight over the sandy streets of the town. The only people who marched here were not campaigners but hundreds of soldiers demonstrating their drill technique at the football stadium on the edge of the market. They traipsed back and forth keeping ragged time. Their boots tramped grey clouds into the air.

Government officials told me later that the display of Sudanese air power had been laid on for a minister visiting from Khartoum. And maybe it was a coincidence that the aircraft responsible for so much death and destruction were overhead on the very day that the rest of the world was taking time to focus on Darfur's tragedy. But from the camp on the edge of town the air show had an altogether more sinister feel.

"When the aeroplanes came it was frightening for the women and the children," said Sheikh Abdallah Sharif Bashir, sitting on a threadbare woollen carpet spread beneath the flimsy grass roof of his community's simple mosque. He spread his bony fingers as he traced their path through the sky. "It's very dangerous but the government wants us to know they are still in charge."

This was 2007, four years into the conflict, and the third Day for Darfur. Organisers claimed events in 200 cities around the world. More than 3000 campaigners gathered in London outside Downing Street where a giant hourglass was filled with red liquid to represent the blood spilled so far in the conflict. Mia Farrow addressed protestors in front of the White House. Boston hosted a mass "die-in". Editorials appeared in newspapers; American college campuses were festooned with posters. All around the world protesters turned hourglasses upside down to demonstrate how time for a solution to be found was running out. Their aim was to remind the world that the killing had not ended in Darfur and to push for the deployment of United Nations peacekeepers. Along with Mia Farrow in Washington, George Clooney, Hugh Grant, Bob Geldof, Don Cheadle, Sir Elton John and Sir Mick Jagger were just some of the celebrities who added star power to the demonstrations or signed letters. Politicians got in on the act too. In Britain, Margaret Beckett, the foreign secretary, announced that Sudan would face tougher sanctions if it did not accept an international peacekeeping force within days, rather than weeks. For one day, the eyes of the Western world were on Darfur.

Thousands of miles from the glitzy rallies, it was business as usual for the residents of Otash, the scruffy camp that has grown into a ragtag suburb of Nyala. The women gathered early at the wells as they always did at that time of year. The waterholes would run dry by mid-morning and things would not ease until the rains arrived in a couple of months time. Then mud, flood water and disease would become the daily problem rather than empty buckets. No-one here knew that thousands of people were marching in their name.

"I do not know this Day for Darfur," said one woman, clutching a plastic jerrycan in a queue for water. Her wrinkled skin and sad eyes captured the broken spirit of someone used to life in a hostile environment, where the sickly smell of sewage and rotting waste is never far away. I tried to explain as best I could, provoking a slightly confused smile.

"This is good that people have not forgotten us," was all she said. She turned away to take her place at the tap. It was just another day at the pumps for her.

The people of Darfur had not been forgotten. This was not one of the world's forgotten crises. Yet there was still no sign of peace.

"It is impossible to go home. It is not safe," said Sheikh Abdallah, who had led forty of his villagers to safety in Otash five months before my visit. Like many of his Zaghawa tribe he carried a dagger strapped beneath the billowing robes of his white jalabiya – protection, he said, against Janjaweed raiders who steal cattle and women from the camp at night. His face was full of pride as he slipped the knife from its sheath the better to show me, but in some ways it was a reminder of the sheikh's impotence rather than a show of power. The camp was not safe and the sheikh knew he was helpless to protect his people. Their life as IDPs was only just beginning.

"We will be here until there is peace," he said sadly, as if knowing that this meant a long, long wait.

The following day my story, a simple piece about warplanes criss-crossing the skies of Darfur and misery in the camps, appeared on page thirty of *The Times*. In fact, it was the sort of thing I might have bashed out on my first trip to Darfur, a bog standard African war tale. Another average day for the people of Darfur. On subsequent trips I would not have even pitched it to my editors. The interviewees had said nothing I hadn't heard before. Theirs were miserable stories, but nothing that hadn't appeared in the papers before. People living in camps and queuing for a muddy bucket of water were not news. The difference, though, was that this was all happening on a Day for Darfur. The story had a hook. My piece was illustrated not with a photograph of women at the water pump or the sheikhs sitting on their threadbare carpet, but with a stark portrait of the actress Thandie Newton – hair tousled, plain white

T-shirt dress showing off her long legs – standing over a broken hourglass, fake blood smeared across the floor. Similar pictures of Matt Damon or Hugh Grant appeared in other newspapers.

It was the closest I'd been to Thandie Newton since we had lived on the same staircase at Downing College, Cambridge, some fifteen years before. I didn't know she shared my interest in Sudan and its civil wars. But none of that really mattered. My mum read the story and sent an email congratulating me on my page lead. I bet a lot of other mums who don't spend long flicking through the world pages also read the story.

If the aid agencies working on the ground in Sudan had been silenced by an oppressive regime in Khartoum and by their own need to maintain access to the region, then here were other voices more than willing to make some noise. Celebrities and the organisers of events like the Day for Darfur were more than making up for the vacuum in policy debate. In fact, they had managed to go much, much further, turning Sudan's desert conflict into the world's favourite African war.

No opportunity for raising funds or attention had been ignored. New forms of activism were even being invented. U2, Green Day and REM were among artists who recorded cover versions of John Lennon songs for the Instant Karma LP put together by Amnesty International. There was an internet computer game, Dying for Darfur, in which players would control a family member dodging Janjaweed raids to collect water. T-shirts, mugs and even underpants emblazoned with messages such as "Think, Act, Save Darfur" or "Empower Darfur" could be bought for a few dollars on the internet. The discerning pet could eat its dinner from a bowl proclaiming, "If we don't speak up we become accomplices." Actors from ER travelled to South Africa to film episodes of the TV drama set in a Darfur aid camp.

This was not one of Africa's obscure conflicts, rumbling on out of sight. Not by a long way. From 2006, Darfur consistently outranked both the Democratic Republic of Congo and Somalia for searches on Google. Never mind that Darfur was only a region of Sudan rather than an entire country, it seemed it was on the minds of internet users more often than other local wars, if my rough and ready analysis of statistics readily available from Google Trends was to be believed. Somalia would occasionally leap ahead – when Islamist militias were sent fleeing from the capital Mogadishu, or if pirates seized a cargo ship or attacked a cruise liner – but then settle back beneath Darfur on the graph. The Democratic Republic of Congo, where five million people had died in a seemingly never ending cycle of civil war, trailed along with a negligible number of searches. The trend was most marked in the US, where searches for Darfur outnumbered Somalia by pretty much two to one.

The same pattern was repeated in news coverage. From 2006, Darfur made the headlines consistently more frequently than Somalia. The same studies showed the Congolese wars rising from the baseline only once, at the end of 2008, when rebels came close to seizing a regional capital.

It was a pattern that journalists and press officers based in Nairobi, the hub for East Africa and the Horn, were all too familiar with. Pitching trips to Somalia or the Congo was fraught with questions over budgets and what stories might be possible. Costs and benefits were closely weighed. Somalia also brought serious risks to personal safety. In contrast, trips to Darfur – which often would last three weeks, including ten days or so in Khartoum, possibly the most expensive city in Africa – were nodded through, safe in the knowledge that this was not some sort of remote, forgotten war only of interest to foreign affairs wonks, but a story that would be read widely. It was particularly frustrating for the public information officers with aid groups or the United Nations. They were desperate to get journalists interested in the latest horrors in northern Uganda, where Joseph Kony's thugs were still at work, or to write about Somalia, even if they couldn't go there.

"If only we could get that sort of coverage," one of my friends who worked on Somalia would say every time Darfur appeared once again on *CNN* or in the papers.

"Maybe we should get George Clooney to visit," she would say, before collapsing in giggles at the absurdity of a movie star taking an interest in Somalia's intractable clan wars.

* * *

It wasn't always like that. The first months of the conflict in 2003 generated all the headlines of any other crisis in a distant land peopled by alien tribes whose blood feuds went back generations. Its confusing tangle of rivalries seemed to shift with the sand. Darfur held no strategic interest: there was no oil and barely any minerals. In fact, it held no interest for the average Western newspaper reader. Coverage of Sudanese affairs was limited to the North-South peace talks, while Darfur's bloodshed was only picked up by specialist publications. That all changed in March 2004.

"The most vicious ethnic cleansing you've never heard of is unfolding here in the south-eastern fringes of the Sahara Desert," wrote Nicholas D. Kristof in an editorial published in *The New York Times*.[14] "It's a campaign of murder, rape and pillage by Sudan's Arab rulers that has forced 700,000 black, African Sudanese to flee their villages. The desert is strewn with the carcasses of cattle and goats, as well as fresh refugee graves that are covered with brush so wild animals will not dig them up."

Kristof knew how to spin a yarn for maximum impact. His readers might not care about a bunch of Africans killing each other, but ethnic cleansing was something different. After Bosnia and Rwanda, it was a term fresh in the memory and a signal that this was the worst kind of murder. The Arab government in Khartoum, explained Kristof, had already been responsible for twenty years of slaughter in the black, African South. "Lately it has armed lighter-skinned Arab raiders, the Janjaweed, who are killing or driving out blacks in the Darfur region near Chad," he continued.

He was picking up on apocalyptic warnings issued by the United Nations humanitarian co-ordinator for Sudan, Mukesh Kapila. He had been trying to raise the alarm for months. His descriptions of a worsening humanitarian crisis, where aid workers were being delayed and harassed, had made little impact. Eric Reeves, professor

---

14 – *Ethnic Cleansing, Again by Nicholas D. Kristof*, New York Times, *March 24, 2004*

of English at Smith College Massachusetts who had written extensively on Southern Sudan, was one of the few foreign observers to notice. Then Kapila went nuclear. In an interview with the BBC he described the government's scorched earth campaign as "ethnic cleansing" and compared the offensive with the Rwanda genocide. He repeated his analysis days later in an interview with the UN's own news service. "The only difference between Rwanda and Darfur now is the numbers involved," was the sensational way he put it.[15]

Kapila should know. He was part of a British team that entered the Rwandan capital of Kigali while the bodies were still fresh. He was speaking out after an attack on the village of Tawilla. There, Arab militiamen had killed seventy-five people, he said, and more than one hundred women were raped. A further 150 women and 200 children were kidnapped in the raid. His words finally forced Darfur into the mainstream media, but also ended Kapila's time in Sudan. Within a month he had been transferred out of the country. Not for the last time the UN – like the NGOs – decided that keeping quiet was preferable to outrage. No matter. A connection with Rwanda had been made and the G-word was being used in newspaper reports. People were sitting up and starting to listen.

Kristof would later talk about trying to find the Darfur puppy, the heart-rending human story with big brown eyes that no-one could ignore. That might have been necessary for other African wars but in Darfur Kristof had already found his puppy. The world had its angle. Journalists had their headline. This was not just another African war like those already under way in Somalia or the Democratic Republic of Congo. This was a genocide. On the tenth anniversary of Rwanda's carnage, the same thing was happening all over again. In a continent of wars without end, of coups and counter-coups, where each conflict seemed to have its roots in an older one, this was a narrative that was easily grasped. Arab

---

15 – *The original story by Irin, the UN news service, is no longer available, but* A Long Day Dying: Critical Moments in Darfur's Genocide *by Eric Reeves and Michael Brassard, The Key Publishing House, offers a detailed account of Kapila's statements*

militias sent by the government were driving out black, African tribes. It was a short step away from describing a battle of good against evil. The impact was immediate.

Thousands of miles from Darfur, prayer meetings and college debating clubs suddenly wanted to hear about the twentieth century's first genocide. Jerry Fowler – then the director of the Committee on Conscience at the United States Holocaust Memorial Museum – found himself in demand. His role was to raise awareness of unfolding tragedies around the world as part of a programme to help remember the Nazi Holocaust by preventing crimes against humanity. He was already a frequent town hall speaker, but as 2004 wore on he was addressing audiences on the topic of Darfur more and more often.

"But I was being invited to come. It was not the museum or anyone else out there doing events trying to get anyone to come. Somehow, spontaneously almost, people were reading about what was happening – and Nick Kristof covered it, he played an important role in that – and it touched off this interest," he told me, five years later. "It was the interest that created the movement, not the movement that created the interest."

Invitations to synagogues and church halls continued to flow. There was a growing appetite to hear about Darfur. It seemed as if genocide was the cause of 2004. The timing could not have been better, for that year marked the tenth anniversary of the Rwandan genocide and brought fresh promises that such a tragedy could never be allowed to happen again. It was also the year when the film *Hotel Rwanda*, starring Don Cheadle, was released. The result was a grass-roots movement, building from the bottom up. For Fowler, the simplicity of Darfur's conflict helped people connect with the suffering in a way they couldn't with Congo or Somalia.

"Set aside issues of the term genocide – there was a high concept in Darfur that was simplistic but had a core truth: that there was a civilian population that was at risk because of extreme violence being used by the government – that kind of basic description," he said in 2009. "Then you need to get into; why is this? What is the context? All of that is very, very important to explain, but people could get their minds around it. In Congo, you can't explain it in that way. People are at risk, but why are they at risk? You're not even into the second sentence before you are really into the complexities of it, the same with Somalia."

The emerging movement came together at what was billed as an "emergency summit" on July 14 2004 in New York. It was the meeting where the Save Darfur Coalition was born. Organised by Fowler and Ruth Messinger, of the American Jewish World Service, it drew on some of the same organisations that had been active on South Sudan. Christian Solidarity International, which had spent millions of dollars buying back slaves, was among the signatories to a unity statement and call to action that followed.

"There wasn't a whole lot of strategy," said Fowler. "It was literally: we feel this crisis is very intense, we think that we need to respond, there are other groups that seem interested – is there a way we can work together, co-ordinate what we are doing?"

Evangelical Christians and Jewish organisations were heavily represented. Nine rabbis were among the seventy-one signatories. But there were also African-American organisations, human rights groups and Muslim charities. There were liberals rubbing shoulders with the Christian right, much like in the earlier South Sudan campaign. Together they urged an end to the fighting, promised to help the relief effort, promote efforts to return the displaced and demanded a United Nations commission of inquiry. The statement was the first issued by the new Save Darfur Coalition. Its preface shaped the narrative that would gain common currency.

"The emergency in Sudan's western region of Darfur presents the starkest challenge to the world since the Rwanda genocide in 1994," it said. "A government-backed Arab militia known as Janjaweed has been engaging in campaigns to displace and wipe out communities of African tribal farmers."

Today Fowler, president of the Save Darfur Coalition, is far more circumspect in his language. He avoids such stark, black and white language. The coalition's website even offers some pointers on Sudanese ethnicity, the problems with terms such as "black" and "Arab", and the shifting nature of tribe. Anyone who has written about Darfur has probably fallen into the same trap. I know I did. At other times my editors have dropped the term "black" liberally into my copy, when I have strenuously tried to avoid it. Over time and having sipped tea with Arabs, I had come to learn that they were every bit as black and African – as Sudanese and Darfuri – as anyone else.

"In anything like this, there's a bit of a learning curve," admitted Fowler, "so if you go back and look at the preface of the unity statement, I might look at it now and think that's not how I'd say it . . . that's only natural."

In some ways though, the damage has been done. At its inception, the Save Darfur Coalition was based on a simplistic analysis of the war. Just as it was for Kristof, whose columns remain influential, the war was one between Arabs and blacks, or Arabs and Africans. (Kristof, incidentally, continues to use these terms and describes the Janjaweed as light-skinned.) In other words, the Janjaweed were foreigners. The Arabs had a different claim to the land than the black Africans, its apparently indigenous population. The dichotomy added power to allegations of ethnic cleansing or genocide. It was false. It was simplistic. But the picture of light-skinned Arabs killing black Africans had built momentum to stop the conflict. Darfur activists were starting groups on American college campuses, church coffee mornings were raising cash – and the world had a new favourite cause.

* * *

Never ask Mia Farrow whether an actress is the right sort of person to lead the fight to bring peace to Darfur. Her soothing voice – with its characteristic hippy tones travelling thousands of miles down the crackly phoneline from the US – hardened ever so slightly, collecting an air of gentle indignation. This was clearly a question she was rather sick of answering.

"I've read every book written on Darfur. I know I'm only an actress, I don't pretend to be more, but I know what I know, and I've seen what I've seen, and I've heard what I've heard," she said. "I've never claimed to be anything else other than what I am.

I've made eleven visits and some very lengthy ones. If I can put that to use, why shouldn't I? I must."

Along with George Clooney, Mia Farrow has become the celebrity face of the world's conscience on Darfur. Others have posed for pictures, signed letters and put their names to fundraisers, but Mia has dirtied herself in the dust of Darfur – on the two occasions the authorities granted her a visa – and Chad, immersing herself in a project to archive the region's tribal identity, its songs, dances and ceremonies. I caught up with her soon after a month-long trip to the aid camps that line the Chadian border. There she had been collecting artefacts for a museum she had promised to build when the refugees are able to return home. She was planning another visit soon. And in a week's time she was due to launch a hunger strike to promote their plight – a hunger strike that lasted 12 days until her doctor warned her she risked serious damage if she continued.

Like so many other campaigners, it was the connection between Darfur and Rwanda that first caught Farrow's attention. An article by Samantha Power in *The New York Times* linked the two, pointing out that both were carried out while the world looked the other way.[16] Farrow realised she had known little about the Rwanda genocide at the time. The American media had been obsessed with the OJ Simpson trial while almost a million Rwandans were murdered.

"The Samantha Power piece drew me to another genocide that was unfolding in a place I had never heard of, the Darfur region of Sudan," she said five years later. "And it was one of those jaw-dropping moments for me – that this time I'm not going to be unaware this is happening, although I had not the slightest clue what my role would be or what it should be, even."

Within weeks, she used her existing role as a Unicef goodwill ambassador to secure a trip to Darfur. It was a chance to see exactly what was happening for herself. It proved to be a life-changing experience. One story in particular has stayed with her, along with

---

16 – *Remember Rwanda, But Take Action in Sudan by Samantha Power,* New York Times, *April 6, 2004*

the hijab – a little leather amulet containing a fragment of the Koran – that hangs around her neck. It was given to her by a woman called Halima for protection, even though it had afforded little hope when the Janjaweed arrived in her Jebel Mara village.

"She described vividly trying to gather her children, trying to run holding her baby in her arms, the baby being torn from her arms, and bayoneted in front of her eyes. Three of her five children were similarly killed on that day and her husband too. Janjaweed, she said, cut them and then threw them in to the well. Then she grabbed my hand and said, 'Tell people what happened here. Tell them we will all be slaughtered; tell them we all need help.'"

And that is pretty much what she has done ever since. Her website holds a comprehensive listing of news on Darfur. It includes photographs and eyewitness accounts of attacks where she beat journalists to the scene. Aid workers, journalists and activists who travelled with her through the region speak admiringly of her drive and grasp of the subject. She has written more than twenty op-ed pieces for British and American newspapers. And her divestment and Olympic campaigns have targeted the companies and countries that bankroll Sudan's war machine. Her letters to Steven Spielberg are credited with persuading the Hollywood director to withdraw from his role directing the Beijing Olympics opening ceremony. She has become a one-woman campaign.

This is the point, though, where some of her critics – and there are plenty – become uncomfortable. It is one thing to bear witness and raise awareness; it is something else to start pushing for solutions. She talks of Suleiman Jamous, a rebel commander, as a friend. Never mind that the rebels often seem to have little regard for the safety of their own people or the humanitarian workers trying to deliver aid – Farrow is clear about who are the good guys and who are the bad guys.

"Wherever you have a lawless land and individuals ranging through it, you are going to have crime and some bad things happen, but the kind of strategic assault against civilians that we've been seeing by the government . . . I don't mean it as black and white . . . but there are some pretty dark shades here."

By dark shades, she means the war is lopsided. Millions of civilians have been crammed into camps, bombed or burned from their homes as the government has pursued its genocidal policies. Even though the slaughter had ebbed by 2009, she said the Sudanese government was still trying to destroy Darfur's tribes, controlling aid and maintaining attacks.

"These are genocidal circumstances," she said. "The fragility of the populations makes them undeniably dependent on the humanitarians and the whim of a government that can expel in whole or in part the humanitarian assistance, the only means of sustaining life."

On a continent where so many deaths go unremarked every day and so many wars are ignored or forgotten, this is Darfur's unique selling point. It was the first genocide of the twenty-first century. And it was being carried out not with machetes but with Chinese-made bombers, like the ones I had seen in the skies of Nyala. But while the advocacy groups were shouting that the world needed to act to stop the genocide, the humanitarian workers on the ground – the ones silenced by Khartoum – were not sure whether they were seeing a genocide or another bloody war. And no-one could even agree on the death toll.

*   *   *

Shock and awe have long been tools in any charity fundraising or awareness campaign. Saving Darfur is no different. The adverts, paid for by the Save Darfur Coalition and the Aegis Trust, that appeared in the British and American press were brutal in their message.

"Slaughter is happening in Darfur. You can help end it. In 2003, Sudanese President Omar al-Bashir moved to crush opposition by unleashing vicious armed militias to slaughter entire villages of his own citizens. After three years, 400,000 innocent men, women and children have been killed," it ran.

Just one problem. No-one really knew exactly how many had died. Researchers had conducted several mortality studies producing a range of possible figures, but all were subject to uncertainty.

The pro-Khartoum lobbyists had an opening. The European Sudanese Public Affairs Council, an organisation funded by Khartoum to defend its interests abroad and run by David Hoile (who worked the back channels during the teddy bear furore), called in Britain's Advertising Authority in 2007 to assess the claim. Were there really 400,000 dead?

The authority ruled against the advert: "Although the claim appeared in a strongly worded campaigning ad, and SDC & AT were entitled to express their opinion about the humanitarian crisis in Darfur in strong terms, we concluded that there was a division of informed opinion about the accuracy of the figure contained in the ad and it should not have been presented in such a definitive way."

The Save Darfur campaigners were instructed to present the figure as opinion rather than fact and to state the source of any statistics in future adverts. It was a reasonable conclusion but deeply embarrassing for the advocates. They had been caught out using an exaggerated figure. Their credibility was now in question.

Death tolls in conflict are always problematic. Reliable estimates are hard to come by. Researchers conducting mortality studies can rarely access much of the war zone area. Instead they have to extrapolate from accessible areas to estimate a total for the entire conflict. But this is fraught with assumptions. It seems unlikely that death tolls in reachable areas are the same as those in remote, more badly affected battlefields. In Darfur, even basic information about population size and death rates in "normal" years was unknown. The best anyone could hope for was a range of possible death tolls for the conflict. So if 400,000 is an unreliable figure, what is the best guess for the number of Darfur's dead?

Much of the discussion of the Save Darfur ads was based on a study conducted by the American Government Accountability Office.[17] A panel of twelve experts was charged with assessing six

---

17 – *Darfur: Death Estimates Demonstrate Severity of Crisis, But Their Accuracy and Credibility Could Be Enhanced by United States Government Accountability Office, November 2006*

different reports and determining the most accurate. The studies under discussion included estimates produced by the US State Department, the World Health Organisation (WHO) and the Center for Research on the Epidemiology of Disasters (CRED), which is affiliated to the WHO. Three more were provided by independent academics: Eric Reeves, the English professor at Smith College, who works full time as a Darfur activist; Jan Coebergh, a doctor who has worked in Darfur; and John Hagan, a sociologist at Northwestern University, who produced an estimate for the Coalition for International Justice. The numbers ranged from between 98,000 and 181,000 according to the State Department, right up to 400,000 in the calculation provided by Dr Hagan – and the one used in the contentious ads.

All the studies had shortcomings, according to the panel of experts. They had most confidence in the estimate provided by CRED, which analysed thirty mortality surveys, and came to a figure of 120,000 deaths attributable to the conflict over seventeen months. The three studies conducted by individuals, which had the three highest estimates, were the ones that raised the most doubt. Ten of the experts rated Dr Hagan's estimate as "too high".

Since then not much has changed. John Hagan and Alberto Palloni published a paper in the journal Science in September 2006, reviewing published mortality studies. They concluded that 170,000–255,000 people had died, but added that this was a conservative figure, and that an upper limit of 400,000 was possible. These figures also do not include a correction for the death rate in the absence of conflict, suggesting they are probably on the high side.

All this uncertainty poses a problem for journalists covering the conflict. How can we write about Darfur when no-one is clear exactly how many people have died? (My own reporting was picked out by a researcher with Arab Media Watch studying coverage of the conflict, who pointed out that I had chopped and changed the death toll from week to week. He was right. I was uncertain and had flip-flopped between two figures until coming to my own conclusion.) The fall-back position is generally to quote a respected authority. In this case, since spring 2008, it has been Sir John Holmes, the United Nations emergency relief co-ordinator, who began using the figure 300,000 in interviews. This is the number that most of my colleagues use now. But even this is problematic. The UN has never provided the calculation used to reach this figure. Rather it seems a sort of "finger in the air approach", adding on a few tens of thousands to the last number to reflect the extra months of conflict.

For its part, the Aegis Trust sounds rather apologetic for the part it played in bringing to light the problem with the numbers.

"Basically it's a big distraction," said Nick Donovan, head of campaigns, policy and research. "An unnecessary distraction at a time when, whichever number you have, these are human beings and what you've got is a complaint about accuracy and it becomes a big distraction in terms of time, energy and resources. Ever since the issue went to the ASA, we always try to use a range. That's the only accurate way of portraying this type of information."

The Aegis Trust now uses a figure compiled by prosecutors at the International Criminal Court of 115,000–300,000. This figure also has the advantage of identifying the number of violent deaths, 35,000, and those caused by the more indirect effects of conflict, 80–265,000.

The lesson is clear. Hundreds of thousands of people are dying in Darfur. That should be enough for the advocates demanding action. But by focusing on high-end estimates and point figures, rather than ranges, the Save Darfur movement handed Khartoum a propaganda victory. Inflating the statistics may have increased the moral outrage and rhetoric, but at the same it hands Sudan's apologists a means of dismissing the condemnation. Khartoum is the victim of activists intent on exaggerating its crimes, Bashir's supporters can argue, while trotting out their own distorted figure of 10,000 dead. By skewing the figures – deliberately or naively – the activists have weakened their claim to the moral high ground.

There are other problems too. Exaggerated numbers will cloud the analysis of what is happening, and skew the debate towards particular interventions. If hundreds of thousands of people are dying in the sort of "slaughter" described by the Darfur saviours, rapid military solutions such as no-fly zones may be necessary to halt the killing. Peacekeepers can protect the victims and separate the warring parties. Above all, immediate action is imperative. There is no time for the slow, laborious process of mediation. On the other hand, tens of thousands of people dying slow deaths from malnutrition and disease would need a rather different kind of help. A genocide unfolding in Sudan's western province will demand one type of solution. A low-intensity conflict, where deaths come in ones and twos, demands a rather different answer. I knew what I was seeing in Darfur and it wasn't a slaughter.

* * *

There was nothing particularly sophisticated or spectacular about the death that rained from the sky over Madu. A Russian-built Antonov cargo plane circled the village of simple stick huts and choking dust. Its rear loading doors opened on the third pass and the villagers watched as two drums were rolled out of the back. The plane had been painted white to resemble a UN aircraft and was low enough for the locals to see the boots of Sudanese airmen who kicked out the improvised bombs. They exploded in the centre of the village. Shards of metal and razor-sharp wire had been packed inside and they formed a deadly rainstorm as the drums detonated. An eight-year-old boy died. A mother and her three-day-old baby were injured by the homemade shrapnel that ripped through their hut as if the walls did not exist. Two donkeys bled to death.

Elders meeting under the shade of a thatched roof know why they were targeted. Madu is in a region controlled by rebels of the Sudan Liberation Army. Their soldiers, with AK-47s over their shoulders and leather amulets around their necks, hovered in the background as the elders met with UN human rights monitors.

"The government thinks that we sympathise with the movements," said Aduma Aduma Ismail, his flowing jalabiya stained the colour of rusted iron. He was squatting in the dust and had to squint as he looked at me despite the shade. "They consider this area to be occupied by rebels which makes all individuals sympathetic and targets."

A crater left by one of the improvised bombs was all that was left of the attack, some ten days before my arrival by helicopter with an assessment team in April 2008. There wasn't much to look at. It was maybe eighteen inches deep and about the same wide. A villager prodded at the hollow with a stick, exposing pieces of steel wire buried in the sand. It was a brutal weapon, indiscriminate in its killing. And it had left behind a paralysing legacy of fear, according to Abubaker Al Yaqoub, the local sheikh.

"After this experience every time we hear an aircraft we go and hide," he said, his eyes half closed against the dust that rolled in from the desiccated ground stretching on all sides. The raging heat sapped all life from the land. Even the air seemed red with clouds of fine particles. Life was already hard here. There were no women and children in sight; only the men were left.

For all the talk of slaughter, this was how the war was being played out in 2008. Government planes were in the skies supporting technicals and Janjaweed horsemen on the ground. But death was arriving in dribs and drabs, bit by bit, life by life. If there had been a scorched earth policy against villages and towns sympathetic to the rebels, starving the insurgency of its support, that was over. The people of Madu were frightened and shocked by the bombing. A boy had died, the victim of a government assault on a civilian target. Yet the violence of the earlier campaign had ebbed. Things had settled into a far more prosaic pattern. The suffering continued and millions were still crammed into camps for fear of what might happen if they returned home. But a slaughter?

My experience in Madu was confirmed by statistics collected by both UNAMID (the joint African Union and United Nations peacekeeping force) and the Genocide Intervention Network (GI-Net) for violent deaths through the year. UNAMID reports a total of 1,551 for the year, while GI-Net has a figure of 1,211 for January up to 8 September. Of those 496 and 359–720 are thought to be civilians respectively. Those killed by aerial bombardment were forty-six or forty-three in total, including combatants and civilians.

A further 640 people died in intertribal fighting, according to UNAMID, making this category the most important factor in violent deaths in Darfur for 2008.[18]

If there was a genocide in Darfur, this didn't look much like it. This looked like a different phase of the shifting war dynamic. People were still dying. People were still hiding in miserable camps too frightened to go home. The government was still making life desperately difficult for the aid workers who were somehow trying to keep disease and hunger at bay. Yet how could this compare with Rwanda where as many as a million people were murdered by Hutu mobs in not more than one hundred days? In Nazi Germany, the murder of Jews was accelerated even as the regime knew the war was lost. In Darfur, the victims had moved into camps around government garrison towns such as Nyala and El Fasher in their hundreds of thousands, bringing them closer to the alleged genocidaires – unimaginable in Rwanda.

But definitions of genocide are not just about the numbers of dead. Mia Farrow, for example, points out that the government had created "genocidal conditions" which remain in place, even if the large scale attacks of 2003 and 2004 have ended.

"I say we are still seeing genocide by attrition," she had told me. "If you deny people their means of sustaining themselves and herd them, force them into wretched camps across Darfur and eastern Chad, and they have no means of sustaining their own lives and the water they drink by and large is not safe, if on firewood missions the women risk being raped and if attacks on the camps continue."

The notion of genocide is enshrined in the 1948 UN Convention on the Prevention and Punishment of the Crime of Genocide which specifies: "Any of the following acts committed with intent to destroy, in whole or in part, a national, ethnical, racial or religious group, as such: killing members of the group; causing serious bodily or mental harm to members of the group; deliberately inflicting on the group conditions of life, calculated to bring about its physical

---

18 – *The figures are compared and analysed by Alex de Waal at http://blogs.ssrc. org/darfur/2009/02/26/data-for-deaths-in-darfur/*

destruction in whole or in part; imposing measures intended to prevent births within the group; [and] forcibly transferring children of the group to another group." The herding of people into camps, denying women the ability to collect firewood and generally destroying livelihoods certainly fits this definition of genocide – so long as the intention is to destroy a particular group of people in whole or in part. This is where things can come unstuck.

Even when the killing was at its peak, there was no consensus that a genocide was taking place. Colin Powell, then US Secretary of State, stuck his neck out in 2004 telling the Senate Foreign Relations Committee: "We concluded that genocide has been committed in Darfur and that the government of Sudan and the Janjaweed bear responsibility and genocide may still be occurring." The conclusion was based on interviews with 1800 refugees who fled across the border into Chad. Many described being attacked by Janjaweed gunmen who hurled racial epithets as they burned villages and wiped out families.

But few governments followed suit. A commission of inquiry set up by the United Nations found that the killing was not motivated by genocidal intent. "Rather, it would seem that those who planned and organised attacks on villages pursued the intent to drive the victims from their homes, primarily for purposes of counter-insurgency warfare," it concluded. Organisations operating in Darfur have also come to a different conclusion than Colin Powell. Médecins Sans Frontières, for example, was one to contradict his findings. "Our teams have not seen evidence of the deliberate intention to kill people of a specific group. We have received reports of massacres, but not of attempts to specifically eliminate all the members of a group," said Jean-Hervé Bradol, president of MSF France. Others have studiously avoided using the term, preferring "ethnic cleansing" or simply "crimes against humanity".

* * *

So what's going on? Is it genocide? It is and it isn't depending on your definition of the word. If your starting point is the 1948

181

convention then it is. There is no doubt that the government and its Janjaweed allies have been intent on wiping out support for the insurgency by targeting civilians and clearing villages that are loyal to the rebels. They have been killing members of the Fur, Zagawa and Masalit in attempts to destroy them "in part". Of that there can be no doubt. And that is enough for this wide definition of genocide.

Others take a different view, preferring a tighter definition that requires an attempt to wipe out a group "in whole".[19] This reserves the term for episodes such as the Holocaust and Rwanda, where there was a clear intent to destroy an *entire* people. In contrast, the wider definition, it seems, could almost refer to any conflict where a particular group is targeted. Killing a unit of enemy soldiers, for example, would represent an attempt to destroy "in part" a national group. Using the stricter terminology avoids this pitfall, and reserves the word for the very worst abuses. A counter-insurgency campaign that targets civilian villages falls outside this view of genocide. That does not mean such a campaign is not a crime against humanity. It should not lessen international revulsion or absolve Khartoum. Calling it genocide, though, weakens the power of the word.

The more time I spent in Darfur, the more time I spent discussing this question with diplomats or aid workers in Khartoum, the more times I saw IDPs leaving their camps in the morning to go and work in government garrison towns, the more I became convinced that the killings were not genocide. Genocides do not wind down after a couple of years, as the slaughter had in Darfur. They end with the victory of one side or the other, when all the victims are dead or the perpetrators are defeated. There is no such thing as half a genocide. Intending to destroy part of a population does not seem to me a valid definition of genocide. The people in Darfur were victims of appalling crimes. I didn't need to call it genocide to make it matter. The word was one of the factors that first generated interest in the region, linking as it did Darfur with Rwanda. Yet its

---

19 – *A full account of different interpretations is offered by Gérard Prunier in* Darfur: The Ambiguous Genocide, *Cornell University Press*

use has been controversial and, like the exaggerated death tolls, has allowed Khartoum to deny the case put together by Save Darfur. It would be more difficult for the Sudanese government to sidestep accusations of murder. Accusations of genocide allowed it all sorts of ways to get off the hook.

Many of those who campaigned so hard on the issue admit now that the debate has become a distraction from the main issue: the suffering of people in Darfur. The Aegis Trust, for example, is dropping its emphasis on genocide and replacing it with a commitment to "preventing crimes against humanity".

*   *   *

It was a young aid worker that I met deep in the Jebel Mara mountains who first captured the dilemma. He was American and working for an evangelical Christian charity, one of the few humanitarian organisations that straddled the advocacy-aid divide by also being a member of the Save Darfur coalition. He was dressed in classic aid worker style: shabby jeans, t-shirt and sandals, looking for all the world as if he had strolled out of a student union bar. He was, however, much better equipped than me. My lunch was another of the flat, gritty bread loafs that are found all over Sudan. His was a plastic tub of pasta with tomato sauce, cooked by magic, or rather by a sachet of chemicals which when mixed with water produced enough heat to warm the dish. I was waiting for the donkey that would take me into the mountains and to the rebels of the SLA, where I would meet the Arab commanders who had joined their struggle. I started to explain my doubts about the war I was reading up on in press releases from advocacy groups. Up close the black and white analysis was starting to break down and I wasn't sure it was a genocide.

"It's not a genocide," he agreed, "but if we call it a genocide then it gets people's attention. People can't ignore it. Something has to be done."

*   *   *

183

One year after smashing their hourglasses, the celebrities were at work once again. Here was an issue they could stand up for without having to get their hands dirty in the minutiae of international politics or risk alienating fans by getting caught up with domestic interests. It was a moral issue not a political cause. There was only one side to be on. This time they were destroying children's toys. Matt Damon took a baseball bat to a dolls' house. Joely Richardson ripped apart a teddy bear. Thandie Newton blowtorched a Barbie. The images were designed to represent the suffering of Darfur's young and were backed up with a letter from superstar children's author JK Rowling.

It is easy to sneer at the role of celebrities – and the use of dolls' houses and Barbies inadvertently highlighted the cultural disconnect between the global North and South; an empty plastic bottle, rags tied into a football or an old-fashioned hoop and stick were the closest things to toys in Darfur – but the impact was immediate. Once again, Darfur's festering war was all over the newspapers.

And once again the power of the lobby was evident. On the eve of demonstrations, Gordon Brown announced a new plan to Save Darfur. His offer to host a fresh round of peace talks led that night's *BBC World Service* news and made all the papers. Only no-one else knew about it. British diplomats in Khartoum and civil servants in London charged with working towards exactly this sort of progress were taken by surprise. Ambassador Rosalind Marsden was on a field trip deep in eastern Sudan and only found out when an official telephoned her after hearing the proposal on the radio. The diplomats had to make frantic calls to Number 10 to find out about the plans, while fending off irate Sudanese ministers, incensed that they had not been consulted about the proposed talks. The first the Foreign and Commonwealth Office heard was when journalists in Khartoum began telephoning for confirmation. There, civil servants would no doubt have pointed out that a peace process was already under way and any new initiative would need to go through the UN and African Union envoys. And herein lies part of the problem with the huge Darfur advocacy movement. With such pressure and noise for progress, politicians have found themselves pushing for a solution – any solution. He was not the first Gordon to be tripped up by Khartoum, but Brown's initiative was hamfisted and ill-considered.

It showed once again how the success of the Save Darfur movement had been to turn the crisis in Sudan's western region into the humanitarian catastrophe that the world could not ignore. It had become a conflict that mattered to millions of people. The huge publicity campaign meant it mattered to enough British voters to make it also matter to Gordon Brown.

Other African wars are deadlier, have raged longer and are more likely to suck in neighbours, destabilising entire regions of the continent. And in Darfur the simplistic analysis of good guys against bad guys simply does not stand up to scrutiny. Fawning portraits of rebel leaders in the press and exaggerated death tolls belie what is happening on the ground. Maybe that does not matter: maybe it is a price worth paying to ensure the conflict stays on the news pages and in politicians' minds.

The casualty, however, has been progress towards peace. For all their hyperbole and visibility, the advocates have not succeeded in their ultimate aim. They have merely succeeded in pushing Khartoum into a corner and reducing the possibility that diplomacy can prevail. Using exaggerated language and inflated death tolls does no-one any favours. It allows the Sudanese government to justify its own nonsensical casualty figure of 10,000 dead. This helps no-one. Diplomats and UN officials will rarely get on to the subject in public, but in private they are frequently scathing of the Save Darfur movement.

"It has polarised the debate to the extent that it plays into Khartoum's hands," explained one diplomat. "It allows the government to accuse the media of bias against them and it also makes it very difficult to take a different position from Save Darfur."

The debate is so polarised that Save Darfur advocates – often people outside the coalition itself – frequently resort to hurling insults at campaigners who adopt a more nuanced approach. Anyone pushing for greater engagement with Sudan as a means of bringing peace is generally referred to as a Khartoum sympathiser. So too aid workers concerned that Save Darfur's hardline stance risks hampering the delivery of aid to millions of Darfuris. Both are reasonable positions to hold. But not if you are John Norris, the chief executive of the Enough Project – a campaign conceived in 2006 to generate "noise and action" to end genocide and other crimes against humanity. In a blog post he launched into a broadside against those who are cautious about the merits of using the International Criminal Court to bring the Sudanese president to heel, under the title "Bashir's best buddies?".

"Somewhat sadly, Bashir's most enduring loyalists may prove to be the arm chair analysts in New York and Washington who have made a cottage industry out of being critical of international justice, activism, or any forward leaning efforts to actually end a crisis rather than simply managing its consequences," he writes.

The insult is ridiculous when the advocacy lobby and the humanitarian agencies are, in theory, both working towards the same end. They probably agree on more than they disagree, but other UN officials and humanitarian workers have described being heckled at meetings held under the Save Darfur banner for adopting a more moderate position, which emphasises that the Sudanese government is not the only problem in Darfur. Suggesting that splits in the rebel movement have contributed to spikes in violence often gets short shrift from activists who can see no further than Khartoum's crimes.

In this febrile atmosphere, the result has been a one-sided debate on the best way to bring peace to Darfur. The humanitarian actors – who by their very nature tend to weigh up costs and benefits, and opt for solutions that work to reduce suffering – have opted out altogether, preferring to maintain access to the war zone. Instead we are left with a more black and white, rights-based analysis often developed thousands of miles from Sudan. That analysis is not just misguided. It is not just inaccurate. It is leading us to the wrong solutions. Sometimes these are almost comical, such as Gordon Brown's bandwagon-esque attempt to kick-start peace talks. But they are also dangerous. By focusing on criminalising a government and making military intervention the top priority, Save Darfur has made peace more elusive and increased the suffering of ordinary Darfuris. Prescriptions based on the wrong diagnosis rarely work.

9. MISSION IMPOSSIBLE

For three days Sudan's creaking fleet of Antonov planes bombed the far western reaches of Darfur – a sun-blasted plain stretching along the Chadian border. Then came the Janjaweed, some on horseback and some in Toyota pickups, sent to do the government's dirty work. They looted and destroyed the dusty town of Siliea. What they couldn't carry they left strewn across the ground where the market used to be. Clay pots were smashed to tiny, useless shards. Then, with the rebels long gone, the locals pacified and resistance beaten from anyone left alive, Sudanese Armed Forces arrived to take control of the town as if they were on a mission to restore law and order. They painted over graffiti proclaiming support for the Justice and Equality Movement and raised the Sudanese flag in the sandy central square.

The operation was just like dozens if not hundreds that had gone before: lumbering Russian-built cargo planes would soften up the target with crude bombs rolled from the loading bay; Khartoum's proxies would do the hard graft of fighting the rebels; and the government troops would finally be handed their prize. But this was February 2008. Attacks like that were not supposed to happen any more. A month earlier the weak and ineffective troops of the African Union had swapped their green helmets for blue ones as part of what became known as a hybrid peacekeeping mission, fulfilling a central demand of the international community as well as those desperate women I had met in the Jebel Mara a year or so earlier. The United Nations had arrived.

They made no difference. They had not been able to stop the Antonovs, the Janjaweed or the government troops who blasted their way through towns and villages along what was known as the Northern Corridor, a strategic route in and out of the regional capital El Geneina. It had been captured by JEM rebels in December then taken back by the government in February. The government assault was the hybrid's first major test and the men and women of Siliea who had stayed behind rather than flee – now living in charred huts or tents donated by aid agencies – were evidence that the blue hats had made no difference. The people of Siliea were defenceless. It was as if the clock had been turned back to the early, "scorched earth" days of the conflict.

A gently bustling town of mudbrick homes covered in thatch, with a football pitch and a school had all been ripped apart. Around the market, the ground crunched underfoot. Sacks of lentils and sorghum grain had been ripped open and their precious contents scattered. A carpet of pulses that would never be eaten replaced the grey volcanic soil. Here and there were batteries, crushed cardboard boxes, crumbling bars of soap, broken padlocks ripped from brick storehouses. Anything that couldn't be carted off had been demolished or made worthless. Nothing had escaped the vandals as they swept through the market. They had left their slogan on a brick wall in the form of graffiti. "Brothers go and destroy," it read. The scene was one of gratuitous destruction, a mad orgy of ruin.

Alhaj Ibrahim Mohamed Jibrin – his ancient face lined so deeply it resembled the grooved bark of an acacia trunk – was sitting on a battered wooden-framed bed in a compound that had once housed the doctors and nurses of Médecins Sans Frontières. The medics had left, but that didn't stop dozens of families moving in, hoping the flags and logos of an international aid agency would offer them protection in the future.

"During the attack there were two Antonovs bombing and two helicopters," said Alhaj, who reckoned he was about seventy-seven but couldn't be certain. "Then more than 1000 horses. That same day twenty-two people were killed. We ran to the Chadian border. Now it's better so we came back."

A crowd had gathered around him as he told his story in Arabic. Some people nodded as he described seeing a neighbour being shot dead on the steps of his home. Others clicked their tongues when he said eighteen more people had been killed the next day. One or two murmured agreement when he said that they had felt much safer when rebels controlled Siliea. But everyone had something to say as he described his disappointment in the UN peacekeepers who had failed to save them.

"Today is the first time we have seen them," he said without anger, only resignation, in his voice.

The Nigerian troops who made up part of the UNAMID patrol were stretching their legs just around the corner. Their armoured personnel carrier was parked in the shade of what locals called a haras tree. Some of the soldiers raced around trying to stop children turning the steel box on wheels – still bearing its old African Mission in Sudan (AMIS) lettering instead of the new UNAMID logo – into a climbing frame. A second armoured car had continued north out of Siliea with a convoy of 4x4s taking aid workers to inspect projects abandoned in December when rebels closed in.

We were part of a long-range patrol from El Geneina, one of the first since government forces had retaken the northern corridor. Our convoy – the two APCs and half a dozen pickups armed with machine guns interspersed with 4x4s carrying aid workers – had set off soon after dawn, but progress was pedestrian. At best the road was a rutted track; at worst it became a shifting, sandy trap as we crossed dried-up wadis. Twice we ground to a halt as our Toyota Land Cruisers got bogged down in the sand and the Nigerian soldiers scrambled around with shovels trying to slide metal tracks under the spinning wheels.

There were reminders of the danger all around. We had to leave the track at one point to skirt a burned-out government car. It had been hit by a JEM ambush. Further on, an undetonated rocket-propelled grenade lay half-buried in the sand. Soldiers and civilian aid workers gathered around the explosive debating what to do. I stayed firmly in my seat and began breathing easily only once we had resumed our journey, the hazard now marked with a pattern of stones in the road.

For three hours we bumped and slithered along the sandy tracks. I shared the hard benches in the back of a Toyota with a couple of Nigerian soldiers and our patrol's translator, Bashir. He was a chatty sort who had worked for several aid agencies before getting a job with much better pay at the UN – a typical career path, but one that was stretching the resources of charities as the new hybrid force gobbled up drivers, translators, guards and admin staff. The two Nigerian soldiers were both coming to the end of their tours and were desperately looking forward to going home. All they wanted to do was keep their heads down, serve their time and keep out of trouble. We talked about football, Nigeria and life far from home.

Bashir had thought to bring along a tape of traditional Sudanese music. On its first airing it made for an interesting lesson in the local culture. By the third and fourth play, its tuneless twangs and wailing began to grate. Twice the car's stereo chewed up the tape. And twice Bashir managed to repair his cassette. On the third occasion, much to my relief, he admitted defeat. The rest of the journey was spent listening to equally jarring recordings of local music he had stored on his fancy new phone bought with his pay increase. (On the return leg I quietly admitted defeat, plugged my iPod into my ears and pretended to doze – a tried and tested method with talkative taxi drivers across the continent.)

Our route was the same one that government forces would have taken as they recaptured territory lost to the rebels. Two hours from El Geneina we reached Sirba. It was a town of ashes where huts used to stand. Donkeys nosed through the blackened ruins. The only other signs of life were at the town's edges, where tumbledown homes gave way to the yellow scrub. Here an aid agency had begun pitching tents for residents only now, more than a month after the attacks, returning home from hiding places in the Jebel Moon mountains to the north or the Chadian border to the west.

Hundreds of men on camel and horseback, wearing khaki uniforms, had ridden into the town as an Antonov and attack helicopters provided air support. About thirty vehicles mounted with machine guns followed them in, firing indiscriminately. The survivors told investigators from Human Rights Watch that they had buried forty-two people killed by gunshots, rockets or bombs. United Nations monitors reported ten cases of rape.

Further on, our convoy passed the turning to Abu Surouj. It had been hit in the same wave of attacks. About thirty people had died as Antonovs bombed and militiamen set fire to homes and shops. They collected mattresses, pots and pans before using matches to set light to the thatched roofs. If their matches didn't work, they used rockets instead. Women were allowed to escape, while their husbands, sons and fathers were cut down. Corpses would not join the rebels.

The prize for the government was the Jebel Moon, a mountainous region to the north of Siliea and a rebel stronghold. JEM fighters had been using the protection of its rocky outcrops and high altitude to cross back and forth to Chad, rearming and resupplying at will. A few months earlier, the guerrillas had moved southwards out of the hills to occupy the Northern Corridor towns, eventually claiming they were poised to take El Geneina itself. But their paymaster in Chad was in trouble. Chadian rebels were closing fast on the capital N'Djamena and the JEM units were called back to help stave off a coup in February. With the Darfuri rebels defending the Chadian government, the Sudanese armed forces seized their chance and rolled back the rebel gains. In all, more than 110 people are thought to have died for the Northern Corridor, little more than a dusty road with prickly scrub on either side. Another 40,000 people fled their homes under the onslaught.

The suffering didn't stop there. With the Sudanese flag replacing that of the JEM rebels, villagers faced a new threat. The towns were now filled with soldiers, police officers and administrators from elsewhere. And men from elsewhere did what they always do in times of war.

In Siliea there were few people left who were able to protect the women. It was a town of old men, women and children. Any men of fighting age were away fighting or dead. The elders sitting in the main square on blankets or sheets of cardboard directed us towards the edge of town where the women had begun sharing houses as protection against the occupying soldiers. I would have asked my Sudanese guide to find me someone who had been raped and spoke English, but I knew it would be pointless. In this sun-beaten part of Sudan, far from mains electricity or paved roads, it would be impossible to find a woman educated in a foreign language.

We hurried off on the route we had been directed, down a hill towards a football pitch that had little in the way of grass and only one set of goalposts. The rest of the convoy would be returning from its recce up the road and we had little time to talk to the town's women. My short-sleeved shirt was wet with sweat by the time we bumped into Mariam Ibrihim Adam headed in the opposite direction. She was wrapped head-to-toe in a salmon pink scarf and had just come from one of the shared houses to fetch water from a well. As usual, I rambled through my opening question, wondering how candid this stranger would be once I finally got past my vague introductory query about the "security situation" and on to the taboo subject of rape. I need not have worried. Mariam knew exactly what I was getting at as soon as my guide translated my first sentence. Soldiers were roaming the town every night looking for sex, she said.

"Three days ago there were women sleeping who were woken by soldiers with guns in the middle of the night," she continued. "I don't know what happened but there were men with women and then all the women ran to the fursha's [mayor's] house for protection."

My guide and translator whispered in my ear that the women had not been raped. They were working as prostitutes, he hissed. It was impossible to know the truth. Rape and prostitution were each the mark of a wanton woman. Rape would have been as difficult to accept for the men of Siliea as the notion that the women were earning money by sleeping with the soldiers. Either way, the women were victims of a militarised society. There was little left of the place Siliea must once have been. On a continent filled with failed states, Siliea had become a failed town. The elders sitting in the dusty square no longer had any power, just like the sheikhs and umdas I had met in the camps. They were a sad reminder of the old order. They could sit and discuss affairs of the day but their way of doing things had gone, replaced by a government commander who controlled the town. Their white jalabiyas turned them into ghosts of who they used to be.

Peacekeepers had failed to stop the government attack. Nor could they stop the daily assault on the town's residents.

"Now the UN cars are here, stood in front of us, we feel safe," said Adam Omar Mohammed, the eighty-eight-year-old faki, or religious man, of the town. He wore a pair of spectacles with a cracked lens, more a sign of standing and education than an aid to vision. He spoke for the town as he expressed his hopes and disappointment that we were about to leave.

"We want the UN to come and stay."

Minutes later the convoy was on its way, scattering chickens and children in our wake. Two hours was as much as it could spare. We pulled past the football pitch on our way out of town and I gazed at its lone set of goalposts. Amid the looting, raping and burning of Siliea, the horsemen had found time to pull down the missing posts. Siliea had been attacked by men who destroyed football pitches. After umpteen stories of rape, Antonovs and gunmen on horseback, somehow this was more shocking than anything else.

* * *

Each year of the conflict in Darfur has had its own dynamic. It began with the uprising of rebels against Khartoum. The government responded by unleashing its Janjaweed militias in a scorched earth policy against civilians. As the 2006 peace talks loomed, the rebel groups fragmented and splintered, threatening what some aid officials privately called the Somaliasation of Darfur – the descent into anarchy with tiny, rival fiefdoms, each controlled by an unstable guerrilla group, often comprising little more than a commander, a car and a satellite phone. This was followed by clashes between Arab tribes, now awash with weapons and in some cases disillusioned with their Khartoum paymasters. Superimposed on all these conflicts – of tribe against tribe, rebels against soldiers, Arab nomads against settled farmers – was a much bigger source of unrest, the not-so-secret war between Sudan and Chad, which came to the fore in 2008. It was this war that claimed the lives of those villagers in Siliea and the other towns of the Northern Corridor.

There was no disguising the Chadian rebels in West Darfur's regional capital of El Geneina. At its best, this was a bleak city. Even the incessant sun couldn't diminish the dreary greyness of its brick buildings, all coated in a thin shroud of dust. At its worst, the desert heat sapped all energy from the body, a reminder that this was reputed to be the point of Africa furthest from the ocean – the very centre of the continent.

Here there were none of the modest comforts of the other Darfur capitals: the pizza restaurant in El Fasher or the Indian hotel in Nyala. There were no iPods in the market, only cheap Chinese torches, plastic sandals and radios that had arrived from Dubai via Chad. Plastic bags seemed to grow on trees. Discarded and shredded, they caught on thorny branches like straggly blue and white checked leaves. The smell of sewage was never far away. The only respite for the town's expat aid workers seemed to be the weekly volleyball game at the World Food Programme's compound where I stayed.

Outside those walls, the town had a Wild West feel. El Geneina was a border town that would have little reason to exist were it not for Chad, only a few miles distant. The markets were stocked by trucks arriving from N'Djamena. Lorries loaded high with animal skins would trundle back in the opposite direction.

There was another border trade – war. Chadian rebels, backed by Khartoum, were frequent visitors to El Geneina. They wore their scarves wrapped around their faces, only sunglasses peeping through the wraps, in typical rebel fashion. It was their distinctive jeeps that made them stand out. Each had its windscreen and roof cut down, exposing the occupants to the desert wind in a style I hadn't seen anywhere else in Sudan. Yet these customised vehicles were a common sight on the ash-grey dust roads of El Geneina, where they came to stock up with provisions at the markets, girls during the night time raids at the aid camps and, no doubt, weapons from their backers in the Sudanese regime. On one occasion my car drove past one of the Chadian jeeps slowly enough to hear words of French being exchanged between rebels, another giveaway that these were not militias from the Sudanese side of the border.

Amid this volatile mix it seemed the hybrid peacekeeping force, barracked on a sandy hill overlooking the town, had been given an all but impossible task. Aid workers told me they had begged the soldiers to intervene once it became clear that government troops were on their way to recapture the Northern Corridor. In the end the people of Siliea were left to fend for themselves, and it was days before an assessment mission arrived to gauge the casualties.

"We feel disappointed," said Colonel Amgad Morsy, chief of staff for UNAMID Sector West, in his prefab office, air-conditioned to the point of chilliness. "We don't have the capability. It's a weekly and daily dispute that IDPs come and say their people are being harassed, their women are raped. What we can do is try to build confidence, but it's still the very minimum we can do."

I wondered what the locals would make of Colonel Morsy's confidence building measures. He was an officer in the Egyptian army. His light skin meant everyone would assume he was an Arab even if they didn't spot the Egyptian flag on his khaki uniform. Anyway, the people in the camps were expecting more than warm words. Six months earlier, the creation of the hybrid force had been announced with much fanfare. It would swallow up the 7000 personnel of the failing African Union deployment, to eventually become the biggest peacekeeping force in the world, comprising some 26,000 uniformed soldiers and police officers. It was granted a Chapter VII mandate by the UN Security Council, enabling the force to protect civilians, as well as humanitarian workers and its own staff. UN resolution 1769 was greeted with enthusiasm by anti-genocide campaigners. The wording might have been watered down to get it past Khartoum, which was entitled to decide who could and couldn't enter its territory, but it was still welcomed as a significant step towards protecting a population which had endured four years of bloodshed and misery.

But when I visited the new force only a handful of extra soldiers and police had been added, bringing the total number of peace-keepers to 9000 in Darfur. In the months to come a few hundred more would arrive – a pathetic number if the aim was to impose themselves on a region about the size of Spain. Colonel Morsy detailed other problems. He needed aerial support if his men were to travel around their whole sector; in the wet season his patrols would struggle to move at all along the remote, dirt lanes that pass for roads; and his communications equipment was woefully inadequate. And there were dozens of anecdotal reports detailing further shortcomings: a lack of ration packs for long-distance patrols; not enough helmets, forcing some soldiers to paint their green AU headgear blue; helicopter patrols unable to touch down because ground forces had missed the rendezvous and failed to secure a landing site.

For years the people of Darfur had been telling me they wanted UN peacekeepers. They expected American and European troops with the latest military training and equipment to come and save them. What they had got was the same African troops, some with blue plastic bags tied over the helmets. Already the people of Siliea had discovered that this was not enough to protect them.

Even as he outlined the problems, Colonel Morsy remained upbeat. It would take time, he admitted, but morale was improving, security had been stepped up around the aid camps and there were more patrols since the UN had taken over. His men went out at night and had begun escorting women to collect firewood, protect-ing them from rape. They had even chased and arrested a handful of Janjaweed raiders as they looted a camp. But looming large were memories of what happened to the African Union mission.

"Everyone in the city will tell you there's been a lot of changes," he said, "but we still have the African Union forces and logistics which caused us to fail."

The longer I spent in Africa, the more I experienced déjà vu. Nothing seemed to change. Nothing seemed to be learnt. Follow any story long enough, and the same excuses, the same mistakes and the same pleas from villagers came around year after year.

* * *

When nine government pickups mounted with 12.7mm cannons swept through their simple wattle and daub homes in 2005, the villagers of Tawilla knew that the African Union soldiers stationed nearby would do nothing to intervene. So they ran from their homes and streamed up to the gates of the AU base a few hundred yards away where they hoped the 241 Rwandan troops would not turn them away. They didn't. As the government vehicles sped through the sandy alleys, kicking up plumes of red dust, the villagers rushed through the gates to safety.

After a tense standoff in front of the base, the government security forces gave up and went home. But not before they had burned dozens of homes. They fired rocket propelled grenades into four small camps for displaced people arrayed around the village. Five bodies were later recovered. Four were elderly man – all farmers. Three women said they had been raped. Days later Sudanese police told AU officials that they had been acting on intelligence that the small town of thatched huts and rickety reed fences in North Darfur was harbouring rebel fighters – their usual excuse for attacking a civilian target.

Inside the base, African soldiers watched from behind their barbed wire fence without intervening. Some grabbed their cameras and photographed the destruction. Their pictures captured plumes of smoke spiralling into the air as another of Darfur's villages burned. The 7000-strong AU force had been sent to protect ceasefire monitors tasked with watching over a truce between government and rebels that had long since collapsed. In addition, they were supposed to protect humanitarian workers and civilians "under imminent threat and in the immediate vicinity, within resources and capability". The civilians in Tawilla were clearly under imminent threat and in the immediate vicinity, but by September 2005 the AU had already lost the resources and capability to venture out in protection.

It was only a year after they had been deployed as part of a much lauded African solution for an African problem. This was to be the shape of things to come. Instead of looking to the United Nations in New York to organise aid and peacekeeping missions, Africa could solve its own problems in Addis Ababa, seat of the AU. The Darfur mission was its first such operation and a test of African resolve to clean up a continent mired in war.

As our AU helicopter circled Tawilla a few weeks after the attack it was obvious that the African solution was not working. Instead of cooking fires, children racing around and chickens scratching at the dirt, I looked down on a town without any people. The ashes of burned homes were obvious among the patches of sun-yellowed thatch. There were so many charred spots it looked like an irregular chessboard. Where were the people? I wondered. Then as we began our descent into the base it became clear. Hundreds of flimsy-looking lean-tos had been built hurriedly around the AU perimeter. The whole town had given up their homes and moved up the hill. The government wouldn't dare touch them here. If soldiers fired a grenade at the homes here, it would be as good as a direct assault on the African force.

From the base, I travelled into the town itself with a company of Rwandan soldiers. These were generally considered some of the best-trained and motivated of the troops donated by African countries. They certainly looked professional enough as we jumped out of the 4x4s and began strolling through the town's streets, soft sand shifting gently underfoot. Like many Darfuri towns – and the vast aid camps that millions now called home – Tawilla was divided up into compounds by thin fences of sticks and reeds. Each would have one or two mud-plastered huts and a dust yard. There should have been the sound of sweeping as women bent double with handleless brooms of twigs tried to keep their enclosures neat. In Tawilla almost all the yards were empty. There was no swish of sticks on sand. There were no donkeys braying.

In the distance we spotted a thin plume of smoke curling into the vast African sky. We hurried past abandoned homes and through empty lanes before finding a cluster of women arranged around a fire. They had ventured back into the town to do their cooking or to check on one or two goats left behind. They stuck together for safety but said they would be back beneath the AU floodlights before sunset.

Fatima Mohamed Adam looked many years older than the twenty-seven she claimed. Her short cropped hair had flecks of grey and everything seemed an effort. She had left three children back in their new hut by the base and brought her two youngest with her as she cooked up a pot of beans. She kept one baby balanced on her hip as she sliced an onion.

"Our house had been burned and we had nowhere to live," she said. "We have no confidence now in the government but we believe that being near the African Union we will be safe."

Up by the base, among shelters that should have been temporary but would soon become permanent, it was the same story.

Ahmed Suileman Khatir summed it up: "Being near the AU keeps us safe. If the government tries to shoot at us then they are shooting at the AU and they will defend us. If we are not here then there is little that they can do."

Our time was running out. It was only a brief visit to Tawilla and I had already upset the sulky Russian crew who were ferrying me around by arriving late for our departure in the morning. They had insisted we stay for only one hour and the engines of their ageing Antonov helicopter were already whining as I managed a quick briefing from the AU officers who were based in the town. They sounded like they had given up.

"We came here to monitor and now we find ourselves ducking bullets," said a South African officer, shouting above the sound of the whirring rotors. "Morale is down. It has got worse in the past two months as it seems the warring parties no longer recognise us. You don't know if the day will end with your life intact."

A few days before I arrived in Tawilla, three African soldiers and two civilian contractors had been killed. They had been captured in a rebel ambush and executed. From then on things would only get worse, as the AU lost the support of a civilian population it couldn't protect and attracted the ire of rebel factions who blamed the peacekeepers for supporting an unpopular peace deal. Month by month through 2006, the death toll rose steadily in ones and twos as ambushes and carjackings continued. The bloodshed culminated in a bloody attack on an AMIS base in Haskanita in 2007. There were only three months to go before the struggling mission was due to be bolstered by UN cash, personnel and expertise, when an estimated 1000 rebel fighters swept into the town. Many of the African soldiers simply fled in terror. By daybreak ten peacekeepers had been killed.

Each time I visited Darfur after that first trip to Tawilla it seemed that AMIS had lost a little more confidence. A force whose green helmets had once been a common sight around each of the three capitals no longer seemed willing to venture out of base. Officer after officer complained their men lacked the night vision equipment, helicopter support and armoured vehicles they needed to bring security. Undermanned and outgunned, they had failed to protect the civilian population and no longer seemed able to protect themselves. They had become targets too.

So what had gone wrong with the African solution for an African problem? In Khartoum an Oxfam press officer, Nicki Bennett, one of the few aid workers willing to speak on the record to journalists, said a 7000-strong force was not nearly big enough to police such a vast area as Darfur – about the size of Spain.

"But soldiers alone will not be enough to put an end to the ongoing violence and attacks: the peacekeepers also need to receive the proper equipment and logistical support to carry out their jobs. AU helicopters and vehicles in Darfur routinely run out of fuel, camps often take weeks to set up and some soldiers barely have enough ammunition to defend themselves – never mind aid operations or civilians under threat," she added.

That was only one part of the problem, according to the civilian who headed the AU presence in Sudan. Ambassador Baba Kingibe, the then AU special representative in Sudan, said the force was doing what it could. Ultimately though, his men could achieve little while all sides flouted the terms of a ceasefire they were supposed to be policing.

"The bottom line is really that there is nothing we or the UN can achieve in Darfur without the willing co-operation of parties to the conflict," he told me.

It's a hoary old cliché, but true nonetheless, that peacekeepers are useless if there is no peace to keep.

As the African Union mission slid closer to failure through 2006, so the dire warnings of death and destruction mounted. The Darfur advocacy movement stepped up its rhetoric and heaped pressure upon the United Nations to send peacekeepers to stop the killing. A UN resolution had already been approved to take over the mission, but was being blocked by Khartoum, which claimed such a move would breach sovereignty. Back at Smith College, Massachusetts, Eric Reeves was busy writing papers and editorials warning that Sudan's government was preparing for a further genocidal push. In an opinion piece published in the Washington Post he concluded that without an intervention "to protect civilians or the humanitarian efforts upon which they depend – mortality in Darfur over the next year could exceed the present death toll of about half a million human beings, some 10,000 people a week".[20] It was an astonishing figure. But it still took an Oscar winner to capture the world's imagination.

George Clooney dominated news broadcasts with a speech before the UN in September 2006 predicting that 2.5m people would die if UN troops did not step in by the end of the month. His address was blunt and emotive, laden with the sort of blockbuster language that no-one could ignore.

"After 30 September, you won't need the UN," Clooney told a special informal session of the UN's Security Council. "You will simply need men with shovels and bleached white linen and head-stones. In many ways it's unfair, but it is nevertheless true, that this genocide will be on your watch. How you deal with it will be your legacy – your Rwanda, your Cambodia, your Auschwitz."

---

20 – *Accommodating Genocide by Eric Reeves,* The Washington Post, *September 3, 2006*

His words, carrying echoes of the twentieth century's darkest moments, were seen around the world. In an unprecedented step the special session was televised, bringing a touch of tinseltown to what would otherwise be a tedious, long-winded, closed doors lobbying session. His message was backed up by interviews explaining his brand of celebrity diplomacy.

"I would feel criminal if I wasn't involved in things that I believe in. I would think that if you are in the position to act or try and bring focus to an issue you think is important and you don't, you have failed miserably in the human race," he told the *BBC*.

A week after his performance, thousands of people around the world took part in the first Day for Darfur, demanding UN military action. Hundreds of protesters marched through London wearing symbolic blue berets. Survivors of the Holocaust joined demonstrators outside the Sudanese embassy, while religious leaders prayed for a resolution. In Kigali, Tutsis who lived through the Rwandan genocide showed their solidarity with Darfuri villagers. Some fifty cities and forty countries joined in the international day of action. For once, the world was standing together to demand action. Spokesmen talked of "staring into the abyss" as the first genocide of the twenty-first century was poised to deteriorate further. Tony Blair wrote letters to other European leaders urging them to heap pressure on Sudan. The momentum was unstoppable. Something, anything, it seemed, had to be done.

The result was UN Security Council Resolution 1769, passed in July 2007. It completed the long mooted transfer of the AMIS deployment to UN command with day-to-day management staying with the AU. This was the hybrid option for a joint force which would retain a predominantly African character. Rather than using troops from Nato nations, it would be a primarily African affair with the existing soldiers swapping their green berets for blue. That was the price extracted by Khartoum for allowing the world's biggest peacekeeping operation on to its soil. Eventually it would comprise 26,000 pairs of boots on the ground – including military, police and civilian personnel.

It was a victory for the global alliance which had demanded a more robust military intervention to stop the killing in Darfur. Yet many people that I had talked to in Sudan remained unconvinced. The new mission seemed to address some of the problems associated with the African Union deployment, but failed to learn the most crucial lesson of all. If the AU had failed through inadequate funding and international support, the bigger UN-backed force costing $1.5bn a year would have a better chance of protecting the civilian population and ensuring humanitarian aid could get through. But there was more. AMIS had constantly been hobbled by opposition from the Khartoum government which obstructed its work at every turn. Vital equipment was delayed for months in Port Sudan, for example. And the AU had failed, as its civilian chief had told me, because it did not have the support of the warring factions. There was no peace deal to police, only a shifting series of conflicts which occasionally came in and out of focus as a conventional two-sided war. How would an intervention force stop a conflict with no clear frontlines? This was not Kosovo, Sierra Leone or East Timor where the battle lines were clear. Comparisons with Somalia's warlord anarchy, where alliances and clan allegiances change daily, seemed closer. And an American-led intervention force had come dramatically unstuck there. These challenges were not lost on the man charged with leading the new force.

"I think first and foremost there should be peace," said General Martin Luther Agwai down a crackly phone line from El Fasher, two months before he would take charge of the UNAMID force. "There should be a peace agreement. That would be the first thing, because the mandate of UNAMID is peacekeeping, meaning that there needs to be a peace agreement to be kept. Second, if all the planning and the agreements on 20,000 troops, 6,000 police and the equipment are met, then I would see UNAMID succeeding. But anything outside that will create a lot of challenges for UNAMID."

One of his main fears, he said, was that expectations were too high. If his men failed to deliver peace, if government and Janjaweed attacks continued into the new year after UNAMID had arrived, opinion in the aid camps and among rebel commanders would turn against them just as it had against the AU forces. UNAMID would become part of the problem rather than the solution. So with no clear idea of when he would have all 26,000 personnel in place or when donors would come up with vitally needed helicopters, the hybrid force was far from assured of success.

Its planners, officials within the UN's Department of Peace Keeping Operations, knew that too. Some gave it a sixty percent chance of working; others more like twenty-five percent. No-one was quite sure how the "hybrid" force would work. Its mention was greeted with rolling of eyeballs and occasional sniggers.

"There was no doubt that it couldn't do any harm," said one later. "It had to be a good thing getting the bodies in there, but there was no guarantee it was going to deliver peace and it also put back progress in peace talks for eighteen months."

Aid workers in Khartoum also complained that the attention being given to UNAMID was a distraction – that the deployment was useful but should be seen as only one element in the quest for peace. The peacekeepers might improve security around camps and provide escorts for aid convoys but the conflict itself seemed no nearer resolution. MSF, Oxfam and others with workers on the ground were aware of the limitations. But they weren't the ones addressing the UN on primetime TV.

At the same time, celebrity activists and advocacy platforms had built up public pressure to find a solution. They had used it up with the push for peacekeepers. Similarly, international political capital had been spent at the UN in bringing China and Sudan to heel. All the jokers had been played and the only tangible result was a bolstered force which would still face the same hurdles that brought its predecessor down.

George Clooney and other celebrity diplomats had kept Darfur on the news pages and made it the African war no-one could ignore. It was an incredible feat. They had oiled the lumbering workings of the vast UN machine with appeals to emotion that were viewed by millions and edged a world towards a solution. Only it was the wrong solution – the product of an analysis that painted the war as a black and white conflict between the government and its proxies and the rebels and their civilian supporters. The war I had seen was not like that. The Arab militias were not a homicidal or genocidal force, intent on destruction. They were often victims of a conflict that was destroying a way of life. Their reaction, in some ways, could be seen as a rational attempt at survival. Some were even fighting the government. Nor were the rebels necessarily the good guys. At times they had done more to hamper the aid effort than their opponents. All sides held pockets of territory, rather than swaths of the country.

The blue helmets might well have a role to play. But not yet. Without attempts to reconcile the nomads and their settled farming neighbours, to find peace within the warring peoples who called themselves Arab, to resolve Sudan and Chad's border conflict, to police the tensions between villages over resources, peacekeepers would find themselves tasked with mission impossible. All they could do for the time being was make the camps a little safer.

* * *

The truck seemed to be moving too fast for the rutted road of dirt and dust. Its headlights streaked through the murky evening gloom at a speed unusual by West Darfur's relaxed pace. Then the lights came to a sudden stop before disappearing. The driver had realised he was in sight of a UNAMID patrol. The dark shadowy shape of his truck was too close to the Krinding aid camps spread around the edges of El Geneina to have a legitimate purpose at nine o'clock in the evening. An armoured personnel carrier escorted by two pickups left our slow moving column and lumbered off towards where we had last seen the lights.

"Chadian rebels," said one of the Nigerian soldiers who made up our night patrol as we waited under the brilliant night sky for the scouts to return. If UNAMID couldn't actually stop the war and if it was still way short of its full complement of soldiers, at least it could start policing the aid camps more effectively, keeping out intruders. Every couple of nights a patrol like this would lurch out of the barracks at dusk and make its rounds before returning at midnight. The APCs caused quite a commotion as they ploughed through the town's narrow streets. At one point the mudbrick buildings closed in on either side to the point where the big white vehicles needed four or five manoeuvres to make it through a right-hand turn. One still managed to pull down a road sign as it cleared the junction.

Darfur nights can have quite a nip to them and it was chilly by the time we had stopped to watch the mysterious truck go about its business. The vast expanse of the three Krinding camps was spread before us in night-time silence. There were few lights and fewer noises. Shadows came and went. Most of the inhabitants would be in their beds. Without the sun their chores would be over and it was safer to stay in doors at night. A Sudanese policeman ambled out of the darkness to find out what we were doing.

"It's all quiet here. Nothing to report," he said, before exchanging pleasantries with our commanding officer and then disappearing back from where he had come, probably to the warmth of a fire.

Eventually the rest of the patrol returned. They had seen the truck do a three-point turn and then speed off into the desert, its driver clearly reluctant to explain himself. We would never know where it had come from or what it was doing, but the joint UN-AU night patrols chalked it up as a small victory in their quest to bring security to Darfur. Their presence had been a deterrent.

Sheikh Abdulrahman Hassan Yussuf was waiting for us as we continued on, through a police checkpoint, and into Krinding 3 camp. For the past five years he had lived in the camps trying to keep his people – members of the Masalit tribe – functioning as the community they had once been. One of his jobs was to manage security of a warehouse where sacks of maize and sorghum were stored, along with cans of cooking oil.

He met us at its entrance, his long white jalabiya and skullcap glowing in the starlight. He looked anxious and immediately began to report a problem. The previous night had been disturbed by gunmen rampaging through the camp, a place that was supposed to be a safe haven for people who had already lost everything.

"They were looking for women," he said, standing in front of the deserted and locked food warehouse. "There were more than twenty of them – Janjaweed. They didn't find any girls young enough so they left."

They may not have been Janjaweed. The word was being increasingly used as a catch-all for bandits or thugs with horses. That wasn't the point. There were similar stories in every camp I had ever visited. At night, many descended into lawless hell holes. Armed factions of all sides moved in and out, recruiting fighters and stocking up on food. Rape was becoming commonplace inside as much as outside the camp perimeters. Gunshots would often echo around the empty paths and alleys as families hunkered down inside their shelters. Around Krinding, though, things were changing. The last time I had visited this camp it was too dangerous for UN personnel to set foot inside. We had to make do with driving slowly around its edge. A UN 4x4 was carjacked an hour or so after we left on the same stretch of road. Now blue-helmeted soldiers were patrolling what had once been a no-go area.

Lieutenant Adeyinka Adeyemo, commander of the patrol, listened intently to the sheikh's story before turning to his translator.

"Ask him how we can catch these people. Tell him I will come to catch them. All he has to do is phone me," said the Nigerian officer, writing down his mobile phone number on a scrap of paper.

The peacekeepers didn't seem able to bring much peace to Darfur. The failings of the AU force had already begun to afflict the hybrid. Khartoum was doing its best to stymie every move. There weren't enough soldiers, and donor countries were struggling to find helicopters. There was no peace deal or frontline to police, just a shifting array of factions which moved as fast as Darfur's desert sands in the wind. The celebrity campaigners and the thousands who marched in support of deploying UN peacekeepers had got what they wanted. But by neglecting the search for a peace deal, the arrival of the blue helmets had failed to save Darfur. What they could do, however, was deploy their resources in ways that gave them maximum impact. Improving the security of the wretched camps was just one such way that they could show Darfuris they were not the same as the hated African force – even though they were the same Senegalese, Nigerian and Rwandan soldiers with different coloured helmets. Even then Sheikh Abdulrahman wasn't sure it was enough for his villagers with no village.

"These are bad men and they are all around. If they see the patrols then they will not be back," he said. "But if they don't see them for a while then they will come back."

Our patrol would not be back to the sheikh's sector for a week. And that was the problem.

10. KHARTOUM'S BACKLASH

There was no celebrating in the camps of Darfur when the International Criminal Court (ICC) issued a warrant for the arrest of President Omar al-Bashir. Government ministers and officials had taken care of that, warning Darfuris that they faced losing a hand if they were caught rejoicing. In fact, the camps were eerily quiet. A day after the court's three judges had made their decision to indict Bashir on charges of war crimes and crimes against humanity, it was almost as if life had been sucked from the sand alleys and shambling huts. Campaigners around the world had hailed the decision as a great victory for international justice. Things were different in Darfur. Here and there, women were walking to water pumps carrying jerry cans and the odd goat picked at scraps of plastic, but the normal hustle and bustle of life was missing.

The reason was clear. Life had just got worse. The aid agencies, which supported so much of everyday existence, were gone. Their brightly coloured flags still flew above reed-roofed offices or clinics, but there was no-one inside. Gates were padlocked and, as I drove through first Abu Shouk and then Al Salaam camps with a detachment of United Nations police, the only aid agency staff we saw was the occasional security guard sitting on squares of cardboard in the shade of locked gates. After bombing more than two million people into the camps, the Sudanese government had responded to the ICC indictments in March 2009 by shutting off vital aid. Officials had begun telephoning thirteen aid agencies within minutes of the court's televised press conference, telling them they were no longer welcome in Sudan.

The results were immediate. At one little hospital, built from plastic sheeting and wooden poles, patients had been sent home and doctors and nurses told not to turn up for work. It may not have been much to look at but it was one of only three hospitals serving Al Salaam's population. Inside three guards were asleep. They said it was closed. No-one knew when or if it would open again.

Outside the hospital – run by the International Rescue Committee until it was ordered out – a mother brushed flies from the face of her daughter. The little bundle of a child was swaddled in a vibrant sheet of reds and blues, a stark contrast to the still eyes that peered from inside the cloth. Her mother had questions that no-one could answer.

"My baby is sick," said Fatima Abdulrahmen. "She has a fever and I brought her here and now I don't know what to do. Who will help me now?"

The people who should have been helping – the staff of thirteen international charities, including Oxfam, Médicins Sans Frontières and Care International – were boarding flights to the capital Khartoum. Officials from the Humanitarian Aid Commission (HAC) were doing the rounds of their offices, collecting millions of dollars worth of equipment – including computers and satellite phones.

Advocacy organisations from New York to London, as well as aid organisations, had spent months debating how President Bashir's government would react to indictments. Would rivals in the regime use the ICC as justification of a palace coup? Would the pressure force the two-decade president into a more conciliatory pose? Or might it back him into a corner? Now the world knew the outcome. He was turning the screw. Millions of people – families who had already lost their homes and faced a daily battle for survival – were much, much worse off.

* * *

Weeks of rumour ended in July 2008. Three years earlier, the UN Security Council had passed the case of Darfur on to the ICC – the world's first permanent war crimes court – allowing its prosecutors to begin gathering evidence that could bring the men responsible for the region's suffering to justice. In 2007, Ali Kosheib, a senior Janjaweed commander, and Ahmed Harun, then an interior minister who held the Darfur brief, were indicted for their alleged role in arming and organising militias. That was not enough for human rights activists, who always believed the buck stopped with the president. Throughout 2008 speculation grew that President Bashir was about to be named as a suspect.

Confirmation came in July when Luis Moreno-Ocampo, the court's chief prosecutor, handed a dossier of evidence to three pre-trial judges tasked with deciding whether there was a case to answer. Essentially the case against Bashir comprised ten charges: three of genocide, five of crimes against humanity and two of war crimes. Ocampo's argument was not that Bashir had been directly involved in the murder and rape of Darfuris, but that as commander-in-chief at the apex of Sudan's military and political structure he was ultimately responsible for the slaughter. Papers presented to the court accused Bashir's armed forces of killing 35,000 people from tribes allied to the rebels. A further 80,000 to 265,000 had died "slow deaths" brought about by conditions in the camps.

"Al Bashir's decision to destroy the target groups developed over time," read an annex to the main case. "He assessed that the Fur, Masalit and Zaghawa ethnic groups, as socially and politically dominant groups in the region, constituted a threat to his power. They challenged the economic and political marginalisation of their region, and members of the three groups engaged in armed rebellions. Al Bashir's motives were largely political. His pretext was a 'counter-insurgency'. His intent was genocide. The goal was not simply to defeat a rebellion, but to destroy those ethnic groups whose members challenged his power."

Like any good prosecutor, Ocampo was prepared to push his case of genocide as far as he could. He had made his name prosecuting members of Argentina's junta and, at one time, even appeared in a reality TV show ruling on private disputes. He knew the power of a well-placed sound bite. In a press conference before the case was unveiled, he compared Darfur with Rwanda, and the actions of the Sudanese government with those of the Nazis.

"These 2.5 million people are in camps. They don't need gas chambers because the desert will kill them," he said.

I had arrived back in Khartoum a day before the case was due to be unveiled. The reaction was immediate. Journalists waiting for Ali Osman Taha, Sudan's vice-president, to hold a press conference were treated to an orchestrated display of government support. We had all been shepherded into an air-conditioned conference room when about 200 people marched past the windows, fists pumping in the air, shouting defiance at the ICC. It would have been a more convincing act had they not been led by a small man in a dark suit and equally dark glasses who was clearly directing the show of anger. It was one of a series of small protests that took place across the city. About thirty women gathered outside the British Embassy, before handing in a petition condemning the action of the court. The French Embassy and the United Nations witnessed similar demonstrations.

It was an uncertain time for foreigners in Khartoum. Aid agencies, the UN and embassies all shut down, ordering staff to work from home for three or four days. No-one quite knew whether there would be an anti-Western backlash. The new coffee shops popular with expats emptied of white faces. Crowds waving ceremonial swords gathered after Friday prayers as the orchestrated demonstrations continued, day after day. At the same time, helicopters buzzed overhead as the Sudanese military laid on a series of security exercises. Diplomats speculated about the chances of a coup if Bashir's allies decided he had become a liability. With tanks already guarding Khartoum's bridges and rumours of a trench being dug around Omdurman as protection against rebel assaults, it felt like a city under siege. Not that it mattered much to the man at the top – when you have taken power in a coup and made your political reputation by sidelining opponents within your own regime, every challenge to your authority can be turned into an opportunity.

The stout man bounding down the steps from his presidential jet did not look much like a person waiting to be indicted for war crimes. In a khaki safari suit and waving his trademark eagle-topped cane, President Bashir looked like a leader at the height his powers.

As his loafers hit the tarmac of El Fasher airport, various local dignitaries handed him three mangy-looking doves. Bashir launched them into the air above his head – grey rather than white feathers flying – only to watch them drop back to earth like stones. In the end, they waddled away from him.

This was President Bashir's peace mission to Darfur, his chance to show the world that he could be trusted to run his own adoring country. In less than forty-eight hours his presidential jet – crammed with ambassadors who perhaps should have known better – would make a whistlestop tour of the region, giving him the chance to open schools, promise hospitals and generally insist that he was not the warmonger of world opinion. Days after the three judges had begun considering the chief prosecutor's evidence, Bashir was making his response with a rare trip to Darfur. Eight months before the indictments themselves would be handed down and the thirteen aid agencies expelled, Bashir was playing the unlikely role of peacemaker. I was one of a handful of foreign journalists along for the ride.

The press plane arrived half an hour or so before Bashir in El Fasher, the airport where the rebels had first shown they were a serious force in Darfur. A brass band, wearing red jackets that were all a size or so too big, was already waiting. So too a crowd of wellwishers, armed with homemade placards, ready to greet their president. "Bashir is the honour of Sudan," read one, while another asked, "Ocampo, where is the justice?" My own favourite was one that declared, "We reject pretension and hegemony."

It was no great surprise that the small, well-behaved crowd was made up predominantly of teachers and civil servants. They had no doubt been ordered to turn out. The minibuses in the airport car park had then delivered them for their propaganda outing.

"We don't want Ocampo to take our president. It's bad. We refuse that," a teacher told me in English. "If my president is bad or good, it is up to us to try him."

The women began ululating as the presidential jet touched down. It was the foreign diplomats who appeared from the doorway first. They filed down the stairs, looking rather sheepish at their role in

Bashir's roadshow. I caught the eye of the British ambassador, Rosalind Marsden. She had the uncanny knack of looking like a Brit wherever she went, dressed in what appeared to be a Marks & Spencer navy blazer and with skin that turned an alarming shade of red in the Sudanese outdoors.

"Good morning. How are you?"

"Oh, arrr, yes," she said, quickening her pace across the apron towards the reception line.

A startled rabbit would possibly have reacted with more composure. But these were always awkward trips for Khartoum's diplomatic corps. While pressure was increasing around the world for action against Bashir, the ambassadors still had their jobs to do in Sudan, quietly trying to do their bit for peace and development. One by one they lined up alongside UN officials, local government officers and sheikhs to greet the president. He might have been accused of war crimes, but there was still protocol to observe. He eventually emerged from his plane to the slightly wonky strains of the national anthem and, having released the reluctant doves, made his way to the line. For all the diplomatic etiquette, it was still a rather sickening sight. Among the one hundred or so dignitaries were aid agency heads of office and peacekeepers, the very people working to protect Darfur's weak and vulnerable from Bashir's murderous regime. General Martin Luther Agwai, head of the joint AU-UN hybrid peacekeeping force, saluted Field Marshal Bashir, one military man to another. It was a vivid reminder of the difficult conditions that anyone working in Sudan had to endure and the compromises that had to be made.

"There's not much else we can do," said one of the Westerners in the line later. "It's not as if we can make a citizen's arrest."

Then the president was off at high speed in a fancy 4x4. Its tinted windows were wound down so he could wave his cane at the supporters who lined the road into El Fasher. The first stop was a dirt parade ground, where thousands of booted feet had flattened the dust into a hardpacked surface. It was ringed with battered Land Rover pickups. Each was piled high with sacks of clothes and thin foam mattresses. Jerry cans and plastic bottles were tied on with string. Families – women clutching babies and snot-nosed children with dirty faces – were arranged on top. These were people on their way home, we were told. Just as soon as the president had offered an encouraging word or two, they would leave the camps that had been their home for the past four or five years and begin the return to their fields. One twenty-five-year-old woman, with two young children, told me she was excited to be leaving the camp. She leaned down to speak to me, chattering excitedly over her shoulder with the other mothers balanced behind her.

"No we are not being forced to go home. I am leaving because I want to go back to cultivating," she said. After some discussion with the other women she admitted the transport had been laid on by the government for her journey of about 120 miles.

There must have been one hundred or so similar vehicles drawn up in a circle around the parade ground. Their passengers smiled and waved at President Bashir as he made a quick circuit, flanked by security agents. Sudanese pop music blasted from a giant set of speakers as he went. There was time for a quick address to the plucky returnees, promising tractors for the farmers who went back to the fields, and then he was off again.

The bus assigned to the travelling media had long since disappeared. So too had our minders – a couple of government press officials who seemed rather more relaxed about leaving their charges behind than the possibility of delaying the presidential party. Their media skills seemed to consist only of shouting at journalists to hurry up and get on the bus. It was something of a relief to see the back of them. On the other hand, I had no intention of getting left behind in a potentially hostile crowd.

Along with another British correspondent and a couple of American journalists, I pushed my way through the crowds on to the other side of the road. Here the party was in full swing. The jumble of white jalabiyas, women's floral wraps and camouflage fatigues disappeared far into the distance, a heaving confusion of colour. The sun was growing stronger in the sky and clouds of dust were kicked up by Bashir's supporters as they danced and sang to traditional rhythms. Somewhere in the far distance an amplified voice was drawing cheers from the audience. Overhead a helicopter covered in posters of Bashir flew in tighter and tighter circles. Soldiers hung from its open doors waving and smiling. Men on camels and horses, AK-47s slung from their shoulders, pushed their way towards the voice. There was not a great deal to do in El Fasher on a Wednesday morning, except perhaps sit and sip tea in the market, and this was clearly the place to be. There were soldiers who looked like they were no older than sixteen, clusters of women selling tea, schoolboys in their military-style uniforms, as well as elders in baggy white robes. This was not the sort of place to find opponents of Bashir's regime. At the edge of the throng, though, standing beside a deep ditch where the roots of an acacia tree showed through the red earth, were a handful of young men who looked slightly less enthusiastic about the day's proceedings.

"We can't say that we support everything the president does," said Mohamed al-Amin, his head covered with a bright white turban as protection from the caustic sunlight. It was as close to criticism as anyone was going to get. "We wanted to come here though to show our support for the president and to oppose the ICC."

It was a familiar argument and one I had heard before from Al Siir. He, like most of his family, was an ardent supporter of the opposition Democratic Unionist Party. Yet before I'd left Khartoum on this latest trip to Darfur he had made clear his anger and frustration at the ICC. He is our president, he had told me over and over again, and it is up to the people of Sudan to decide what to do with him. Al Siir was desperately proud of Sudan and its history. He did not want outsiders telling him who should or who shouldn't be running the country. This was one of the concerns about an ICC intervention. If Al Siir, no great fan of his own president, could be persuaded to defend Bashir, might an indictment not cement support for the man who had ruled the country with an iron fist since 1989?

None of that mattered as we struggled through the hordes of people assembled on the plain beside El Fasher airport. An aid

217

worker told me later they had heard that some of the crowd had been paid to attend. Most, though, seemed to be ardent admirers. They were here to listen to Bashir speak. They watched a succession of leaders from the Zaghawa, Fur and Masalit tribes clamber on to a podium – a truck covered in black sheeting – to publicly profess their allegiance to the president, despite the fact that each came from a people that has spawned rebel armies. These were sheikhs who had been bought off by the government and were now happy to endorse their president.

It wasn't long before the main act himself appeared. As President Bashir hauled his podgy frame up the steps and on to a table, a pop song burst from the speakers, electrifying the 10,000-strong crowd. Zaghawa tribesmen on camels raised their whips in the air and a sea of fists extended as far back as the ramshackle huts somewhere near the horizon. The first sitting head of state to face prosecution by the ICC decided this would be a good time to dance. Bashir began to swing his ample frame from side to side lifting one foot and then the other as his makeshift platform seemed to sway dangerously. It was a sickening display from a man revelling in his notoriety. I was close enough beneath him on the ground to see sweat dripping from his forehead in the 35°C heat. He would switch his clothes twice in the course of the day, changing from one khaki outfit to another identical one.

"We are for peace and the president, Bashir is our leader," ran the song's cumbersome chorus.

The cheesy synthesiser pop seemed to run on forever. No-one in the carefully stage-managed crowd appeared to get tired of cheering and singing along until its strains finally died away to be replaced by Bashir's voice.

He told his audience of government supporters that the court had no right to investigate him and that he was dedicated to finding peace in the war-ravaged region. He slipped into colloquial Arabic, peppered with references to Koranic verse and local Darfur traditions, which were lost on me despite the help of a government translator. He avoided specific mention of the allegations against him, but insisted Sudan was the victim of foreign powers intent on destabilising the country. "They attack us with false allegations," was his verdict.

But he also seemed to hold out something of an olive branch, acknowledging that people in Darfur were facing injustice, and said all political parties were welcome at peace talks. He wasn't going to admit that his government was responsible for many of the problems, but he was at least using rather more conciliatory language.

"Yes, we all know that there have been problems in Darfur and we know that there have been injustices," he said. "But we, from day one, sought to bring peace for all the people of Darfur. I'm committed to solving the problems of Darfur by providing security."

He also promised schools, electricity and roads for one of the country's most under-developed areas. They were the right words if he wanted to show himself as a peacemaker. There was no anti-Western rhetoric or threats against foreigners. It was restrained by Sudan's hostile standards.

The heat was now intense. The crowd had closed in all around on the temporary podium. Dozens of women had fainted and had to be carried away by Red Crescent volunteers. Somewhere behind us I could see a white canopy where the diplomats were watching the speech seated on leather armchairs. Their role, like ours, was to ensure the rest of the world saw President Bashir's display of bluster in the face of possible criminal sanctions. Their verdict was that he had said all the right things. Now it was a question of whether he would do the right things. Africa was full of clever leaders – Uganda's Yoweri Museveni, Ethiopia's Meles Zenawi and Rwanda's Paul Kagame – who had a neat line in espousing democratic principles when addressing foreign donors, but whose record at home, or in neighbouring countries, suggested their words were often hollow. Bashir's words may have struck the right note, but would it actually make any difference to the people of Darfur? (I learned later that some of the diplomats had been lured by the promise that Bashir was to make a significant announcement. Not for the first time it seemed, they had been duped by a master tactician into tagging along for an extended photo op.)

The crowds had begun drifting away, making it easier to find our bus. It took us past the parade ground where the rows of pickups had been waiting with their human cargo. The place was deserted. It was impossible to know whether the families who had waved and cheered President Bashir earlier in the morning were really on their way home. Maybe they had simply been returned to huts and shelters around the town, their role over in the presidential PR campaign. Even if they had been driven back to their fields, what would they find? It was impossible to imagine them resuming their old lives without any sort of peace deal.

Our next stop was a government office where lunch was laid on for the hacks. It arrived on a vast silver platter. Bowls filled with sweet, roasted hunks of lamb jostled for space with plates of stuffed tomatoes and dishes of watery soup. The president was being entertained elsewhere, so it was a welcome chance to start transferring details from notebook to laptop before being shepherded once again on to the bus ready for our flight down to Nyala, the second stop on our tour.

It was late afternoon by the time we arrived in the capital of South Darfur. Both myself and Barney Jopson, *The Financial Times* correspondent, were struggling to file our copy. My sat-phone was being temperamental and seemed unwilling to transmit emails. Meanwhile, Barney had resorted to sending his story in twenty-word bursts by text message – a desperately laborious business. The Bashir battle bus dropped us at the downtown football stadium where his next rally was due to take place. I left Barney hunched over his mobile and flagged down a motor rickshaw to drive me to a United Nations office where I knew there was wireless internet access. The office was shut for the day as a precaution against anti-Western violence, but a friendly security guard allowed me in nonetheless. I arrived back at the stadium – my 700 words already with the sub-editors – just as everyone was leaving. Bashir had given much the same speech, apparently, accompanied by much the same song and dance routine.

It had been a long day, starting in Khartoum airport's VIP suite sipping glasses of karkadeh tea at six in the morning. The cool morning had given way to desperate heat as the day wore on and it was with a great deal of relief that we arrived at the villa where we would spend the night. It seemed to be some sort of government guest house. Its neatly painted pink and white walls held half a dozen bedrooms, each laid out dorm style with camp beds in rows. Fresh pairs of flip-flops were arranged on each bed and the bathroom had been newly stocked with packets of Imperial Leather soap. The local journalists seemed to know the score rather better than the English visitors, and so it was that Barney and I found ourselves eyeing a couple of beds in the gravel-filled courtyard. Every single one inside had been bagged. Still, the day had been blisteringly hot and a cool open-air bed seemed like the place to be.

And it was. A gentle breeze wafting across my face eased my weary body to sleep. Until about midnight when a Sudanese TV crew set up a mixing desk somewhere near my head. An hour later someone tugged at my leg offering me a bowl of ful for dinner. Then at about two o'clock I was woken by a smattering of raindrops. Utterly defeated, we dragged our mattresses into an outbuilding. It turned out to be a kitchen. Someone started making tea at five, even before the sun had made its first appearance.

Day two continued badly. It started with breakfast of assida – the same dry brown porridge favoured by JEM fighters – followed by a visit to a school, where we barely had time to get off the bus before President Bashir had declared the classrooms open. The girls, dressed in baggy blue uniforms with a camouflage pattern, had not even finished their song of greeting before he was on his way again. Somewhere along the way a power station and a hospital were also opened before we arrived at the airport for the short hop on to El Geneina.

There, another vast crowd had assembled to hear the president speak. Mounted tribesmen with red headbands chanted "Allahu Akhbar" as their leader appeared before them. I had taken up a position right at the front, beneath the platform, with only a thin line of policemen behind me keeping the surging mass back. But there was little they could do when Sudan's commander in chief took the stage and waved the crowd forward. Thousands of people pushed forward to get as close as possible, trapping me in a sweaty maelstrom of humanity. Children disappeared underfoot and women pushed me aside as I battled to stay upright. By the time an agency photographer hauled me on to a trailer set aside for the media, my Thuraya satellite phone had disappeared from my bag. I swear the president was looking at me when he waved the crowd forward.

In some ways the trip was obscene. Darfur was suffering under President Bashir's rule, but he had chosen the very region where his allies mounted their scorched earth assault to deliver his riposte to his critics around the world and the prosecutors of the ICC. He had been careful to avoid the aid camps where he would have faced the seething victims of his oppression. Instead he jigged in front of carefully orchestrated crowds of supporters. He had not called for a Jihad or war against the West. He had not ordered the United Nations or the aid agencies to leave. Instead, he had declared himself a man of peace committed to solving Darfur's problems. He even invited "all parties" to fresh talks.

It did not take long to discover his words were hollow. A day after returning to Khartoum, UN officials announced they were investigating reports that warplanes were bombing Darfur even as President Bashir was releasing his unwilling doves into the air.

*　*　*

Things in Khartoum settled into an uneasy calm as the world waited to find out if Bashir would be indicted. The Sudanese government kept a low-level of anti-Western and anti-ICC rhetoric bubbling away in the state controlled media, but overall its reaction had been sensible. There had been no knee-jerk reaction. No diplomatic or charity expulsions. Gradually the UN and humanitarian agencies went back to work. Even the aid worker parties resumed. Within a couple of days I found myself in an embassy swimming pool at the end of a long night with half a dozen expat women wearing only their underwear. It was a chance to unwind after the stresses of the week before.

Still the matter of Bashir's possible indictment was at the forefront of everyone's minds. No-one knew quite when it was coming and its timing became a favourite topic of after-dinner debate. Khawajas stocked up on bottled water and tinned food. Embassies dusted off evacuation plans and generally prepared for the worst. British officials even kept a speed boat fuelled after realising that many of their diplomats were living on the wrong side of the river. Closing Khartoum's bridges was always one of the regime's first defence measures.

Far from the city itself, the debate over the wisdom of indicting Bashir dominated discussion among Sudan watchers. Critics pointed out that an arrest warrant would be unenforceable. With no police force of its own, the ICC would be making a grand gesture with little chance of actually bringing Bashir to The Hague for trial. At the same time as offering few benefits, the costs could be catastrophic. My chats with Al Siir as we stuttered through Khartoum's heavy traffic had demonstrated how ordinary Sudanese people had rallied behind a leader who was far from universally popular. With the threat of a trial hanging over him, might Bashir feel the time was right to go on an all out offensive to find a military solution in Darfur? Or might the rebels, emboldened by apparent justification for their war against the regime, launch a fresh assault on the capital, further deepening the conflict?

The aid agencies, in particular, felt vulnerable. They had repeatedly been accused of spying for the West and seen senior officials kicked out time and time again. If Bashir needed an easy target for reprisals they would be high on his list, while any escalation in the fighting would also have a huge impact on their operations as they struggled to keep staff safe.

And what about Southern Sudan, where more than two million people had died during a long-running civil war? The man who had signed a peace deal was about to be labelled a criminal. The Comprehensive Peace Agreement had endured a short, faltering life so far. Relations between the former rebels of the SPLM and their new partners in government had been up and down. Could the relationship survive if Bashir was named a suspected war criminal? For anyone who wanted to see a negotiated settlement in Darfur along with progress in the South, using the ICC seemed to choke off any diplomatic options. The nuclear button had been pressed.

One Western diplomat compared it with the Northern Ireland peace process: "It would be like arresting Martin McGuinness during the Good Friday negotiations."

Most often the debate was framed in terms of peace versus justice. Opponents of the ICC warned that seeking justice by taking Bashir to The Hague (or at least issuing an arrest warrant) would undermine the chances of finding peace. Joseph Kony, himself at times a pawn in Khartoum's power play in the South, had repeatedly failed to lay down arms for fear that he would wind up in a prison cell. On the other side, the Save Darfur movement argued that a real and lasting peace had to start with justice. Without it the result would be a sham deal with the man responsible for the war still in power, and millions of his victims still living in fear. Ending the culture of impunity had to be the first step. And anyway, the search for peace was not going so well, they would argue.

In some ways the differences were differences of worldview. The Save Darfur lobby was dominated by faith groups and human rights organisations which tended to take a rather black and white view of life, never mind the Darfur conflict. Their ethical norms were based on rights or duties. For them it was about right and wrong. Seeking justice was the right thing to do. The alternative was a consequentialist approach that focused on outcomes, ends rather than means. If that meant letting a man responsible for war crimes off the hook in the interests of maintaining access to the aid camps or keeping Southern Sudan from war then so be it. This was the position I encountered more often in the Lebanese restaurant or American-style coffee shop in Khartoum itself: the UN officials, humanitarian groups and people tasked with engaging the regime on a daily basis tended to take the more pragmatic view.

There was another factor as well. The further you went from Darfur itself the more likely the search for perfect solutions. Principles of justice, rights and responsibilities made sense in New York.

They added emphasis to noisy press releases or addresses to crowds of students on global days of protest. Calls to action drafted in absolute terms tend to work better. From that vantage point, the nitty-gritty of the conflict was more difficult to make out. Inside Sudan, messy reality tended to get in the way of crystal clear principles. It was less obvious who were the good guys and who were the bad guys. Tackling Bashir seemed to be only one element in the search for peace.

Years spent covering Africa's untidy wars had coloured my own perception. The Kenyan election violence of 2008 was a personal watershed. More than 1500 people died after it became clear that widespread rigging was under way. Opposition supporters took to the streets in a series of violent protests, targeting members of tribes loyal to the government. As the death toll rose, and hundreds of thousands of people fled their homes, members of the president's tribe began forming their own death squads. Both sides were guilty of the worst atrocities, burning down churches packed with opponents or clearing villages of their tribal rivals. The violence ended only with a shabby peace deal. The man whose supporters fixed the figures kept his job as president. The opposition leaders whose supporters burned Kenya in a display of fury were rewarded with ministerial cars and salaries. Everyone got their turn to feed at the trough of corruption. Peace talks that were supposed to heal tribal rifts over land stalled as soon as the negotiators got their government jobs. No-one believed the new "grand coalition" would last until the next election. But none of that mattered. It may have been a discredited, ugly deal without a hint of justice – but at least it had stopped the killing.

The more time I spent in Africa, covering its complicated deadly wars, the more my worldview changed. Imperfect solutions – even if they stored up problems later down the road – seemed preferable to no solution at all.

This debate was being played out several thousand miles from Darfur itself. While the Sudanese diaspora has been heavily involved with the Save Darfur movement, it was difficult to gauge exactly where ordinary Darfuris came down on the argument. Their voice was silent as newspaper op-ed pages and dozens of blogs buzzed with angry exchanges between people claiming to have their best interests at heart.

I was back in Darfur just a week or so before the ICC arrest warrant was expected in March 2009. This was my chance to find out the mood in the camps. After a few quiet months, world attention was swinging back to Sudan. I had arrived just as George Clooney and Nicholas Kristof, the *New York Times* columnist, had finished a brief visit to the camps on the Chadian side of the border (or the "Darfur region", as Kristof insisted on calling it). They came away, apparently, with calls for justice ringing in their ears. Refugee after refugee had insisted that they wanted the man responsible for forcing them into Chad to be brought to book.

Things were not so clear on my side of the border. Few of the people here had time for the debate. Few had heard of the ICC. Those that had were too frightened to discuss the matter openly. They were worried the government would come down hard on anyone celebrating Bashir's indictment and most seemed to be more interested in trying to get home than anything else. At the risk of putting words in their mouths, it seemed they were putting peace ahead of justice. In Otash camp one young man was prepared to speak up.

"All the people have got to work together to have peace," said Ali Hassan in neat English, as he sat on a brick ball. "All the people who make problems and all the people who did not make problems – all have to work together."

There were similar sentiments in Zam Zam camp outside El Fasher. More than 20,000 had arrived there just before me as they fled fighting around the town of Muhajiriya. One corner of the camp had been given over to the new arrivals, who were living beneath plastic sheets. The sun-blasted sandscape had a post-apocalyptic feel. Shelters stretched in all directions, disappearing far into the desert. Mariam Ahmed Abu, who claimed to be sixty but could have passed for one hundred, stood next to her pathetic tent. She had nothing. There was no bundle of clothes, cooking pot or jerry can tucked inside the rickety construction of sticks and plastic that was now her home; its roof was barely a metre off the ground. She began to tell me her story, opening her thin lips to reveal a bare set of gums. She had survived six years of war, but left when she realised she no longer had any children living left to care for her. A dozen or so other elderly women made the same journey. They had all run out of children. I asked her if she wanted justice for her suffering

"This is what happened and now we have to live and to forget it," was all she wanted to say.

She had lost pretty much everything, yet her sad eyes did not burn with the anger of the injustice. She just wanted to go home. Then again, there had been the women and children in the Jebel Mara who had created a dust storm as they marched in front of me, demanding international justice with their handwritten signs.

As I stood among the newly displaced families, their small tents filling with smoke from cooking fires, it seemed to me that issuing a warrant for Bashir's arrest would be more of a victory for the activists around the world than it would be for the people of Darfur. They had already been victims of the regime once and were still at Bashir's mercy. There were conflicting opinions about the wisdom of indicting a sitting head of state, but the public debate failed to reflect the concerns. The discussions were one-sided. The sceptics among the diplomats and aid workers in the field had to stay silent. Several academics, including Alex de Waal, a noted Sudan scholar, were doing their best to urge caution. But how could they compete with the self-appointed Save Darfur lobby? Within days of returning from Chad, George Clooney was discussing his trip with President Barack Obama and any TV anchor that would have him. And he didn't really seem to get it.

I'll let Nicholas Kristof, his roommate and tutor during their trip to Chad, have the last word on the debate. A week or so before the ICC was expected to announce its decision, Kristof, one of the main cheerleaders for the Save Darfur position, used his *New York Times* column to discuss the issue. Amid references to Janjaweed militias attacking black, African villages (as if there were any other sort), he dismissed concerns about the risk to the North-South peace deal and the prospect of Bashir lashing out and expelling aid workers.

His considered conclusion? "I think all these fears are over-blown."[21]

* * *

First came the armoured personnel carriers, soldiers hanging from gun turrets and door handles. Then came the technicals, pickups converted into battlewagons armed with heavy machine guns and anti-aircraft guns. Some carried rocket tubes. Behind them were the trucks crammed with soldiers, some wearing balaclavas, others with scarves wrapped around their faces – all shouting "Allahu Akhbar". Tyres screeched as the deadly motorcade accelerated through the centre of El Fasher to whoops from onlookers gathered around the market.

It was a chilling display of Sudan's war machine, a deadly arsenal that had killed, raped and burned its way across Darfur's scorched land. This was the day that the three ICC judges would make their decision on whether to issue an arrest warrant for President Bashir. The message to the people of El Fasher was clear. Whatever happened later that afternoon, President Omar al-Bashir, the country's commander-in-chief, was still the man with his finger on the trigger.

"This is to show that the government is still in control of the town and if any of the rebel movements think they can try something then they should think again," said Elesail Abdul Munim, a local journalist watching the parade of almost 200 military trucks.

I was not really supposed to be there. My white face was conspicuous in the crowd and United Nations officials had warned me that my presence would startle the men with AK-47s. But I knew I was the only Western journalist in Darfur and the chance to see Khartoum's military muscle up close was too much to resist. I wasn't going to stay put in a UN office and pass up the chance of

---

21 – *Africa's "Obama" School by Nicholas D. Kristof*, New York Times, *February 26, 2009.*

a great piece in *The Times*, particularly with my competitors stuck in Kenya unable to get a visa or a travel permit from Khartoum.

My presence was quickly noted. As the trucks made their second pass through the market, where I had sat drinking tea a few minutes earlier, one or two of the gunmen began chanting "khawaja". They were smiling and laughing, but it made for an uncomfortable experience nonetheless. When one soldier lowered the barrel of his rifle to point it in my direction it was clearly time to leave. The procession of trucks was just coming to an end anyway.

As their engines faded, the sound of air force jets ripped through the air. Two Russian-designed Sukhoi ground-attack planes passed low and fast over the town, almost brushing the twin minarets of El Fasher's central mosque.

The day had arrived. Everyone knew the indictments were coming but no-one knew quite what else would follow. The Sudanese government, with its show of strength and a demonstration planned for the afternoon, was already preparing its reaction. The market was quieter than usual as traders shut up shop. Taxi drivers ended their shifts at lunchtime to be with their families. There had been a gunfight at the hospital a couple of days earlier and the city almost smelled of violence, like a wild west frontier town. At the UNAMID base on the edge of town, staff were going into lockdown mode. Non-essential workers were going home early. Those that had to stay had brought sleeping bags and toothbrushes as they prepared to spend forty-eight hours in their prefab offices.

The aid agencies already had an inkling of what might come next. At least six, including Oxfam and MSF, had already been ordered to pull international staff out of Darfur. Aid workers had been forced to abandon camps and towns filled with thousands of people in need. Doctors and nurses treating two meningitis outbreaks were among them. The agencies were advised it was for their own safety during an uncertain time, but there was a nagging suspicion that ordering nationals back to Khartoum was simply the prelude to full expulsion. Yet there was little resistance. The United Nations seemed to be in denial. One official told me the government had given assurances that the measure was temporary and had eventually offered a compromise, allowing the workers to stay in the three regional capitals. It may be that this was the start of full expulsions, he admitted to me, but for now the government was getting the benefit of the doubt.

The ICC announcement came a couple of minutes after 4.00pm. All doubt vanished seconds later as the first expulsions followed. Even as the press conference continued in The Hague, government officials began telephoning the Khartoum headquarters of aid agencies to tell them their licenses to operate in Sudan had been terminated. The goons from HAC had waited until the court announced that its judges had issued an arrest warrant for President Bashir before moving. There was a small victory for Khartoum: the charges of genocide had not stuck. Instead, he was charged with seven counts of crimes against humanity and war crimes. That didn't really matter. As the day wore on, my list of expelled NGOs was growing by the hour. First it was the same six who had been pulled back earlier in the week. Then it was ten. By the time I had finished filing from the UN guesthouse I was sharing with a grumpy Russian helicopter crew, thirteen international NGOs were on their way home.

The next morning the impact of those phonecalls was clear. This was no negotiating tactic or game of brinkmanship. There was a shiny pickup and two motorbikes parked outside the Oxfam compound. The motorbikes were the giveaway. Security heavies must already be inside.

They were. A young British aid worker, dressed in jeans, t-shirt and sandals, was running around the courtyard doing his best to keep them happy. He looked nervous and was slightly too eager to help the surly officials as they looked for loot. A journalist was the last thing he wanted.

"Look I really can't talk now," he said. "These guys are from HAC and National Security and this is really not a good time."

They were putting together an inventory of equipment they would seize. The pickup was waiting to cart away Oxfam computers and other equipment paid for with British taxpayers' money or fundraising jumble sales. Satellite phones, mobile phones, cars . . .

everything had to be turned over to the government. Programmes that had been built up over the past five years were being picked apart in minutes.

It was the same scene across town at the Action Contre La Faim offices. Stunned workers wondered whether they could find other agencies who might be able to take over their therapeutic feeding centres, where dozens of mothers and their stick-thin children depended on daily helpings of a nutritious peanut paste. Wages were hurriedly being totted up for local staff, even as Sudanese officials marched back and forth, scouring desks, drawers and files.

"They are here with their clipboards and just making lists of everything they are going to take," said one international member of staff, who looked as if he could not believe what was happening. He stood in the shade of a spindly tree radiating an air of defiance whenever a Sudanese official walked past.

Driving around the camps that afternoon the impact was clear. Logos of the thirteen expelled organisations were everywhere: posters, flags, brands painted on fences. Oxfam, two branches of MSF, Care International, Action Contre La Faim, Solidarités, two branches of Save The Children, The International Rescue Committee (IRC), Padco, Norwegian Refugee Council, CHF International and Mercy Corps were all out. The organisations targeted were drawn predominantly from Britain, America and France. Sudan believed these were the nations responsible for pushing the indictment. But the charities were also the big hitters, the ones providing a disproportionate amount of services. The list was a who's who of the NGOs that mattered. Three local organisations were also shut down for good measure.

Adam Mahmoud, chief umda of Al Salaam camp – its most senior tribal leader – pointed one way and then the next as he tried to pick out facilities that were now padlocked. "International NGOs help us with food, water and many daily needs, blankets, shelters and things," he said, reeling off a list of aid workers' acronyms that had been absorbed into camp language. "The most important is Oxfam. It provides the people with so many things. Even the camp co-ordinator is from CHF. This hospital is run by IRC. It's very helpful for us as IDPs."

His was a short, chubby frame with the sort of face that probably used to smile. His jalabiya was dirty and stained red from the sand. He was still waiting for some sort of confirmation that the rumours he was hearing were true. As I explained what I had seen in El Fasher, the HAC officials seizing equipment and harassing aid workers, his body sagged. He had already helped his people escape one onslaught. Now they would have to fend for themselves again. I felt awkward that I was the one to break the bad news.

"If these organisations leave then there is no doubt that we will all suffer again," he said. "It will be a disaster."

Some 6500 staff – or forty percent of the humanitarian workforce – were suspended at a stroke. Four of the agencies were partners of the UN's World Food Programme, responsible for delivering sacks of maize and pulses to the camps. Without them, more than one million people would go hungry. Oxfam and Solidarités were known for their water and sanitation expertise. Without them, a million people were at risk of losing drinkable supplies. One and a half million had seen health care disappear overnight. Almost five million people – whether surviving in camps or clinging on to life in villages – needed aid which was now being withheld.

The government said the NGOs had gone beyond their humanitarian mandate, supplying evidence to the ICC. It was the same old argument: the NGOs were spying. There was next to no evidence to support the allegation of a co-ordinated campaign. The best Khartoum could come up with was an internal IRC memo which concluded that it would not be appropriate to co-operate with prosecutors in The Hague. Government stooges pointed journalists to the website of a paediatrician who once worked for MSF in Kalma. He explained how he had collected drawings from children showing Antonovs bombing villages, smuggled them out of Sudan and on to the ICC. And there were no doubt other cases of idealistic individuals who used their experience as humanitarian workers in Darfur as part of the advocacy campaign. And that was about it. There were dozens of secret files, I was told, but no, I couldn't see them.

The advocacy lobby, which had worked so hard to push the ICC, reacted with shock. Withholding aid was further evidence of Sudan's role as a genocidal state, they argued. To the more cautious voices, the aid agencies and the Sudan academics – people who had followed the workings of Bashir's regime up close – the expulsions were sadly inevitable. They had warned of a backlash. They had warned that an arrest warrant was the nuclear option with potentially devastating fall-out for Darfur's civilian population. They would take little satisfaction in being proven right.

Ultimately, there was only one person responsible for ordering out the NGOs – Bashir himself. At the same time, though, it seemed that in ignoring the widely predicted consequences, the ICC and its supporters were in part to blame for the shutdown in aid. They had pushed for justice all along, disregarding the concerns of people like Alex de Waal (too often labelled a Khartoum sympathiser) that in so doing the chances of peace would be reduced and the chances of an anti-Western backlash would increase. As usual, the debate had been one-sided. Apart from off-the-record briefings, press officers from NGOs had to stay silent about their fears as the Save Darfur juggernaut powered on. They could not compete with Clooney's power.

Jerry Fowler, of the Save Darfur Coalition, is not impressed by allegations that his stance was in some way to blame. According to him, the movement's position was more nuanced than simply demanding the arrest of Bashir.

"I wouldn't say that Save Darfur was pushing for the indictments," he said. "My personal position is that there needs to be a comprehensive solution to the whole problem. Accountability is part of it. Not even international justice, but accountability is part of a comprehensive approach. It's not a solution in and of itself."

In other words, choosing peace or choosing to hold Bashir to account was a false dichotomy. They could go hand in hand. In fact, they should go hand in hand as part of a full and lasting settlement. Only that seemed to miss the point his opponents were making. The search for the perfect solution, incorporating justice along with peace, did not fit with what we knew about Bashir's Sudan. It seemed to me that issuing a warrant for the arrest of the leader of one side or another was inevitably going to reduce the chances of a comprehensive settlement. When that leader also had power over the people of Darfur and was the commander-in-chief of Sudan, the impact at ground level was always going to be negative. Nothing else made sense. It made the distance between the advocates – the self-professed saviours of Darfur – and the reality of Sudan's misery all the more stark.

I'll never forget the pitiful sight of the dozen or so men clustered around a borehole in Abu Shouk. I had been in and out of these camps, their sandy narrow lanes and tidy compounds, for the best part of four years. The people here were hardy and visitors were always struck by the strength of spirit they showed. The existence of the rambling aid cities was depressing, yet the camps themselves always seemed to be proof that life would go on. Conditions may have been miserable, but there was something strangely uplifting about them. Until now. The men in front of me hadn't given up, but the hopelessness of their predicament felt suddenly overwhelming. They were hammering at a water pump, trying to draw cold, clear liquid from the dusty ground. Fixing it should have been the work of Oxfam engineers – but they were gone. The elders, who had responsibility for looking after the 50,000 people in the camp, were doing their best.

"We don't know how to fix it," said one, wielding a foot-long spanner which he had clearly never used before, "but we are thirsty."

AFTERWORD: SOLVING DARFUR

After five years I was exhausted. Gradually the travel, the stories and the stress wore me down. It was time to go home. My little apartment in Nairobi was emptying. The sitting room looked bare without its piles of books and carved wooden couches. The cat had gone to a neighbour. My pictures, souvenirs from my travels, were coming back with me but everything else had been sold or was sitting in boxes. I was left with a television in the corner and a couple of camping chairs arranged so I could look through the French windows to the wooded valley slopes beyond, and watch monkeys swinging through the garden each evening.

It had been a couple of months since my last visit to Sudan, an illegal crossing from Chad, and I wondered whether I'd ever see Al Siir again. Darfur had affected me in a way I never expected. It was not the miserable stories of suffering that I would take home. It wasn't so much the women who had been raped or the piles of stones where villages once stood. It wasn't the rambling aid cities that had been transformed from tented cities to shanty towns of lean-tos and finally into mudbrick cities with an air of sad permanence. It wasn't the death toll. I wasn't outraged by the lies of Sudanese ministers anymore or the inability of the UN to intervene. No, a melancholy ache struck when I least expected it, perhaps when my guard was down: the futile optimism of the old woman in the Jebel Mara who thought the world would ride to her aid; the football pitch destroyed needlessly by Janjaweed horsemen; the proud umdas and sheikhs who still carried their canes as symbols of authority but who seemed lost in the camps. It was often the prosaic nature, the sheer ordinariness, of the suffering that hit home.

235

These were elements that I might not have noticed if I had just jetted in once or twice. Of all the miserable conflicts in my patch, this was the one I had started to care about. I guess it had become my favourite African war. More than that, it had become personal. I would miss Al Siir, of course, but dozens of contacts had become friends as I returned time and time again: the aid workers expelled from Khartoum whom I now bumped into at the supermarket in Nairobi, or the rebel commanders that I slept alongside, or the diplomats who kept me in gin but were powerless to make a difference.

It was late on a Friday evening. The monkeys who regularly pinched bananas from my kitchen had already swung through the garden on the way to wherever it was they slept. It was dark outside, silent except for the occasional buzz of a mosquito or froggy croak. I'd left Sky News twittering in the background as I fiddled around on my computer. The word Darfur caught my eye as it rolled across the yellow breaking news ticker. I had to wait for it to swing around again to read the whole thing: "Irish aid worker kidnapped in Darfur."

I might have been about to leave but the place had one last reminder that I was intertwined with the story. As the evening wore on I managed to piece together what had happened down the phone line from contacts in Khartoum and Darfur. Armed gunmen had broken into the compound of the Irish aid agency Goal in the town of Kutum, snatching two women and a security guard from the neat brick buildings where I remembered drinking tea during a visit a couple of years earlier. The Sudanese security guard was soon released. But there was no word of the two women, a Ugandan called Hilda Kawuki and an Irish woman, Sharon Commins.

I knew Sharon. We had met at a crowded bar in Nairobi a couple of years earlier. Over ice-cold bottles of Tusker beer she had ummed and ahhed about leaving her desk job in Dublin, where she worked as an information officer with Goal, to work in the field. She had been sending me press releases and we had swapped emails for a couple of years before that. Her pretty blond hair and clear ivory skin kept me in the bar rather longer than I had planned. The beer and an occasional flash of her long eyelashes encouraged me to recount some of the adventures I'd had that year in Darfur, all suitably embellished. A few weeks later, in an email overflowing with excitement, she wrote to say she was on her way to Khartoum. Since then I hadn't heard much. Each time I was in Khartoum she would be out in Darfur or vice versa. A couple of days after she was kidnapped, her photo and name popped up on my computer screen as I logged on to Facebook. Our network of mutual contacts had prompted an anonymous server somewhere to flag her up as a potential friend.

It was the third similar kidnapping since Khartoum had expelled the thirteen international agencies. Before that, despite all the banditry, the guns and fighting, foreign workers had rarely been targeted. In the two previous cases, Sudanese officials had managed to negotiate the release of the hostages. There seemed to be political motives at work. The first abduction was carried out by The Eagles of Bashir, apparently in protest at the ICC's indictment of the president. The second was claimed by the Falcons for the Liberation of Africa, who snatched workers in revenge for the actions of Zoe's Arc, a French charity caught trying to smuggle children from Chad. The stories may have been true. Or they may have been a cover for renegade government militias trying to win money from their backers in Khartoum. The kidnappings could even have been ordered by regional authorities keen to demonstrate their ability to rescue aid workers in trouble. Darfur had become that complicated, that messy, that opaque.

Despite this backdrop of instability, some of the expelled aid organisations were preparing to return. Scott Gration, Barack Obama's newly appointed special envoy to Sudan, returned from discussions in Khartoum with a deal allowing American charities to go back under different names and with different logos. My friends, the ones who had been detained, harassed and then finally expelled couldn't believe the naivety of the deal. Each charity had lost millions of pounds in vehicles, computers and phones. They had been forced to pay six months' severance pay to their local staff. International staff had been kept in Khartoum as unofficial hostages, denied exit visas and unable to leave until the cash was handed over. Now they were going back with no guarantees that the same thing wouldn't happen all over again. Up close it seemed a ridiculous thing to do, but once again voices far from Sudan itself were deciding policy. The deal suited a new regime in Washington and a new envoy keen to prove his worth, and it suited the charity headquarters where jobs and programmes were supported by millions of dollars in funding attracted by one, simple word: Darfur.

In five years, nothing much had changed. None of the pressure generated by the lobbyists had managed to improve conditions for the humanitarian agencies. They were limping back piecemeal – changing their names not clearing them – rather than sticking together and negotiating terms. Yet again, President Bashir had outmanoeuvred the opposition.

It was the same every time. He could count on the support – or at least the silence – of the Arab world. Turning the conflict into one between Arabs and Africans allowed him to tap into a powerful bloc of support. What Arab League president would want to denounce Sudan, and thereby stand alongside a mass movement founded by Jewish and evangelical Christian groups? The heat and noise generated by the Save Darfur Coalition worked well in the US, but seemed counter-productive overseas.

Similarly the ICC's arrest warrant had won President Bashir the support of other African presidents, no doubt mindful of their own chequered records on human rights. The African Union announced that its members would not try to arrest the Sudanese president if he visited.

After five years, President Bashir's position still appeared impregnable: his hold on power was absolute and the urgency to solve Darfur seemed to be fading. The new war that I was desperate to cover when I arrived in Africa had become a part of the land-scape. Just as my successor, picking up my assortment of newspaper strings, would see Darfur as another African war, so too would world leaders wondering how they might make their mark. George W Bush, Tony Blair and Kofi Annan had watched the conflict develop on their watch, and I wondered whether they felt an extra responsibility to help clean it up. But they had given way to Barack

Obama, Gordon Brown and Ban ki-Moon. Would each now wonder whether Sudan's complicated network of conflicts was as intractable as Somalia or the Democratic Republic of Congo, which seemed likely to fester forever.

Even the activists were wondering what their five years of action had achieved. Blogs and newspaper columns began to fill with debates over what direction to take. For Mia Farrow, who had poured so much time and energy into the dusty Chadian refugee camps, her museum, where she eventually wanted to display Darfuri history and culture, took on a new importance. It was one concrete achievement she would be able to point to amid years of fruitless campaigns.

"As you may imagine, after this many years it's pretty frustrating because I think the bottom line is that it's not clear what advocacy has accomplished," she told me. "The people of Darfur are still suffering, and things have been ratcheted up considerably."

Of course, we don't know how much worse the death toll may have been if people like her and George Clooney had not done so much to raise awareness. The slaughter of the early period of the conflict gave way to a lower intensity war, no doubt partly as a result of media attention. But I also think she is wrong on the broader point. Advocacy has achieved a lot. The campaigners pushed Darfur on to the political agenda at a time, in our post-Cold War world, when African wars don't matter much. They had won plenty of what was on their banners. African peacekeepers were wearing blue hats, world leaders were discussing no-fly zones and President Bashir was a wanted man.

But it was all based on a flawed analysis of the problem. Of course, we journalists had not done much better. At times we had dropped our neutrality and given in to the rebels' slick PR operations. Clearly, they were fighting an unpleasant regime in Khartoum, but occasionally we had let our scrutiny of JEM and the SLA become too relaxed. Had we not learned the lesson of rebel leaders in Uganda and Ethiopia, who won power only to rule their countries in the same way they kept control of their armed movements: through an obnoxious mixture of paranoia and ruthlessness.

And we had lapped up the Save Darfur position, offering as it did a grand narrative to explain a messy war. We could fit details – the stories of women raped by Janjaweed – into the bigger picture of an Arab genocide directed against Africans. It turned a convoluted, complicated conflict into something we could understand. If the humanitarians did not want to speak to us, then there was always a campaigner in London or New York who would give us a pithy sound-bite. Genocide always makes a better headline.

But the more I travelled through Darfur the more it seemed everything I knew about it was wrong. The tribal and ethnic distinctions were artificial, arbitrary and unhelpful in trying to seek peace. It was only one element of a complicated war. To complete the picture took journeys to Southern Sudan, the Democratic Republic of Congo, Chad and Uganda. Only then did the many different factors come into focus.

Reaching for solutions means grasping the true nature of Darfur's multi-faceted battleground. There can be no quick fixes or silver bullets. Bringing peace to Darfur means tackling all the underlying causes of the multiple conflicts that have sometimes resembled a single war. Darfur has been used as a battleground between Chad and Sudan, between rebels and government, Arabs and Africans and within individual tribes. The widely understood picture of an Arab genocide directed against African tribes fails to capture the reality of Darfur – and it is no surprise that this black and white analysis has failed to bring a solution. It misses all but one of the factors that pushed more than two million people into aid camps.

The relationship between Sudan and Chad, their support for opposing sets of rebels and their proxy war, needs to be addressed. Darfur's relationship with Khartoum, the marginalisation of its people – from whichever tribe – has to be put on a new footing. The impact of climate change, and what this means for disputes between herders and farmers, needs to be understood. If the landscape is changing, then lives will have to adapt. The old mechanisms for resolving disputes between villages, clans and tribes need to be repaired and updated. Everyone needs a stake in the land.

None of this is rocket science. In fact, none of this is new. Too often, though, attempts at peace have failed because pressure has too often been applied in the wrong places. Talks have been unrepresentative, including only rebels with enough power to fight their way to the negotiating table. Who speaks for the Arab tribes who have no part in the war and who say they do not want to be represented by Khartoum? Who speaks for the Janjaweed? Peace talks that have focused on bringing the rebels and government together ignored too many other stakeholders.

The starting point for solving Darfur has to be an inter-tribal discussion forum, bringing together grassroots representatives of all the people of the region. There are many genuine grievances that have not been addressed by previous talks. One promising solution is offered by Mandate Darfur, set up by expat Sudanese telecoms entrepreneur Mo Ibrahim. It was due to bring together about 400 delegates from all ethnic groups in Addis Ababa in May 2009. It had to be cancelled when the Sudanese government, perhaps recognising the danger of genuine bridge-building, began harassing some participants and withdrawing passports from others. The episode shows that promoting dialogue between all of Darfur's people will not be easy, but this is exactly the sort of forum that can start discussions on the sort of grazing disputes, climate concerns and land clashes that have been manipulated by Khartoum. The outcome would be a coherent set of principles, a people's mandate, which might then be used as the starting point for peace talks between the warring factions. A second attempt in Doha, Qatar, at the end of 2009 showed that just such an approach might bear fruit. Representatives from the three states of Darfur, from Khartoum and from Darfuris abroad agreed a single, unified statement of principles and priorities for building a just peace. Their Doha Declaration set out the need for proper security arrangements and spelled out a basis for power and wealth sharing – exactly the sort of things that should feed into peace talks between government and rebels.

The success of the Save Darfur Coalition has been to turn this crisis into one the world could not ignore. Its mobilisation of support, its underpants and use of celebrities offers a model for other advocacy efforts. Its failure, though, has been to channel its pressure in the wrong directions. Its need for simple slogans and concrete successes – peacekeepers on the ground, no-fly zones, arrest warrants – has distracted attention from the slow business of a negotiated peace.

Every UN Security Council resolution requires a bit of arm twisting. Russia and China have to be brought on board. This costs political capital – something in short supply as the international community continues to agonise over Afghanistan, Iraq, North Korea and Iran. The advocates may have made Darfur matter, but it still doesn't matter quite enough. So every mistaken solution means there is less goodwill to use on the right ways to save Darfur. If Mia Farrow is frustrated it is because we have had the wrong sort of advocacy.

Now is not the time to give up on Darfur. Sudan-wide elections are planned for 2010 and the South is due to vote on independence the following year as part of its own peace deal. Both could have desperate implications for Khartoum's empire built on sand. If the South votes to break away then a government whose main motivation is clinging on to power at all costs is unlikely to give in without a fight. Proxies never quite go away. The peace with the South is already fragile. A yes vote in the plebiscite could plunge the region back into a war that has already claimed two million lives, dwarfing Darfur's death toll. In the same way, any threat to Bashir's presidency and the position of his National Congress Party in elections could provoke a fresh round of repression and reprisals. There are already questions about whether a ballot will be possible in Darfur at all. Continuing insecurity and poor communications present major logistical difficulties. Add in a volatile mix of rivalries and the chances of a free and fair vote, representing all of the region's people, seem slim.

At the same time, the elections and independence referendum also offer a potential solution to Sudan's problems. They were conceived as part of the Comprehensive Peace Agreement to end civil war and a chance to redraw Sudan's political map, overturning the

Northern, riverine elite's hold on power and giving one part of the periphery a chance to stand on its own two feet. The Sudan-wide elections bring an historic opportunity to reshape Khartoum's relationship with its country, turning an empire into a state and sharing power and wealth more widely. The implications for the marginalised people of Darfur, whose poverty and problems cut across differences of tribe, are obvious.

Encouraging successful elections and a fair referendum are now where international efforts should be focused. President Bashir is a wanted man, yet his Antonovs continue to bomb Darfur. He has used humanitarian agencies as pawns in his game, and does not seem like a man to willingly cede power to his opposition. So that is where advocacy and diplomacy must now be concentrated. Solving Darfur means solving Sudan.

The further away from Africa you travel, the more clear-cut the solutions tend to look. Dig beneath the surface, talk with Arabs in the aid camps, see the exhausted eyes of captured Sudanese soldiers, or try to draw a family tree of the rebel groups and nothing seems so simple any more. It was the apparent simplicity of Darfur's problems that first caught the eye. A genocide unfolding ten years after Rwanda's horror triggered an unprecedented response. It generated headlines and drew in celebrities. Up close though – when you can feel the sand between your toes or smell the woodsmoke of the camps, or when you are cowering from Antonovs overhead or clinging to a donkey – things looked rather different. Or rather they looked familiar. Dig beneath the surface and its changing cast of rebel commanders, government stooges and proxy militias started to remind me of other African wars. There was regional politics at work. Land and water brought simmering tensions between tribes to the boil. Guns were readily available. It only took the tribal trigger of Arab supremacy to ignite a war. In some ways there was nothing very different about Darfur.

Sharon and Hilda were freed after three and a half months. They had been spirited across the border with Chad and held in one mountainous hideout after another. There, they often went days without food, endured freezing nights and were subjected to a terrifying mock execution. They never knew if the next day might be their last. For weeks, messages passed back and forth between tribal intermediaries negotiating for their release. Several times, hopes were raised of a deal only to be dashed within hours. In the end, the key to their freedom was my old quarry, Musa Hilal, who claimed to have broken the deadlock by handing over more than $200,000 to their kidnappers. The Sudanese, Irish and Ugandan governments all denied paying a ransom, but then again their writ does not run far into Darfur's deserts, where deals are lubricated with copious amounts of sweet tea and hours of chit chat about camels or cows. Nor was it ever any clearer who took the aid workers. Maybe it was a gang with a political motive, maybe it was just about the cash, maybe it was a combination of the two. Or maybe the whole thing was dreamed up by Hilal in an attempt to demonstrate his influence, and carried out by his son – one of the leading theories.

We will probably never know the truth except that, in Darfur, nothing is ever quite as it seems.

ACKNOWLEDGEMENTS

Sudan is not the sort of place where ordinary people can speak freely to a foreign journalist. Informants and security officers lurk everywhere. Despite the risks, countless Darfuris in the aid camps or in Khartoum answered my questions, offered me telephone numbers or encouraged me in my research. They cannot be named but I am deeply indebted to them all.

This book would also not have been possible without the help of dozens of aid workers, diplomats and activists who took risks on my behalf. They know who they are. In Khartoum, Alun McDonald, Liz McLaughlin and Dawn Blalock all helped me better understand Sudan and became firm friends in the process. Opheera McDoom never lost her patience with my stupid questions. Amber Henshaw and Andrew Heavens opened their home to me, ensuring I remained sane through eight of the craziest days of my life. Catriona Laing and Clive Bates always ensured a lively debate at dinner and helped formulate some of the ideas that appear in these pages. Jennie Matthew offered coffee and advice in generous measures, as well as commenting on the draft of this book. Professor Elteyb Hag Ateya, Ghazi Suleiman and Dr Ghazi Salahuddin Atabani talked me through the workings of Sudanese society and government time and time again. Fouad Hikmat performed the same invaluable role in Nairobi.

In Darfur, Jason Benham and Stuart Price bailed me out when others were ready to wash their hands of an interfering journalist. Kemal Saiki and Josephine Guerrero organised access to the UN/AU hybrid peacekeeping force.

In Chad, Ettie Higgins drugged my stomach into submission while Celeste Hicks opened up her contacts book. And Kate Holt took me on a wild ride – by motorbike and chartered plane – deep into the Congolese jungle.

Bec Hamilton provided thoughtful discussion on the role of international justice and advocacy.

Alex Perry spent longer than he should have done in helping revise this manuscript and he has my deepest thanks.

My editors all deserve special praise. Richard Beeston at *The Times*, Paddy Smyth at *The Irish Times* and Matt Clark at *The Christian Science Monitor* each allowed me to return to Darfur more times than was strictly necessary.

At Reportage Press my thanks go to Jennifer Sandford, Laura Keeling and Rosie Whitehouse, who turned my idea into a book.

One man – and his battered yellow taxi – deserves my particular and enduring gratitude. Were it not for Al Siir Sabil Nasr, I would never have met half the characters in this book, eaten fried fish in Omdurman or fallen in love with the mishmash of people and places that make up the vast country of Sudan.

DONATION

The Dart Centre for Trauma and Journalism aims to equip journalists with the tools they need to report effectively and responsibly on violence, conflict and trauma – be it street crime, natural disasters or war. It brings together news professionals, researchers and clinicians, offering training and discussion of the issues surrounding tragedy. As well as tips for handling sensitive situations, it offers support to journalists affected by the horrors they have seen. It is just the sort of place that I should have liked to have known about before I left for Africa.

Five per cent of the proceeds from *Saving Darfur: Everyone's Favourite African War* will be donated to the Dart Centre Europe, to help it continue its work.

REPORTAGE PRESS

REPORTAGE PRESS is a new publishing house specialising in books on foreign affairs or set in foreign countries; nonfiction, fiction, essays, travel books, or just books written from a stranger's viewpoint. Good books like this are now hard to come by – largely because British publishers have become frightened of publishing books that will not guarantee massive sales.

At REPORTAGE PRESS we are not averse to taking risks in order to bring to our readers the books they want to read. Visit our website: www.reportagepress.com. A percentage of the profits from each of our books go to a relevant charity chosen by the author.

The DESPATCHES series brings back into print classic pieces of journalism from the past.

You can buy further copies of *Saving Darfur: Everyone's Favourite African War* directly from the website, www.reportagepress.com, where you can find out more about our authors and upcoming titles.

Reportage Press is now on Facebook! Come and join our online community to discuss the issues raised by our books and read our press features and reviews.

REPORTAGE PRESS

ALSO FROM REPORTAGE PRESS

Something is Going to Fall Like Rain
By Ros Wynne-Jones

"An authentic, well-written and deeply-felt portrait of the tragedy that is South Sudan" – John Le Carre

"A book of meat and emotion, blood and fire – it is a story of our time. And a masterpiece" – Tony Parsons

In Adek, a tiny village in the sprawling desert of Southern Sudan, a community lives on a knife-edge of starvation and war, at the mercy of the bombs that fall from the sky like rain. When three western aidworkers are stranded here – a place where poets carry Kalashnikovs and rebel commanders wear pink dressing gowns – their presence brings hope and danger in equal measure. An ominous ode to Africa's violent beauty, *Something is Going to Fall Like Rain* is also a life-affirming reminder that love and happiness can co-exist with famine and conflict.

Part of the proceeds from *Something is Going to Fall Like Rain* go to Oxfam.

Paperback £12.99

ALSO FROM REPORTAGE PRESS

Genocide: My Stolen Rwanda
By Révérien Rurangwa

"The eyes of your assassin. They stay in your mind's eye until death."

Rwanda, April 1994. For thirteen days Révérien Rurangwa hid in silence with his family in a hut on the hillside in Mugina. Eventually they were hunted down by their Hutu neighbours and in minutes forty-three members of his family were massacred before his eyes.

Révérien was the only one to escape, missing a hand and an eye. He was just fifteen years old. In this extraordinary memoir he reflects upon his experience as a survivor uprooted in exile, and attempts to confront the enigmatic power of evil which has steered the course of his life.

Part of the proceeds from *Genocide: My Stolen Rwanda* go to Ibuka – Memory and Justice.

Paperback £8.99

COMING SOON FROM REPORTAGE PRESS

Crossing Qalandiya: Exchanges Across the Israeli/Palestinian Divide
By Shireen Anabtawi and Daniela Norris

Two women meet by accident at a party – both mothers, both a similar age. One is Israeli, the other Palestinian. So divided by fear and hatred are their two countries, they realise they will never be able to visit one another at home, despite living less than 100km apart. So, they begin to exchange letters. As their friendship grows they discuss not only their families, childcare and recipes, but also the wars and ethnic tensions that have shaped their lives.

Their exchange is fraught with challenge, but also a sincere desire on each side to understand the thinking and grievances of the other. This is a moving and illuminating exchange of ideas – at once accessible and profound, personal and political – and a beacon of hope in the wilderness of the Israeli/Palestinian conflict.

Part of the proceeds from *Crossing Qalandiya* will go to Children of Peace.

Paperback £8.99